A CENTURY OF
WINE

THE STORY OF A WINE REVOLUTION

A CENTURY OF

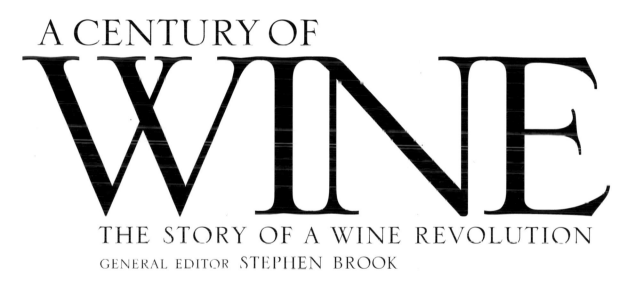

WINE

THE STORY OF A WINE REVOLUTION

GENERAL EDITOR STEPHEN BROOK

Contributions from the world's finest wine writers
FOREWORD BY HUGH JOHNSON

A Century of Wine
General Editor Stephen Brook

First published in Great Britain in 2000 by
Mitchell Beazley, an imprint of Octopus Publishing
Group Limited, 2–4 Heron Quays, London E14 4JP.

A CIP catalogue record for this book is available from
the British Library.

ISBN: 1 84000 253 0

The author and publishers will be grateful for any
information which will assist them in keeping future
editions up to date. Although all reasonable care has
been taken in the preparation of this book, neither the
publishers nor the author can accept any liability for
any consequences arising from the use thereof, or the
information contained therein.

Commissioning Editor: Rebecca Spry
Executive Art Editor: Tracy Killick
Managing Editor: Hilary Lumsden
Design: Sarah Williams
Editor: Diane Pengelley
Picture Research: Helen Stallion, Khali Dhillon
Production: Nancy Roberts
Index: Hilary Bird

Typeset in Caslon

Printed and bound by Toppan Printing
Company in China

ACKNOWLEDGEMENTS
The general editor and staff at Mitchell Beazley
would like to thank Bodegas Torres, Bodegas Domecq,
Compania Vinicola del Morte de España SA, Sherry
Information Service, Bodegas Marqués de Riscal,
Domaine Marquis d'Angerville, Domaine Henri Gouges
and Maison J Faiveley for their kind help in supplying
archive photographs for this book.

Foreword by Hugh Johnson

Every generation reinvents the world, and there have been two generations since wine began its recovery – from almost half a century of stagnation – after the Second World War. This book is an inventory of the multiple revolutions that have brought us, at the start of the 3rd millennium (and with six millennia, at least, of wine history behind us) to a paradise of good drinking, unimaginable in any previous age. In the boom times of today it is hard to recall, or even believe, that for most of the first half of the 20th century a wine estate was more of a liability than an asset. Two world wars, revolution and The Great Depression brought wine-growers almost to penury, and Prohibition did not help. Three vintages of memorable quality ushered in the peace, but it was not until 1955that buyers returned with any enthusiasm, at first to Bordeaux. Then, in 1959, the news of a great vintage made it onto the front page of *The New York Times*. Young as I was, I remember thinking 'we're off'. And we were.

Whatever else the 1960s are remembered for, they saw wine back on the agenda of the western world. The decade started with the first new Napa winery since Prohibition: Heitz Cellars. By 1966 Robert Mondavi had launched what is still the Napa Valley's flagship. In 1960 Penfolds disclosed their secret: Grange – Australia's first great red wine, which Max Schubert had been perfecting since his one historic visit to Bordeaux ten years earlier. And back in Bordeaux, Château Haut-Brion made the momentous decision to install stainless-steel vats.

Modern times were coming. Italy's reaction was a fit of housekeeping – the birth of her DOC regulations. Spain and Portugal slumbered on. But the countdown had started.

Is wine driven by taste, or does technology provide the momentum? I have often pondered, watching the evolution of what we drink. The last time the wine world saw a revolution was in the 17th century. Wine had reigned unrivalled since Creation – unique, as harmless inebriant, medicine and antiseptic – when suddenly rivals appeared. Within 100 years spirits, hop-stabilized ale, chocolate, coffee and tea all burst on the scene as fashionable alternatives. It is no coincidence that wine-growers raised their game. The 'New French Clarets', the *crus* of Burgundy, sparkling Champagne, the first botrytis wine, Tokaji, and port all made their appearances between 1650 and 1700. True, politics played a part, but inventiveness was the key; 250 years later there had only been modifications and extensions to the repertoire that was in place as the 18th century began.

The 20th century revolution was different. Nobody was looking for new and better tastes. The classic wine list had been burnished to perfection and the best grapes found for each kind of wine. But now it was being imitated in new countries and regions where conditions were not the same. Listen to the prophet Bleasdale (the Rev John) soothsaying in Melbourne in 1867: 'Whatever the wine is, sweet or dry, one thing is certain: that in hot climates you can never produce wines with the perfume peculiar to those of colder regions... if you are to have the perfumed wine of France... you must also have the other conditions, especially slow, long-continued fermentation at a low temperature.' He had realized, long before others, that Europe's best vineyards are just at the margin of ripening, in climates where vintage time is relatively cool and winter extremely so. In countries like Australia and California, nothing could be done until means were found to cool the fermentation. Refrigeration was the first revolution of 20th century wine. The second was an understanding of its chemistry, begun by Pasteur and built up in laboratories around the world, but led, above all, by the Bordeaux team of Professors Ribereau-Gayon and Peynaud. This is a revolution that will revolve for ever. The third, and the single thing after refrigeration that made New World wines directly comparable with Old, was the realization – first made in California in the later 1950s – that French oak gives wine a French taste.

Each of these could be described as a leap in technology. We are still looking for ways to perfect certain flavours that started with European grapes in European soils. The roll-call of grapes scarcely alters; just where they are planted. On the other hand each technological advance introduces new possibilities for a different emphasis. More alcohol, for example, more oak, more pure fruit flavours, softer acidity, softer tannins – all these, or combinations of them, are easily arranged. At this point it does become a matter of taste. The winemaker has a bewildering set of alternatives: which does he choose?

What a chance for the marketing department. Mass sampling will tell you which taste sells most at a given price. Business logic could take it from there – with catastrophic results for diversity. We have seen the reality of a bland sameness creeping in, above all with Chardonnays. But we have also, thank goodness, seen it retreat.

Diversity is the soul of wine. It is also the soul of competition. How do you compete in the market with just another Chardonnay? It won't work, and wine-growers round the world are seeing the challenge of the new century as establishing their own territorial taste. In the end his land, its soil and climate, in a word his terroir, is the only unique proposition a wine-grower has to offer.

A Century of Wine is the first book to survey the achievements of the busiest period in wine's history. Stephen Brook has brilliantly brought together the specialists who can plot each detail of its multiple revolutions, and make their protagonists come to life. The revolutions are by no means over. They never will be. Future generations will find new pleasures in new wines. But the 20th century opened up this infinite potential – and its story makes fascinating reading.

WINE
REVOLUTION

Fashion, gastronomy, religion and culture have all had a dramatic influence on wine styles in the 20th century. No longer defined entirely by regional idiosyncracies, wines from the world over are now influenced by international markets and global concerns.

Wine, Food, Style & Pleasure

Stephen Brook

At the beginning of the 21st century, alcohol consumption continues to be influenced by national culture. Wine's civilizing influence is taken for granted by many Europeans: it has a role to play in celebration and good eating, and lubricates conversation in all kinds of social contexts. In several Mediterranean cultures wine is more often seen on the dining table than the bar counter. Yet many such countries, including Greece and Italy, record low rates of alcoholism – this in spite of the fact that until a few decades ago, wine (or beer) was often safer to imbibe than water in these particular countries.

But wine has also been a battlefield on which wars of moral principle, taste and medical opinion have been fought.

In chillier parts of Europe, where the need to keep out the cold traditionally takes precedence over mere gustatory considerations, wine usually takes second place to spirits. Outside Europe, in Japan, North America, Australia and South America, heavy drinking is tolerated within certain contexts, such as business entertaining in Japan and carnivals in South America. In the Caucasus, the Georgians drink on an epic scale

on occasions, but usually as a liquid backdrop to prolonged banquets. In 1979, during an earlier career as an academic editor, I endured an instructive week in Russia negotiating contracts, a process that involved downing copious toasts of brandy to seal each stage of the *rapprochement*. Drinking, in these countries, can be a form of social bonding.

But wine has also been a battlefield on which wars of moral principle, taste and medical opinion have been fought. It was the obscure borderline between alcohol-induced well-being and blind drunkenness that precipitated the forces of Prohibitionism in 1919.

Concern about drunkenness was, of course, nothing new. Strong spirits, such as gin, cheap and ruinous, had wreaked damage in Britain for centuries. Drinking habits in the 18th and 19th centuries would make most steady drinkers of our own day quake. Inevitably there was a reaction in the form of temperance movements, which brought moral fervour to the cause, and such movements flourished – as did the enemy they fought against – in cultures given to drinking outside the context of meals and religious practice.

It was not the dining tables of France, but the saloon-bar culture of America, with its *pichet* of

red wine drawn from the barrel, that provoked the founding of the world's first temperance movement in 1826.

Concern about the effect of alcohol consumption during periods of war gave some intellectual justification to Prohibitionist sentiment right through the First World War, and temperance reached its apotheosis in 1919, with the enactment of Prohibition in the United States.

No doubt there were plenty of alcoholics in Europe, but for the most part the limits of

socially acceptable consumption were thought to be understood. It would be stretching a point to argue that the centrality of wine to the rite of Holy Communion in Roman Catholic and some other churches has made its consumption acceptable, but at the very least this has prevented it from being seen as aberrant. Similarly, religions such as Judaism require the tasting and limited consumption of wine as part of the ritual. The Sabbath is ushered in with a family meal, which is begun only after the wine and food have been

△ Throughout the century the auction house offered the most efficient and profitable way to trade fine wines; here at Sotheby's bottles of 100-year-old sherry are 'hammered' down to the highest bidder.

△ Nothing has yet been devised to beat the ideal conditions of a hole in the ground such as this *cave*, which offers a cool, even temperature, dark, calm and a certain degree of humidity.

blessed. The great Seder feast, consumed on two successive nights during the Passover festival, requires the consumption (or at least the sipping) of four glasses of wine. Wine within Judaism is presented as celebratory, and Jews in Poland or Canada, far removed from the Levantine origins of their religion, have effortlessly absorbed wine into their rituals. This may partly explain why rates of alcoholism among Jews remain low.

EXCESS AND ALCOHOL CONSUMPTION

In countries with more austere religious and social traditions, echoes of temperance linger: in the more remote Welsh and Scottish valleys, in the English licensing laws, in the restrictive selling practices of countries such as Canada, and in the dry corners of the United States.

In 1983, compelled to visit the Texan city of Lubbock, I discovered to my dismay that it was 'dry'. Fortunately, wetness lapped at the city boundaries, and just beyond them sprawled half

a dozen liquor markets, some offering an admirable wine selection. Northern countries, such as Scandinavia and Russia, which from time to time have legislated to reduce alcohol consumption, nonetheless suffer from high rates of alcoholism, although this may also be related to the prevalence of spirits rather than wine, and to a tendency towards binge-drinking, a phenomenon virtually unknown in Mediterranean cultures.

However, a fondness throughout much of the world for 'recreational' narcotics has meant that there is less dependency on alcohol as a stimulant than might otherwise be the case.

The drinking of fine wine has been ennobled by connoisseurship. However, in the 18th and 19th centuries, when liver-crippling quantities of port and other fortified wines were consumed as a matter of course by the British upper classes, wine was routinely abused as a stimulant. But it was not the only alcohol to be abused. The memoirs of some of Britain's more heroic 20th-century drinkers – Evelyn Waugh and

George Melly, for example – report prodigious consumption of gin, brandy and sometimes Champagne, but rarely of fine wine. Americans tended to favour the high-strength bourbon or cocktails, while among the less affluent classes there was a fondness for cheap fortified wines.

EDUCATION AND CONNOISSEURSHIP

More than most spirits or beers, wine has been accorded respect, even awe. The wine books of the 1930s and 1950s were meditations on taste and aroma, their authors rich connoisseurs who indulged a passion for mature wine in a club-like atmosphere. An understanding of wine – in those days largely limited to Bordeaux, white burgundy, port, and madeira – was part of a gentleman's education. This was especially true in countries that were not zones of production. Wine in Italy or Greece was almost always a local brew drawn from the barrel; bottling was a recent innovation except for the most highly prized growths. In France, too, it was customary to purchase wine in bulk. As a teenager staying with a French family in Nice, one of my chores was to take the demijohns down to the local cellars to fill them with wine purchased on the basis of colour and strength. In Britain or Belgium, wine was usually purchased in bottle (although the bottling was originally undertaken by importers rather than producers); its price and the necessity to choose between hundreds of competing regions, châteaux and styles, encouraged the growth of connoisseurship.

STYLE REVOLUTION

The fine points of wine enjoyment counted for little in many areas of production, where it was taken for granted that the local wine would have an almost mystical rapport with local cuisines. This association still exists. The bracing white wines of the Loire admirably accompany river fish such as *sandre* (a kind of perch) and the strong flavours of *andouillette* (tripe sausages). Is there a better combination than a juicy Dolcetto with a dish of pasta in a rich Genoese or Piemontese sauce? A good Provençal *rosé* is delicious with *salade niçoise* or a dish of grilled peppers. How better to cut through the tart substantiality of *sauerkraut*, with its pork garnish, than with a tangy Alsace Riesling or Pinot Blanc? The almost astringent acidity of Chianti mellows alongside a platter of grilled birds on a Sienese terrace, and Argentina's deep flavoursome Malbecs seem tailor-made to complement the country's superlative beef.

Yet nobody would deny that there has been a stylistic evolution since the 1960s. Once wine – especially wines other than the French classics – began to be exported, producers had to start thinking about the tastes of potential customers elsewhere. It didn't take the Chileans or the Portuguese long to realize that tired oxidized white wines were not going to go down a treat in the smart restaurants of New York or London.

A lot of bad wine – mostly the inexpensive but widely available brands – was once considered acceptable by the north European or American wine trade and its customers. But by the 1970s the public was more sophisticated and less willing to be fobbed off with mediocrity.

Up to the 1950s wine had been relatively expensive outside the wine-producing regions and in some markets, notably Scandinavia, high taxes kept prices artificially high. Thus regular consumption was limited to the wealthy and to institutions. In Britain, high-quality wine was routinely served at college high tables and in officers' messes and gentlemen's clubs. In America, South Africa and the Antipodes, wine was a minority interest, and most bottles

▽ Conviviality and celebration: wine adds sparkle and zest to any social gathering, such as this election party night at the Bow Wine Vaults in London.

◁ A toast to the fruit of the vine at a family picnic. Wine forms a central part of the Mediterranean diet, as it has for centuries.

▷ In 1932, the leisure classes worldwide couldn't get by without Champagne: easy to enjoy and a timeless fashion statement.

◁ Even a country picnic can be enhanced by good wine, encouraging a complex interaction of aroma, flavour, and texture.

▷ The wine bar and the pub-turned-restaurant creations of the 1970s and '90s confirmed wine's popularity as an everyday companion to wholesome cooking.

George Melly, for example – report prodigious consumption of gin, brandy and sometimes Champagne, but rarely of fine wine. Americans tended to favour the high-strength bourbon or cocktails, while among the less affluent classes there was a fondness for cheap fortified wines.

EDUCATION AND CONNOISSEURSHIP

More than most spirits or beers, wine has been accorded respect, even awe. The wine books of the 1930s and 1950s were meditations on taste and aroma, their authors rich connoisseurs who indulged a passion for mature wine in a club-like atmosphere. An understanding of wine – in those days largely limited to Bordeaux, white burgundy, port, and madeira – was part of a gentleman's education. This was especially true in countries that were not zones of production. Wine in Italy or Greece was almost always a local brew drawn from the barrel; bottling was a recent innovation except for the most highly prized growths. In France, too, it was customary to purchase wine in bulk. As a teenager staying with a French family in Nice, one of my chores was to take the demijohns down to the local cellars to fill them with wine purchased on the basis of colour and strength. In Britain or Belgium, wine was usually purchased in bottle (although the bottling was originally undertaken by importers rather than producers); its price and the necessity to choose between hundreds of competing regions, châteaux and styles, encouraged the growth of connoisseurship.

STYLE REVOLUTION

The fine points of wine enjoyment counted for little in many areas of production, where it was taken for granted that the local wine would have an almost mystical rapport with local cuisines. This association still exists. The bracing white wines of the Loire admirably accompany river fish such as *sandre* (a kind of perch) and the strong flavours of *andouillette* (tripe sausages). Is there a better combination than a juicy Dolcetto with a dish of pasta in a rich Genoese or Piemontese sauce? A good Provençal *rosé* is delicious with *salade niçoise* or a dish of grilled

peppers. How better to cut through the tart substantiality of *sauerkraut*, with its pork garnish, than with a tangy Alsace Riesling or Pinot Blanc? The almost astringent acidity of Chianti mellows alongside a platter of grilled birds on a Sienese terrace, and Argentina's deep flavoursome Malbecs seem tailor-made to complement the country's superlative beef.

Yet nobody would deny that there has been a stylistic evolution since the 1960s. Once wine – especially wines other than the French classics – began to be exported, producers had to start thinking about the tastes of potential customers elsewhere. It didn't take the Chileans or the Portuguese long to realize that tired oxidized white wines were not going to go down a treat in the smart restaurants of New York or London.

A lot of bad wine – mostly the inexpensive but widely available brands – was once considered acceptable by the north European or American wine trade and its customers. But by the 1970s the public was more sophisticated and less willing to be fobbed off with mediocrity.

Up to the 1950s wine had been relatively expensive outside the wine-producing regions and in some markets, notably Scandinavia, high taxes kept prices artificially high. Thus regular consumption was limited to the wealthy and to institutions. In Britain, high-quality wine was routinely served at college high tables and in officers' messes and gentlemen's clubs. In America, South Africa and the Antipodes, wine was a minority interest, and most bottles

▽ Conviviality and celebration: wine adds sparkle and zest to any social gathering, such as this election party night at the Bow Wine Vaults in London.

produced domestically were cheap fortified
styles, drunk more for their stupor-inducing
qualities than for their taste. This degrading of
the domestic market helped to repress the
positive image of wine. After the Second World
War these attitudes began to change, and in
Britain middle-class households began to broach
the occasional bottle. Sherry and port, although
often of mediocre quality, remained popular,
but table wines also gained in popularity.
Sadly, their quality was often doubtful. Good
wine was sold by independent wine merchants
who, in London at any rate, can still be
intimidating to the uninitiated. The alternative
source was the off-licence, which stocked mostly
importer-bottled generic wines and brands,

including many dire blends under names such as Hirondelle and Rocamar. Wine is all about variety and subtlety. Branded wines offered the opposite: consistency and blandness. Lax or non-existent regulations meant that labelling counted for little, and the disreputable practice of blending Algerian wines into red burgundies, which continued until the early 1970s, was legal. Occasional scandals in Bordeaux made it clear that some underhand, often illegal, blending was going on there too.

RE-EVALUATING 'TRADITION'

By the 1970s and early 1980s 'traditional' wines were on the defensive. With technological advances in winemaking that led to the creation of 'fruit-driven' wines, wine-lovers began to question whether rasping levels of tannin and a distinct lack of fruitiness were really intrinsic to Bordeaux. Was burgundy, as old-fashioned British connoisseurs maintained, a dark, heady brew (thanks in no small measure to a *dosage* of Algerian wines), or an intensely ethereal and perfumed wine emphasizing delicacy, subtlety and finesse at the expense of power? 'Tradition' had to be re-evaluated.

Italy, in particular, had appellation rules that demanded protracted ageing of most red wines in large barrels. Brunello di Montalcino had to be aged for three years or more, regardless of the effect this might have on the quality of the wine. By the 1980s the rule was being broken by many leading estates in the interests of better quality.

There is a raging dispute in Tokaj in eastern Hungary, where the fresher, fruitier, more intense sweet wines, produced by the companies who have revived the region since 1990, are being condemned as atypical by wine authorities accustomed to the more oxidized wines of the communist era. These were a clumsy cocktail of wine, must concentrate and added alcohol, sealed by flash pasteurization. But internationalization has led to the overall amelioration of wine quality in the 20th century. There are some wine-lovers, especially those English and Americans termed 'necrophiliacs' because of their partiality to very old vintages, who rave about the unparalleled splendour of ancient claret. Anyone lucky enough to have tasted a 1929 or 1961 can attest to the wonder of these wines, but the champions of old wines tend to forget that most wine produced in Bordeaux in, say, the 1930s or 1950s was fairly nasty stuff.

Wine is all about variety and subtlety. Branded wines offered the opposite: consistency and blandness.

Practices in vineyard and cellar that we now take for granted, and which can help salvage even a tricky vintage, were unknown then. Bunch-thinning, canopy management, and above all the relegation of poorer lots of wine to the second label, leaving only the best for the *grand vin* – such forms of quality control would have been undertaken by only a tiny minority of châteaux. More scrupulous and better controlled practices in vineyard and cellar have assured that most high-priced clarets are now, at the very least, clean and balanced.

Clonal selection, although open to abuse, ensured a degree of resistance to disease; rootstocks are now better adapted to local conditions; hybrids and crossings, once adopted with enthusiasm in Canada and Germany, have to a large extent been replaced by classic varieties. Temperature-controlled fermentation and hygienic bottling lines and filtration systems have done wonders for the balance and stability of all wines, especially those that are mass produced. Problems such as volatility and musty flavours derived from bad-quality wood have become very much the exception. The major challenge remaining to the wine industry is to eliminate cork taint.

Champions of old wines tend to forget that most wine produced in Bordeaux in, say, the 1930s or 1950s was fairly nasty stuff.

Everyone accepts that countries not previously known for the quality of their table wine – such as Portugal and Austria – have made enormous strides in the last two decades, raising some of their wines to world-class levels. But many critics would argue that the internationalization that has improved overall quality has also led to

◁ A toast to the fruit of the vine at a family picnic. Wine forms a central part of the Mediterranean diet, as it has for centuries.

▷ In 1932, the leisure classes worldwide couldn't get by without Champagne: easy to enjoy and a timeless fashion statement.

◁ Even a country picnic can be enhanced by good wine, encouraging a complex interaction of aroma, flavour, and texture.

▷ The wine bar and the pub-turned-restaurant creations of the 1970s and '90s confirmed wine's popularity as an everyday companion to wholesome cooking.

△ Wine may have been rationed at home, but the importance of supplying 'Dutch courage' and an alcohol-induced sense of well-being was lost on few who commanded front-line soldiers.

◁ The ritual significance of wine – established thousands of years ago in some cultures – still persists today, with a central role in celebratory and formal rites the world over.

standardization, so that a Cabernet Sauvignon from Austria is scarcely distinguishable from one produced in Spain, the Languedoc or Chile.

The emergence of 'flying winemakers' who, it is claimed, impose their styles on alien traditions, has abetted this standardization. Yet in Europe especially, but also in Australia and other New World wine regions, tradition remains firmly embedded. It will, I am sure, take decades before the Grüner Veltliner of Austria is seriously threatened by Chardonnay or Sauvignon Blanc. Sangiovese is deeply entrenched in Tuscany, despite the fashion for

The emergence of 'flying winemakers' who, it is claimed, impose their styles on alien traditions, has abetted this standardization.

Bordeaux-style 'Super Tuscan' blends. There's Baga in Bairrada, Chasselas in Switzerland, Tannat in Madiran, Nielluccio in Corsica – the list of wines with a distinct regional identity is endless. The same is true of the New World, if to a less emphatic extent. I associate Sonoma Valley with Zinfandel, Barossa with Shiraz, Stellenbosch with Pinotage. There's no point trying to grow Cabernet Sauvignon in Oregon's Willamette Valley, and even Chardonnay is rarely as successful there as Pinot Gris.

MATCHING WINE AND FOOD

If wine variety is still inevitably dictated by climatic conditions, style is a matter of choice. No wine illustrates the fickleness of style more than California Chardonnay. The pioneers of this relative newcomer to California made the wine in a distinctive fashion: they blocked the malolactic fermentation to retain acidity, and aged but did not ferment the wine in older barrels. Then some of the winemakers travelled to Burgundy. As a result, in came *barrique* fermentation and malolactic fermentation.

By the late 1970s the 'French-style' whites, both Chardonnay and Sauvignon Blanc, were massive wines, powerful in alcohol, thickly textured and intensely oaky – magnificent if not exactly subtle. Then the West Coast began to take food seriously, and restaurateurs and foodies alike realized these splendidly monstrous wines overwhelmed most dishes. California Chardonnay was reinvented as a leaner, more discreet wine, but after a decade it became, to many tastes, nondescript. Back came the bigger, fatter styles, and the mantra of 'optimal ripeness' from late-picked grapes resulted in wines with high alcohol. No doubt by the time this book is published there will be yet another twist in style. A similar progression can be traced in the fortunes of California Zinfandel.

This continual revision of wine styles became a dominant trend at the same time as a more self-conscious notion of gastronomy arose. In the 19th century, dinner parties were served *à la Française*, which meant that all dishes were served more or less simultaneously, as is still the custom with Chinese food. By the end of the century this mode of presentation was replaced by service *à la Russe* – dishes assembled on a sideboard and served one at a time.

This encouraged a proliferation of wines where formerly a single wine would have sufficed. Soup would have been accompanied by sherry and madeira. Fish courses would have been offered with Sauternes, Graves, Chablis or sherry. Meat courses called for burgundy or claret, while Champagne refreshed the palate after the meat or roast dish (or was sometimes served with it), and hock would have been poured with vegetable *entremets* or side dishes. Port made its appearance with desserts, and gentlemen would drink more wine once the ladies had withdrawn.

The dwindling numbers of domestic staff in all but the greatest houses meant that such elaborate dining gradually became obsolete, although traditional food and drink matches persisted. During the inter-war period, formal dinner parties became far less routine and other forms of entertainment blossomed. In the 19th century few British people would have taken a drink before a meal, but by the 1920s the cocktail party was in fashion, with copious consumption of modish concoctions, often followed by a relatively swift meal in a restaurant.

I recall large parties given in the 1960s by a wealthy host in deepest Gloucestershire. Dinner would be delayed until the guests had consumed mind-blowing quantities of pre-prandial spirits. At table, only the cheapest Chilean wines were poured. 'No point serving anything decent,' my host confided in me, 'as they're all too smashed to tell the difference.'

A MATCHMAKING CRUSADE

The return to prosperity in the 1950s and 1960s led to a renewed interest in food and wine, spearheaded by the cookbooks of Elizabeth David and Robert Carrier in the United Kingdom, and of Julia Child and James Beard in the United States.

Foreign travel introduced the middle classes to the wines of Spain and Italy as well as those of France. As cooking styles continued to expand, embracing a range of oriental cuisines, the matching of food and wine was no longer a matter of instinct or ancient custom, but took on more analytical overtones. In the United States, one of the first American Masters of Wine, Tim Hanni, embarked on a personal crusade to untangle the mysteries, focusing on primary taste sensations such as sweetness and saltiness, and introducing the Japanese notion of *umami*, which gives an illusion of sweetness in the absence of sugar: it is *umami* that explains the 'sweetness' of scallops. Hanni also demonstrated that the sauce accompanying any dish was as important – if not more so – than the primary ingredient. Choices of wine needed to take all these factors into consideration. Under Hanni's influence, certain wine lists were reorganized to facilitate a suitable choice of wine for any dish.

It became fashionable for the wine press to organize 'food and wine' tastings. The ever curious Paul Levy, then writing for *The Observer*, routinely laid on such tastings, in which the invited guests tested, for example, *salade niçoise* against some 20 wines. Levy himself made no claims for scientific exactitude. Others followed where Paul Levy led, and by the late 1990s entire books were being devoted to the matching or pairing of wine with food.

There was a simple explanation for this sudden explosion of interest in the subject – the gastronomic certainties of the past were under attack as new culinary influences made themselves felt. The British fondness for Indian food (or what it took for Indian food), the French embrace of Vietnamese cooking, the Californian discovery of Pacific Rim cuisine with Oriental and Hispanic influences – all these muddied the waters. Fashionable chefs jettisoned classic sauces and traditional recipes, and introduced a whole panoply of flavours and textures: some coriander here, a dab of salsa there, horseradish in the purée, a drizzle of Thai fish sauce in the reduction.

'Fusion' cooking blew a hole in the armour of traditional food and wine matches, and a new generation of experts stepped into the breach. Since there are infinite numbers of food and wine combinations, especially given the subtleties of sauces, spices and herbs, an entire new form of punditry emerged. (It all seemed of little practical use, especially in the setting of a restaurant, where each member of a party might be eating a different dish.)

THE HUMAN TOUCH

The wine glass became a further source of anxiety. The Austrian glass manufacturer Georg Riedel decided to do away with the dimples, tints, and other embellishments sometimes associated with fine glassware, and focused solely on the shape of the bowl, lip and stem. He staged exhaustive tastings to establish which shape of bowl would most flatter the intrinsic qualities of a white burgundy or a vintage port.

Chefs jettisoned classic sauces and traditional recipes, and introduced a whole panoply of flavours and textures.

Ever more extensive ranges of glassware were produced by Riedel and his imitators, so that any well-equipped pantry would have had to stock a minimum of 80 crystal glasses to ensure that a formal dinner party could be certain of having the appropriate glass at each stage of the meal.

The *sommelier*, too, has taken on fresh importance. In the past the customer, presented

with a good wine list, would have had a shrewd idea of what to order and it was the *sommelier's* task to decant if required, taste, and pour the wine. The modern host in a restaurant, except in traditional French restaurants and regional European ones, is likely to be presented with a list so eclectic that he falls helplessly on the mercies of the *sommelier* to suggest and advise. Some friends of mine went to a celebrated

Until quite recently, wine-drinking seemed to carry more risks than benefits to health.

restaurant for an anniversary dinner. The *sommelier* looked after them handsomely, advising impeccably as to the best style and the best vintage to complement their dishes – but when they saw the wine bill, they nearly fainted. The main role of the modern *sommelier* is to sell as much wine – and water – as possible, and at the highest possible price, as well as to advise.

Although medicinal claims have been made for some wines – most famously for Tokaji Eszencia – and the efficacy of alcohol as a pick-me-up was well-known, until the 1990s health was seldom considered an important issue

in relation to wine consumption. It was recognized that too much alcohol, especially if fortified, led to short-term distress and that excessive consumption could be fatal. Spirits were favoured over wine for medicinal purposes, especially since the process of distillation was seen as an extraction of the most beneficial elements of plants and herbs, giving rise to monastic potions such as Chartreuse. But the idea that wine could be good for your health (as opposed to your morale) was never taken too seriously – wine was not considered compatible with a clear head or a sound liver. It was accepted that given moderate consumption, alcohol would do little damage and could give considerable pleasure, but until quite recently, wine-drinking seemed to carry more risks than benefits to health.

It was the incompatibility of drinking alcohol and driving – a motor vehicle, Boeing jet or TGV train – safely that preoccupied the mind. What, drivers wondered, were 'safe' limits? Our instincts, it soon became clear, were not to be trusted. National governments and police forces offered their own definitions, which were programmed into their testing systems. A driver returning home from a restaurant in Glasgow could be safely within the proscribed UK limit; a driver in France with the same proportion of alcohol in the blood could be locked up; and a motorist found in Hungary with any trace of alcohol in the blood whatsoever could be placed under arrest. Alongside the legitimate concerns about drink-driving were worries about when and how the long-term damage to health would manifest itself. Where precisely did those boundaries lie?

In 1987, the UK government established 'safe limits' and the number of 'units' that could be consumed without risk, although some of those involved in creating such limits subsequently admitted that their findings had little scientific basis and were mostly intended to deter excessive consumption. Jancis Robinson's 'self-help guide to sensible drinking' *The Demon Drink* (Mitchell Beazley, 1988) examined this very issue, although her sober assessment has been somewhat obscured by excitement over subsequent studies of wine's 'health-giving' properties.

At about this same time many winemakers were making wines of what the Napa producer Jayson Pahlmeyer happily calls 'industrial strength'. A glass of Pahlmeyer's Chardonnay (15 per cent) or Turley's Zinfandel (17.5 per cent) will help set you on the path to breathalyser hell, obliging each car load at a party to elect a 'designated driver' to stick to the Dr Pepper while everybody else indulges.

The French, always alert to any threat to their national interest, have ridden to the rescue. In 1991, French scientists, notably Serge Renaud, discovered that wine, especially red wine, was good for you and was a positive factor in combating heart disease. This explained why the French, tucking into a diet rich in animal fats, nonetheless enjoyed remarkable life-expectancy. This sensational discovery was reported on the CBS television programme *60 Minutes* and, dubbed 'The French Paradox', entered the history books. Almost overnight, patterns of wine consumption changed. American sales of red wines went through the roof. The King of Thailand, formerly partial to the occasional whisky, abandoned the habit of a lifetime and switched to red wine. (Unfortunately the Thai economy would soon prove less healthy than a magnum of Lafite.) The effect of the 'French Paradox' on consumption was profound. White wine had

been fashionable in the 1980s. In Britain in 1970 it represented 49 per cent of imported wine; by the mid-90s that proportion had soared to 70 per cent. Ladies who lunched could even spurt soda water into it. It was thought to be 'light' (in the manner of 'lite' beer, one supposes). After the 'French Paradox' hit the

Thus fashion... has come to influence not merely the style of wine production, but the very colour of the wine.

headlines, all this changed. Airlines had to alter their wine lists to reflect the growing popularity of red over white. Countries such as South Africa must have thought they were sitting pretty when, at the end of the apartheid era, they re-entered the modern world with 87 per cent of their vineyards planted with white wine varieties. Two years later nobody wanted their mega-hectolitres of Chenin Blanc and the international market was clamouring for red wines that represented only a small fraction of South African production. Thus fashion, whether prompted by modishness or health issues, has come to influence not merely the style of wine production, but the very colour of the wine.

THE POPULARIZATION OF WINE

In the course of this century wine has grown in international popularity, spreading not just laterally across national and continental boundaries, but vertically through the social classes. Until quite recently wine was a luxury item in many countries, but today it is as affordable as beer. Foreign travel played a large part in democratizing wine consumption, although only over the last two decades in Britain has wine-drinking started to lose its class associations. Only in a deeply class-obsessed country could a politician be pilloried for his fondness for claret as Lord Roy Jenkins was in the 1970s. It is hard to imagine the councillors of a communist-run city such as Bologna in Italy being derided for enjoying wine. When, in the mid-1980s, I became the first wine columnist of the *New Statesman*, people found it odd that a

◁ In the 1980s fine old vintages, hitherto curiosities for connoisseurs, became highly valuable and much-traded commodities.

socialist journal should take an interest in what was still widely perceived as a 'toff's tipple'.

All this changed as millions of tourists, American as well as British, chose to spend their holidays in wine- as well as sun-drenched corners of Europe. An earlier generation of national servicemen had acquired a fondness for

It's hard to imagine the councillors of a communist-run city, such as Bologna in Italy, being derided for enjoying good wine.

German wines after postings to military bases in Germany, and now holidaymakers along the Spanish coast began to realize there was an alternative to bitter and lager. Travellers used to be deterred from buying wine abroad on the ground that it 'doesn't travel', and in some cases that was true, in the sense that faulty or mediocre wines were hardly improved by a prolonged journey in an airline locker or a stifling car boot. But with technological improvements in winemaking it became apparent that wine travelled very well indeed; and, in the 1990s, the abolition of duty barriers on wine imported into Britain from the EU for personal consumption meant that ever-growing quantities of wine caught the travel bug.

The burgeoning wine press on both sides of the Atlantic provided potential wine-lovers with precisely the information they needed.

At the same time the wine bar came into being, and was particularly well received in Britain. Although simple food, often from a buffet, was on offer, for many regular customers, especially women, the wine bar became a substitute for the pub, which was often perceived as grubby, noisy and smoky. The wine bar also became fashionable in American and European cities, where they often catered as much to the couple sharing a bottle of Muscadet after work as to the wine-lover keen to taste a range of interesting wines by the glass.

Wine became more accessible as a result of the commercial success of New World varietal

wines. The enjoyment and understanding of most European wines was enhanced by a little scholarship: a knowledge of the regions of production and the styles associated with them. No such worries with an Australian Chardonnay or a Chilean Merlot. With the emphasis switched from the secondary characteristics of aroma and flavour acquired after prolonged bottle-age to primary fruit quality, wine became immediately broachable and easily comprehensible. The snobbish connotations, albeit unintended, of French classifications and German quality levels could be safely ignored. But even if the mass of younger wine-drinkers were fervent consumers of varietal wines, the traditional European wines styles were not superseded.

Wine had always been a status symbol, and its role as such was intensified by the broadening base of wine consumption. The burgeoning wine press on both sides of the Atlantic provided potential wine-lovers with precisely the kind of information they needed to accumulate a private cellar. Wine books such as *Hugh Johnson's Pocket Wine Book* (Mitchell Beazley, 1977) sold millions of copies in over a dozen languages. The invention of the 100-point scale and other forms of precision assessment offered consumers certainties in an uncertain world. As the prestige and track record of critics such as Robert Parker and the *Wine Spectator* grew, wine became viable as an investment. Each vintage yielded a small crop of blue-chip wines.

Investment in wine was a hazardous business, of course, and many a cellar built up in the 1980s was dispatched to the auction block in the early 1990s after the worldwide recession had struck.

A TRADABLE COMMODITY

Wine's popularity as a status symbol, fashion accessory, investment, and occasionally drink, spread across the world, especially to the Far East. The Asian market has had its ups and downs, but by the end of the 1990s the Japanese were still the major purchasers of Bordeaux in terms of value. The explosion of the restaurant industry worldwide also helped to reinforce the image of fine wine. You are as likely to encounter ancient vintages of Latour and Pétrus in Singapore as in Paris.

In 1998, staying in a small dusty town on the border between Thailand and Burma, I found bottles of Haut-Brion and La Tâche in a grocery store across from my hotel. Major European cities have always had grand and expensive restaurants with impressive wine lists, as have gloomy country house hotels in Scotland and the depths of France. But by the 1990s even rollicking Las Vegas was being acclaimed for the quality of its restaurants, and London was being hailed as restaurant capital of the world. With every restaurant came a wine list, on which the grandest French and Italian wines cohabited with sleek, brash bottles from the New World.

By this time wine had become accessible to all, regardless of where you lived, as long as you had a reasonably large disposable income. The wine market had become competitive, and producers, whether in Bordeaux or Napa, jostled for position in the marketplace by pricing their wines, if they dared, at points higher than those of their neighbours. In fashionable regions such as Burgundy and Napa Valley, the price of land also jacked up the price of the bottle, even if the quality was not always as fine as the price implied. Prices also rose in regions such as the northern Rhône, where the delimited areas of the top appellations were too small to meet the new demand.

But all was not lost for the impecunious. Supermarkets and high-street chains competed fiercely to source inexpensive but palatable wines, and largely succeeded.

EMERGENCE AND TRANSFORMATION

But there is no shortage of wealth in North America, northern Italy, and many other pockets of the world. The new prominence of wine was sustained by the activities of the auction houses, who vied aggressively with each other to sell the most dazzling cellars. Online auctions, especially in the United States, offered new forms of trading. Businesses devoted to temperature-controlled secure cellarage came to the aid of urban wine collectors with no cellars of

their own. By the end of the 20th century everything was in place for wine to emerge as a mature commodity – one intended to be drunk, to be sure, but also capable of being aged and traded.

The explosion of the restaurant industry worldwide also helped to reinforce the image of fine wine.

Indeed, the growing prominence of the 'wine collector' was one of the more depressing side-effects of the worldwide fashionability of wine. Consumer magazines such as the *Wine Spectator* often feature glowing articles about professors/investment bankers/sports personalities who have got their hands on a few prized magnums of sought-after wines. Yet a wine in a cellar bin is never quite as impressive as wine in a glass.

True, rich men in the past also collected wines, but in order to secure a steady supply of the stuff for their often large households. The European aristocracy, with their vast houses and heavy-duty entertaining obligations, had to maintain big cellars, replacing consumed vintages with their successors. The emergence of 'trophy wines' and of 'collectability ratings' can only aid the transformation of wine from a drink into a commodity.

Supermarkets and high street chains competed fiercely to source inexpensive but palatable wines, and largely succeeded.

Yet wine has proved its ability to survive all manner of abuses: snobbery, bouts of adulteration, over-valuation and under-valuation, the chasing after 'trophy wines', the excesses of drunkenness on one hand and Prohibitionism on the other, and attempts by certain social classes to claim a unique understanding of the beverage. Wine, good wine, is now drunk by a wider cross-section of the world's population than ever before, and cultures that were previously ignorant of its pleasures are taking to it with enthusiastic delight.

Phylloxera brought devastation; two world wars caused mass destruction; and the Depression and Prohibition meant economic disaster for winemakers. Yet as the century progressed, increasing global wealth brought ever greater individuality and quality to wine.

Wine, Politics & Economics

Giles MacDonogh

With some notable exceptions, wines served an essentially local community until the coming of the railway. With the advent of rapid travel, wine-drinking was transformed: the people of a small Norman town could experience the fermented juice of sun-ripened grapes rather than the sour and weedy liquid that passed for wine in their local taverns. Parisians could throw off that locally made Suresnes wine which had been a byword for nastiness for so many centuries, while the vast new warehouses at Bercy filled with big, strong reds from the deep south.

Paradise seemed to have arrived at last – but it was short-lived. Phylloxera struck. The aphid brought catastrophe for all those whose lives hinged on wine, but some of the plague's

The people of a small Norman town could experience the fermented juice of sun-ripened grapes rather than the sour and weedy liquid that passed for wine in their local taverns.

repercussions were eventually positive, leading to the transformation of Europe's vineyards. Only the fittest survived. Bad vineyards and under-performing grape varieties were uprooted and better uses were found for the land. Some

of France's best butter and cheese, for example, is now made from cows that graze on Charentais soil which was covered with vines a century ago. *Cuvées* were also standardized. This was particularly important in creating certain wines as we now know them. Champagne and Bordeaux finally achieved the grape mix which defines them today.

In Bordeaux, the 19th century ended with a glorious vintage and the 20th started with another. But Margaux 1899 and Lafite 1900 were small compensation for the traumas of the previous 20 years. However, the region maintained some kind of stability in the harvests preceding the First World War. Elsewhere it was a lingering, slow change; replanting on American rootstock was not as rapid a process as some might imagine. Grafting virtually every vine in Europe took time. Romanée-Conti, for example, was not grown on American rootstock until after 1945.

At the end of the 19th century the newly classified wines which brought fame to Bordeaux were virtually the same as those produced in the region at the start of the 18th century. Things were changing, however. With rail travel and bridges over the Garonne, merchants could shop in Saint-Emilion. From

En France

En Allemagne

the pages of Somerville and Ross' *In the Vine Country* (WH Allen, 1893) it is clear that the London-based merchants, Gilbeys, were buying wine for their blends in Saint-Emilion. Pomerol's reputation is generally thought to have been established later, though in fact Pétrus was already one of the most expensive wines sold at the Paris grocers Fauchon at the start of the 20th century.

The immediate pre-war period saw perhaps the last heydays of the elegant merchant families on the Pavé des Chartrons in Bordeaux, with their Anglo-Saxon-style coaches and fours:

Bartons, Guestiers, Johnstons, Lawtons, Schröders, Schylers and De Luzes; socially pretentious traders heartily mocked in the novels of François Mauriac, who came from their *milieu* and knew them well.

Based in London and from relatively humble stock, the Gilbeys never properly broke into this set, although they survived for longer. From 1875 they based their operations on Château Loudenne, beyond Saint-Estèphe. With its view across five kilometres of the Gironde Estuary they decided it reminded them of Cliveden, on the Thames.

After the First World War the foreign names in France were replaced by horse-traders from Corrèze, men careful to ape the manners and sartorial style of their predecessors. Tweeds and cords, kilts and loden coats, hunting with hounds, shooting on the islands of the Gironde Estuary, yachts, English gardens and even the odd English locution are still thought to represent correct form in the Médoc today, although the noblemen who first planted the vines in the 18th century are recalled only by the estate names.

Also around this time, big red wines drew the admiration of the wine trade. They were useful for proprietory blends, and they suited the French internal market too, as they were often drunk cut with water. The Gilbeys thought Algerian wine might prove the salvation of the wine trade in the face of the ropey stuff that was being eked out of the Midi's ravaged vines in the aftermath of phylloxera.

Some of it was *piquette*: a wine with a strength of about six degrees made from refermenting the husks and pips together with a few handfuls of raisins. According to a Gilbey diary the North African wine, by contrast, was 'far superior to anything now produced in the Midi, the Hérault and other parts of France'.

Phylloxera and slim pickings had sounded the knell for the Languedoc-Roussillon's *noblesse du bouchon*, merchant dynasties that had acquired châteaux and huge estates on the proceeds of selling cheap wine to the industrial north. Soon they found delegations of disgruntled vineyard workers at their gates. The army had to be called in to control riots.

Armies had an unquenchable thirst for alcohol...
'plonk' is believed to be Tommy's attempt
to pronounce 'vin blanc'.

There was a partial recovery, but the Midi took decades to achieve any form of respectability. *Le gros rouge qui tache*, or the 'big red stainers', survived into the 1980s, when the low-lying vineyards which had caused so many heartaches to so many French administrations were finally grafted over to *vins de cépage*. 'Plonk' was transformed into Chardonnay.

In 1911 similar riots broke out in Champagne. The men of the Aube in the south of the historical region resented the fact that although Champagne merchants were supplementing their meagre crops with the Aube's wines, the Aubois could not officially label their own wines 'Champagne'. The merchants of Reims and Epernay may have had a point, since chiefly Gamay grew in the Aube. Again troops had to be called in to put down violent demonstrations which led to the sacking of the small town of Aÿ. The Aubois achieved real success only much later and it was not until the 1950s that the Aube was substantially replanted with the Pinots Noir and Meunier that made it attractive to producers based in Champagne's traditional regions.

WORLD WAR

Dreams of recovery were shattered by the First World War. Labour was short in the vineyards as the men went off to the Front. There was some fighting in the vineyards of Alsace. Much more serious was the great German offensive of 1918.

The opening artillery barrage blasted away the vines above the River Marne. They were fully replanted only after the Second World War. Champagne was particularly badly hit. The Germans took Reims, reducing the great coronation city to a heap of rubble. For a few memorable moments the soldiers found themselves in the great cellars of the Champagne houses and gorged themselves on the contents – but the wine was still on its lees, and the effect was dramatic. Bitter experience taught them it was better by far to wait until the wines were disgorged before you drank them.

Not everybody lost out during the war. That extraordinary Hollywood-style villa, Masia Bach in the Penedès region of Catalonia, was built by a brace of tailors on the proceeds of massive sales of military uniforms to both sides.

Armies had an unquenchable thirst for alcohol and the military authorities had every interest in making sure they were liberally supplied with 'Dutch courage'; 'plonk' is believed to be Tommy's attempt to pronounce 'vin blanc'. When the war ended the Treaty of Versailles redrew Europe's borders.

Hungary may have gained independence from Austria, but it lost Transylvania with its vines to Romania, which had fought on the victorious side. It lost out in Burgenland too, as Austria successfully pursued its claims to represent the German-speaking majority in the border province. In 1921, Hungary was left with a tiny piece of the cake around the town of Ödenburg (or Sopron).

That was not enough to save Austria from becoming little more than a tourist trap for Germans, who came in search of a comforting draught of sweet *Gemütlichkeit*. Serbia finally realized the ambition that had caused the war in the first place: to control the rest of the southern Slavic provinces of the Austro-Hungarian Empire. The Jugoslavian state now had a chance to make a go of the Croatian wine 'Grk' and others like it.

THE RISE OF PROHIBITION
President Woodrow Wilson had been behind the 'principle of nationality' which had such

lamentable consequences for Europe. Some would say his effect at home was even worse: he imposed the 18th (Volstead) Amendment to the American Constitution on July 1st, 1919. This enacted Prohibition. The measure had been mooted in Europe in the first years of the century and to some degree imposed in Sweden and Norway to counter the rising tide of heavy drinking. Lloyd George considered it for wartime Britain – which had been the original argument in the United States too – but imposed draconian licensing laws instead, which have to some extent survived into our own time.

Prohibition not only destroyed the hard liquor companies and the bourbon distilleries in the south, it encouraged smugglers and gangsters. It also nipped the new California vineyards in the bud. Fortunately many of the vines survived as companies such as Mondavi took to selling grapes to anyone who wanted them. What the purchaser did with them was not the producer's responsibility, after all.

△ Reims cathedral, built between the 13th and 15th centuries, was virtually destroyed during the First World War, but has been rebuilt by the tenacious Champenois – its magnificent stained glass an assemblage of old and new.

△ Perverse puritan
pleasures: the deliberate
destruction in Boston,
Massachusetts of wines
and spirits during
Prohibition.

Italian immigrants in particular made wine surreptitiously, but they favoured the thick-skinned, staining grape varieties which, some writers argue, set back the development of quality wine in the Napa Valley until the 1970s. The reluctance of growers to uproot vines has nonetheless preserved some of the finest Zinfandel and Mourvèdre vineyards in California. It allows us today to enjoy wines made from vines planted in the late 19th century, just after the end of the Gold Rush.

The loss of good markets after 1918 was a further serious blow to the wine industry. The aristocrats of Czarist Russia had consumed vast quantities of sweet Champagne, Tokaji and Château d'Yquem, and developed their own vines in the Crimea. All this was gone after the Revolution. Similar uprisings in Central Europe, followed by a wide ranging Depression throughout the 1920s and '30s, were hardly conducive to trade. Merchants drummed their fingers on their desks as vineyards withered.

EARLY COOPERATIVES

The first cooperative cellars developed at the beginning of the century, allowing small growers an alternative to selling their grapes to merchants. In Bulgaria they more or less created the national wine industry since there were no large feudal estates to offer a lead as there were in Hungary, for example. The country was a hopelessly confused patchwork of peasant holdings. Cooperatives provided strip farmers with the necessary encouragement to plant grapes, and a desire to adhere to Western rather than Eastern styles meant planting the varieties that would later sell at export.

Most of the German cooperatives were created in the 1920s and '30s when growers got together to fight the merchants who paid a pittance for their grapes and wines. As a result they flocked to Nazism. Hitler, of course, did not approve of wine any more than his friend Mussolini did, although he is supposed to have made an exception in the case of some sparkling *Trockenbeerenauslese*. Not all his cronies were so puritanical. Göring protected the restaurateur Otto Horcher so long as he supplied cases of port for the Reichsmarschall's cellar. Foreign Minister Ribbentrop was married to Anneliese Henckel from the sparkling wine company of that name. Before graduating to diplomacy he had been the German agent for Pommery Champagne.

Economic depression had set in after the war and sales of Bordeaux slumped. As Bordeaux's *noblesse du bouchon* sold out, their estates were knocked down to their suppliers, creditors or lawyers whose descendants held on to them until they too were bought out by insurance companies from the 1970s onward. In a bid to combat fraud, which was still endemic, there was a gradual creation of a system of *Appellations d'Origine Contrôlées* or AOCs. These protective measures were first mooted in 1925, but it was not for another decade that the French began to define their wines by variety, *terroir* and yield.

THE FIRST APPELLATIONS

The man who is often credited with developing AOCs is Baron Le Roy of Château Fortia in Châteauneuf-du-Pape. He isolated 13 grape varieties which he believed to have been at the core of the best wines before phylloxera, and had them enshrined in new legislation as early as 1923. It is unlikely that those 13 represented the true image of the *cru* in the 19th century, but the statute added to the carefully doctored image of Châteauneuf. But Le Roy's mix has its apologists, and AOCs in our day have prevented the whole of France being turned over to easy-selling Cabernet Sauvignon and Chardonnay. Many people (especially those who see their future in Chardonnay and Cabernet Sauvignon) see the French system as too constricting.

The desire to define wines according to type and protect their image on the home and export markets was not confined to France. The regions of Tuscany reputed to produce classical Chianti – to some extent the invention of united Italy's second Prime Minister, Bettino Ricasoli – were shielded from such an affront in the 1920s. In the following decade the zones were legally recognized under the banners of *gallo nero* and

There was a seemingly unquenchable thirst for Champagne among the officer corps. Bubbles kept them going on the Eastern Front.

putto. These fixed recipes for wine in Chianti have been criticized in recent years: growers want the liberty to create their own recipes. The Super Tuscans of the 1970s and '80s flouted the rules of DOC (*Denominazione di Origine Controllata*), or DOCG (plus '*e Garantita*': guaranteed) as it later became.

THE OCCUPATION OF FRANCE

At the beginning of the German Occupation in France in 1940, the behaviour of some of the occupying forces was almost anarchic – they grabbed what they could. Later, the Champagne and Bordeaux trades were effectively policed by former wine merchants who made sure that most transactions were above board. The Germans paid for their wine in 'occupation marks' and even left a healthy balance in the account of Ronald Barton of Château Langoa when they departed in 1944 – despite the fact that he was a British Army officer.

At this time in Bordeaux, Adolph Segnitz, a Bremen wine merchant, managed to reclaim Château Chasse-Spleen, a property confiscated in 1914. And the German house of Mumm, which had been seized as a *bien d'ennemi* in 1914, was restored to its original owners. In 1944 it was re-nationalized. A year later, one of the Mumms, Herbert Mumm von Schwarzenstein, was dispatched with a shot in the back of his head for instigating a plot to kill Hitler. The Soviet Army had already entered Berlin.

The German Army was a good market. There was a seemingly unquenchable thirst for Champagne among the officer corps. Bubbles kept them going on the Eastern Front and the general staff thought nothing of sending planes from Stalingrad to fetch fresh supplies. When the Front collapsed and the armies streamed back to Central Europe, it was as though there was a contest to see who could drink up the contents of cellars first. The Russian need proved the greater. They drank virtually every drop of wine in store between Tokaj and Lower Austria and machine gunned the barrels they had emptied. Before their arrival there were desperate efforts made to hang on to a few prize bottles. These were lodged deep in wells, or in empty barrels so that Russian tapping revealed

Frau von Schubert... went down to the cellars and concealed a few of the choicer bottles under her voluminous skirts to bear them to safety.

only hollowness. In some instances, alleys of cellars were bricked up and disguised so that a few precious vintages were spared.

The creation of new nation states after the war meant the end of wine production in certain areas. Poland was shifted westward to let the Russians acquire some of its land in the east. The Poles took over Silesia with its small plot of vineyards around the town of Grünberg, which was best known for its Sylvaner Sekt. The table wines had been a metaphor for acid for centuries. The Poles decided not to continue to cultivate the vineyards and today Grünberg – or Zielona Góra as it is now – is better known for its vodka.

Liberation wasn't good news for everyone. Some wine merchants who had done business with the German forces had an uncomfortable time. The Bordeaux trader 'Onkel' Louis Eschenauer was thrown weeping into prison because he was related to a number of Germans who ran the city during the war.

The Western Allies behaved marginally better than the Russians. Although American soldiers made deep inroads into the historic cellars in the port of Bremen, they failed to drink up the casks of 17th- and 18th-century wine. Billeted on the estates on the Rhine and Mosel, American, British and French officers and men took what they could out of the cellars. Often they evicted the estate owners. This was

the case at Maximin Grünhaus, where Frau von Schubert found the occasional pretext to visit her house to fetch some vital object. While she was there she went down to the cellars and concealed a few of the choicer bottles under her voluminous skirts to bear them to safety.

Conquerors and conquered shared a sweet tooth: the Americans because they had been brought up on cola, and the Germans and Austrians because sugar had become a rarity. Wine was seen as a sugar-substitute. In Baden, Ruländer and in Austria, Neuburger grapes were popular because of their ability to condense sugar in their berries. After the *Wirtschaftswunder* or 'economic miracle', such wines fell into disrepute. It is said German and Austrian wines got sweeter across the board after the war, a metamorphosis that has contributed to their decline in an age when dry means good, and half-dry is an admission of lack of sophistication.

The post-war scene was fairly bleak. The literature of the 1950s depicts drab characters drinking 'harvest burgundy' from Australia and the Cape or Spanish 'sauterne'. Wines from the New World were made in imitative styles, even when the grapes were not to hand: Clare Riesling was made from Crouchen; Hermitage was correctly made from Shiraz, but so was Australian claret, burgundy and port. On the all-important Australian medal circuit there was a wine which had won a gold as a claret and years later, once it had become mellow, another as a burgundy. It was made from 100 per cent Shiraz.

RISE OF THE NEW WORLD

The first Australian wine to stake a claim to originality was Grange Hermitage, which, as its name implies, was still constrained by the same imitative terminology. It was created largely by mistake when a Barossa-*Deutsche*, Max Schubert, returned from a trip to Bordeaux with a desire to make something like a top-flight claret, a venture in which he had received encouragement from the Cruse family. The problem was that he didn't have the grapes, and he didn't have the wood. So his 'claret' was once again made from Shiraz and housed in cheap 100 per cent American oak barrels. A similar story created Portugal's most famous red wine, Barca Velha, which is another 'claret' made in a sweltering climate from local grapes.

As recently as 1990 the Chileans were making Pommard and Saint-Emilion. In the United States they continue to call many still white wines 'chablee' and sparkling wines Champagne. This behaviour has led to the *Comité Interprofessionnel du Vin de Champagne* (CIVC) taking drastic measures to protect the image of the world's most famous sparkler. It has taken a manufacturer of elderflower cordial, a scent producer and a cigar company to court to date. The *Comité* has not been alone in this litigiousness. The Sherry Institute has seen off the men of the Cape and has tried – largely unsuccessfully – to put a stop to 'Foxhunter', 'QC' and other British 'sherries'.

Port producers have left Australian fortified winemakers in a quandary as to what to call their imitations, and the Portuguese recently persecuted the makers of Austria's first port-style wine (not, incidentally, made with Blauer Portugieser). Not surprisingly, the United States has learned this game too: Gallo has endeavoured to convince Chianti producers it alone has the right to write *gallo nero* on bottles.

A new mood of optimism was slow in coming after the war. A higher degree of professionalism led to the creation of the Institute of Masters of Wine in 1953 and the election of the first six MWs. The Institute has gone through several incarnations since then, breaking out of the narrow purlieus of the British trade to offer the most famous international qualification available. Training still centres on London and most of the Institute's members are British, which suggests the old expertise is not entirely lost to the country.

POST-WAR BORDEAUX

The end of the war was greeted with jubilation in Bordeaux. Just as the ends of the War of the Spanish Succession in 1713, the Seven Years' War in 1763 and the Napoleonic Wars in 1815 raised expectations in the port region, 1945 seemed to promise much. The mood was helped by the quality of the wine at that time,

which had been concentrated by late frosts thinning the bunches of grapes on the vines. One of the best wines was Mouton, which encouraged Baron Philippe de Rothschild in his campaign to elevate his second growth to first, despite the fact it had always figured as second or even third *cru* on brokers' lists until then.

Baron Philippe launched an attack on the stranglehold then practised by the Bordeaux trade with their subscription system, which bound estates to sell their wines at a fixed price for a number of years. To make château-bottling the rule was another of his aims, something first performed at his cousins' property, Lafite. Certain wines, such as Pontet-Canet, were notorious for the variations caused by their range of bottling places. Rothschild and his supporters argued that filling at source would abolish time-honoured fraud and improve the reputation of classed-growth claret. In 1973 Baron Philippe finally managed to secure a revision of the 1855 Médoc classification, and his second growth was promoted to a first. No one has managed such a coup since, but there have been revisions of other Bordeaux classifications.

A higher degree of professionalism led to the creation of the Institute of Masters of Wine in 1953 and the election of the first six MWs.

The frost which ravaged Bordeaux vineyards in 1956 possibly caused more damage than any since 1709. A massive replanting exercise was required using new, more productive clones. The famous 1961 vintage, which yielded only 11 hectolitres per hectare, was possibly the last of old Bordeaux. By 1964 or 1966, the new vines had come on stream, and these days it is rare that production falls below 60 hectolitres per hectare.

A new expertise developed at around the same time. Once proud vineyard owners asked for help. Emile Peynaud had graduated from being a laboratory assistant to a professorship at the University of Bordeaux. By the time he retired he was the uncontested 'Pope of Bordeaux', receiving fees to advise two thirds of the classed growths and to tell producers how to get the best from their grapes.

◁ During the Second World War in Holland, two Nazi agents uncover a hoard of wine hidden by a Dutch householder.

▽ French nuns welcome American rescuers towards the end of the Second World War – with 'liquid hospitality'.

◁ In 1944 weary German infantrymen find brief respite in a southern French vineyard.

▷ While heavy bombing in Germany during the Second World War impaired the wine industry, the Americans discovered that German wines appealed to their sweet tooth.

◁ Bombing, shelling and the German occupation of France during the Second World War disrupted the wine industry – but liberation was not good news for merchants who had done business with the Germans.

▷ Bonhomie in a bottle: actress Clare Luce bolsters the fighting spirit at a soldiers' canteen in London in 1939.

Despite decent vintages, Bordeaux's post-war doldrums lasted until 1972, when at long last the market began to boom – but the dream was shattered when it was discovered a merchant called Pierre Bert had reverted to fraudulent blending to stretch his meagre product before delivering it to the market place. Bert was working with the Cruse family, one of the most distinguished dynasties among the Chartronnais. The scandal led to his imprisonment. The Cruses were let off with suspended sentences but the shame was too much for Hermann Cruse: he threw himself off a bridge into the Garonne.

POST-WAR PORTUGAL AND SPAIN

In Oporto, the depression also lasted until the 1970s. The bottom dropped out of the vintage port market and it was no longer thought worthwhile to despatch the wines to London for bottling. During the post-war decades port families were obliged to shed valuable *quintas* in the Douro Valley which they are only now managing to buy back. It was the time for the Symingtons of Vila Nova de Gaia to consolidate their position. They mopped up Dow, Warre and Graham, and successfully fought off the multinationals which bought up all but the Taylor-Fonseca group among the better-known 'English' lodges. In the 1980s, Johnny Graham managed to reverse the process a little and stage a comeback. His company, Churchill, was the first new growth on the Oporto vine in decades.

The Symingtons... mopped up Dows, Warres and Grahams and fought off the multi-nationals which bought up all but the Taylor-Fonseca group.

A similar process led to the fall of most of the great houses in Jerez in Spain, which were acquired by multinationals. A decline of sales at export led to desperate measures: 'cream' sherry was invented to please a rapidly ageing public which still enjoyed sweet, fortified wines. Despite well-meaning efforts, it is still a problem finding an enlightened market for the great wines of the area, the *finos* and *manzanillas*, the dry *amontillados* and *olorosos*.

VARIETY BACK IN VOGUE

As the world's economy picked up, buyers went farther afield to stock their warehouses. Despite the antiquity of wines such as Côte-Rôtie and Hermitage, the Rhône Valley was rediscovered only in the late 1970s. In 1978, at the same time as Rhône wines made their reappearance in Paris, John Livingstone-Learmonth and Melvyn Master brought out the first edition of *The Wines of the Rhône* (Faber). Robert Parker's even more influential *Wine Buyer's Guide* (Dorling Kindersley, 1989) came out a decade later.

Steven Spurrier, a Paris-based wine merchant in the late '70s, claimed responsibility for spreading the fame of many French local wines, including such staples of current restaurant wine lists as Sancerre. Spurrier also held the first formal comparative tasting between the top growths of France and California. Napa Chardonnays were pitted against white burgundies; Cabernets against Médocs. Several American wines achieved positions ahead of the holiest of holies. The top wine was the 1973 Stag's Leap Cabernet Sauvignon. It signalled the moment of awakening for Napa after the long post-Prohibition sleep.

The Mondavi family and later the Gallos poured money into public relations campaigns that sought to underline the findings of Spurrier's Paris tasting. There was a scramble to buy up the remaining plots of land in Napa and Sonoma counties. Henceforth they would become status symbols for upwardly mobile dermatologists, dentists, film-makers and property developers. As the French had always said: *le vin anoblit*.

From California, Brian Croser carried the message to Australia and created Petaluma. He joined a group of pioneers which included Len Evans, the surgeon Max Lake and a lawyer-turned-journalist and winemaker, James Halliday. Roseworthy Agricultural College became their equivalent of the University of California at Davis; healthy grapes and modern viti-vinicultural technology their gods. Cabernet and Chardonnay swept the board. Australians brought up by the new creed went to Europe. Many sniffed at the old-fashioned ways they saw there. Others became 'flying winemakers', applying their slick technological know-how to making wines for supermarkets and other retail multiples. With their help the new wine-drinking public got their tongues round concepts such as new oak and stainless steel. For those who couldn't rise to the price of a new oak cask there were oak chips, which could invoke more economically the flavour the public had come to crave in wine.

Marketing helped. Beaujolais attracted attention through its annual *nouveau* race, but lost ground when several other regions began to market their wines *en primeur*. Burgundy cleaned up its act and stopped colouring its wines with imported stainers from Morocco or the Midi. The Midi learned to value its hillside sites. With a little help from quality grapes such as Syrah, Grenache and Mourvèdre, the Midi produced a new classic blend on the *coteaux*. Down on the plains a sea of gut-rot was transformed into an ocean of *vins de cépages*.

In 1985 a scandal erupted in Austria after it was discovered that some producers had been lacing their wines with dyethelene glycol to fatten and sweeten them for German tourists holidaying in Burgenland. The scandal proved an effective watershed. It virtually closed down the Austrian wine trade and drove many of the older winemakers into retirement. Younger generations were determined to do better. Ten years later it had become clear that Austria could produce dry white and nobly sweet wines as good as any in Europe, and that there was a potential for red wines too. The scandal eventually had an extremely beneficial result.

As wine-drinking outside producing countries expanded in the 1980s, red wines began to threaten the supremacy of whites. This started with Rioja and took in Bulgarian wines and Fitou in the 1980s. By the 1990s Australian and Chilean reds had become fashionable in their turn. This development was aided by the discovery by scientists that grape tannins could help prevent wasting diseases, cardiac arrest and cancer. With the EU encouraging producers to grub up vines there was, by the end of the 1990s, a shortage of quality red wine. Meanwhile former best sellers such as Liebfraumilch went into decline, dragging the image of good German wines down with it.

The fashionable wines were not all red. New Zealand wines were also a discovery of the 1980s

when the trade first encountered powerful Sauvignon Blancs and Cloudy Bay achieved the status of a classic. Gorbachev's decision to ban drinking in the Soviet Communist Party flooded western markets, the British in particular, with cheap Bulgarian wines.

COMMUNISM AND APARTHEID

In 1989, the Iron Curtain collapsed. For the wine trade it proved a mixed blessing. For many years it was unclear who actually owned the land, and the communists had planted the big state cooperatives in the plains where they were easiest to farm. To return to quality, vineyards had to be replanted on the south-facing hillside sites.

Others became 'flying winemakers'... With their help the new wine-drinking public got their tongues round concepts such as new oak and stainless steel.

In the confusion, the area under vines in countries such as Bulgaria, Romania and Hungary began to shrink. When everyone had land there was no value in vines. Only in Hungary were positive developments clear by the end of the millennium: in Villany, the descendants of Germans settled in southern Hungary by Maria Theresa had begun to secure high prices for their red wines. More promising by far was Tokaj in the east. Here foreign investment completely reformed the vineyards: Spanish, Austrian, German, French and British money contributed to putting the regions wine back on the wine-lover's map. One of the major players has been the British wine writer Hugh Johnson and his Royal Tokaji Wine Company.

After communism lost its grip in Europe, apartheid was slowly wound up in South Africa between 1985 and 1993, ending a period of isolation felt by most South African growers. A depressed rand had put their wines at a disadvantage, condemning them to backward technology; growers had a limited knowledge of the outside world, and didn't know the wines to emulate; and there had been an informal boycott of South African wine by most of the

△ The Lebanese wine industry has struggled to survive years of civil war. Producer Serge Hochar surveys the momentous damage inflicted in the 1980s in Beirut, just south of his Bekaa Valley vineyards.

▷ A collaboration of talent, expertise and dedication at the Spice Route Wine Company on the newly fashionable Cape west coast promises to make an inspiring contribution to Thabo Mbeki's 'South African Renaissance'.

British wine press. In the 1990s, low prices assured South Africa of a large market and recognition for its white wines above all. It remains to be seen whether the attractive prices will be maintained in years to come, or whether South Africa can make reds with real gravitas.

One of the great forces for change in modern wine has been the American lawyer-turned-critic, Robert Parker. His consumer guide *The Wine Advocate* rates the world's wines on a controversial 100-point scale in which no wine worthy of the name earns under 75, and the best are awarded more than 90. The chief accusation levelled at Parker is that he induces producers to fashion wines that conform to his own tastes, which may be crudely defined as oak, tannin, colour and alcohol. Praise by Parker can double, triple or quadruple a wine's price, so it pays to heed his opinions.

In Bordeaux the effect of Parker has been to downgrade Cabernet Sauvignon in favour of the deeper, stronger Merlot and to encourage use of as much new oak as possible. Some Saint-Emilions are now '200 per cent' new oak, since a second new set of barrels is bought for when the wine is racked in the spring. But Parker's effect is not limited to Bordeaux. It is felt in Burgundy, the Rhône, indeed anywhere top wines are made.

At the turn of the 20th century the shortage of quality red wines, a global market and the enthusiasms of Parker and his ilk have meant that areas which scarcely figured on the wine map a decade ago are charging a small fortune for some bottles. In Spain's Ribera del Duero and Priorato, for example, certain properties demand the prices that some over-hyped Napa Valley wines fetch at the cellar door.

The prices of top burgundies have begun to look modest by comparison. Any wine which receives between 90 and 100 points from Parker or the *Wine Spectator* is effectively removed from the open market. This happened to Etienne Guigal's Côte-Rôtie *crus* in the 1980s when they were awarded a round 100. English merchants who enjoyed the privilege of a small allocation made a killing by sending it straight across to the United States. Few loyal customers had the chance to acquire a bottle.

CONFIDENCE STARTS TO PAY OFF

By the end of the century quality wines came from countries which had never been known for such a thing in the past. Serge Hochar alerted the world to the Lebanon with his Château Musar; properly made Greek red began to replace the image left by Retsina; Argentina revealed itself as a waking giant. Even England showed that it could produce decent stuff, in spite of the truculent weather.

Winemakers could now see farther than the fence at the bottom of their gardens. Most of the present generation has been away to school or viticultural college. They are keen to try their hands at different styles and to vinify grapes which are not necessarily approved of in their own areas. Everywhere the narrow system of controlled appellations is being challenged, especially where it appears to favour under-performing wines over real quality, as in Italy, for example, where *vini da tavola* often fetch higher prices than Barolos, Chiantis or Brunellos. The election of Albano di Romagna as Italy's first white DOCG (the highest accolade) caused despair in some quarters, although since then its strong, sweet *passito* wines made from dried grapes have partially repaired the image.

Everywhere the narrow system of controlled appellations is being challenged, especially where it appears to favour under-performing wines over real quality.

Britain has lost much of its traditional role. There is demand for the world's great wine from every corner of the globe, but Britain must make do with a limited allocation like everyone else. In the early 1990s the economic recession killed off much of the historic trade. The lion's share of buying passed into the hands of the supermarkets and high-street multiples. It is no longer true that British merchants bring in the world's most precious wines for a small number of connoisseurs. If anything they supply decent bulk from mass-producers to a rapidly expanding number of wine drinkers.

Wine is no longer what it was to many people in 1900 – a fortifying draught to relieve the strains of heavy manual work. Mediterranean factory and farm workers are now more likely to drink beer. It has become the province of a large number of men and women to enjoy a glass of wine with their meal, and wine is now more of an aspirational drink than it has ever been. Some historical cycles, however, seem more difficult to break.

As I write, phylloxera has cut a swathe through the new vineyards of California. Replanting is well under way with the new vines on the hillsides, and not just on the valley floors as it tended to be in the past. Growers have emerged from the experience with their knowledge enhanced and their eyes wide open.

Our experience of wine was once cruelly curtailed by geography and the vagaries of transport. Expensive imports often lost their integrity – or worse – in transit, so the choice was either local or doubtful. The 20th century's journey towards consistency of quality has been a bumpy ride.

Wine, Geography & Transport

Andrew Jefford

A tyrannical superior has misjudged you. Your true worth has come to his attention and he wishes to buy you a gift; he knows of your affection for wine and has researched, with unusual thoughtfulness, your tastes. Five cases arrive on your doorstep: third-growth Médoc from the last great vintage; a case of young Rhine wine from a sunny site in Eltville; Zinfandel from Napa; Carmenère from Chile; Shiraz from the Barossa. The year is 1900.

The most significant development affecting the transport of wine is the now ubiquitous practice of bottling quality wines at source.

Impossible? Yes and no. Very little wine was sold under grape-variety names in 1900, and in general exports from the southern hemisphere and from California were uncommon, with the scale of quality-wine production in these countries still modest. Yet such a gift was, at least theoretically, transmittable. The greatest wines of the Médoc and of Germany were staples of the international fine-wine trade (and fine hock was a much pricier commodity than it is now); the phylloxera pest in both regions was not yet defeated, but it was in hand. Bottles

from either region with 1893 on their labels would have been most acceptable.

California's plantings had surged in the second half of the 19th century, Napa's 6,700 hectares (in 1887) reflecting the fact that it was already considered one of the state's most promising locations. Phylloxera took its toll, but there were still over 1,200 hectares of vines there by the end of the century. Chile's wine industry, too, was burgeoning in 1900, thanks both to the classic French grape varieties collected and brought back to Chile in 1851 by Silvestre Ochagavia Echazarreta, and to the country's triumphantly phylloxera-free status. There are living Shiraz vines in the Barossa today which would have been well-established in 1900. South Australia, too, was already on track to become Australia's chief wine state, since it largely escaped phylloxera which was then cutting a swathe through Victoria's vineyards. In other words, the potential was there, even if the practicalities remained prohibitive.

In 2000, of course, nothing could be easier than arranging the swift delivery of these five cases. What has changed?

There were two great transport revolutions in the 20th century. One had almost no impact on wine itself, but was highly significant in

◁ Wine leaves the winery by ox-cart at the turn of the last century in Germany's Pfalz region. The first vines were planted here by the Romans, and quality wine production was underway by 1717.

improving winemaking skills and standards, as we will discover later. Wine, a liquid that cannot be concentrated and that is customarily packed in glass bottles, is too heavy to be efficiently and economically transported by air.

The other revolution, by contrast, has been of enormous significance. Road transport by motor vehicle offers far more speed and flexibility for heavy goods like wine than horse drawn transport ever could; even the iron horse, far more important for the movement of goods in 1900 than it is today, was quickly superseded by lorry transport in the often remote regions where wine is grown.

Of our five modern cases, though, only two might remain in the back of a lorry for the entire journey from producer's back door to recipient's front door: the case of Bordeaux and the case of Rhine wine. Indeed, even these could easily take the traditional route to market, the route by which wines have journeyed since Homer's days: stowed in the hold of a barge or a ship. Wine leaving California, Chile and Australia for Europe has and always will travel by water. This is a most unrevolutionary form of transport, still slow (six weeks from Adelaide to London), though now

speedier and more reliable than a century ago. Sea transport is relatively secure and stable, too.

The most significant development affecting the transport of wine in the 20th century, though, is the now ubiquitous practice of bottling quality wines at source. Had these five wines arrived on your doorstep in 1900, all would have been shipped in cask and bottled by a wine merchant on, or shortly after, arrival. The transport of wine in casks or tuns was

Wine, a liquid that cannot be concentrated and that is customarily packed in glass bottles.

always hazardous and accident-prone; so, too, was bottling in a large variety of cellar locations at the wine's eventual destination. Quality control was impossible to achieve. This is evident even at the highest levels, as a tasting of six bottles of Château Pétrus 1947 (five of them Belgian merchant bottlings) held in Bordeaux in March 1999 showed. Only the château-bottled version lived up to its reputation; the other five wines had partly or wholly disintegrated. Any tasting of pre-1970 burgundy, meanwhile, must always address the issue of possible inauthenticity. For ordinary wines, transport-related quality variations would have been greater still. The insistence on château-bottling by Baron Philippe de Rothschild for Château Mouton-Rothschild as early as 1924 was prescient. Château-bottling, surprisingly enough, only became obligatory for classed-

The introduction of bottling at source has, indeed, been so significant that it has changed the pattern of wine consumption.

growth Bordeaux in 1972, and merchants' reputations for the first half of the 20th century were established as much by the quality of their bottlings as by their purchasing astuteness. It is hard, at the end of the century, to understand the fierce resistance Rothschild met when he first suggested château-bottling. 'Why, then,' he wrote in his 'autobiography' *Milady Vine* by Joan Littlewood, (Jonathan Cape, 1984) 'were we shipping the wines at the most critical period of their lives? Anything might become of them in the wine merchants' sheds. Three years' maturation in a strange environment, at the very time we were responsible for nursing the precious juice. Had we ever known exactly what was going into those bottles which carried our labels? It wasn't good enough.'

Bordeaux *négociant* Christian Cruse declared that the Baron's plan for château-bottling would mean 'the ruination of the wine trade'; Berry Bros & Rudd, London's oldest merchants, declared that their reputation had been impugned by the proposal. Yet, winemaking advances aside, it is the single element that has most improved the quality of good wine during the 20th century.

A PIPE ON THE QUAYSIDE

The introduction of bottling at source has, indeed, been so significant that it has changed the pattern of wine consumption.

One of the most vivid of 19th century wine controversies came to a head in 1844. *A Word or Two about Port Wine* was the pamphlet's innocuous title. Its author was Baron Joseph James Forrester, 'Douro Farmer and British Merchant'. Forrester accused his fellow port producers of defiling the pure, natural, unfortified and unsweetened wine of the Douro with poor-quality brandy and elderberry juice. The truest port, Forrester argued, was what (this is my example, not his) Samuel Johnson and James Boswell had enjoyed on the night of June 25th to 26th, 1763. Between nine o'clock in the evening and one-thirty in the morning, they drank two bottles between them in London's Mitre tavern while discussing whether or not Colly Cibber was a blockhead, Johnson's belief in ghosts, and Boswell's possible perambulation of Spain. We would call it Douro table wine.

More popular by Forrester's day was port as we now know it, fortified part-way through fermentation, thereby arresting the yeast's activities and leaving the wine toothsomely sweet. It is generally assumed that Forrester lost his side of the argument because drinkers preferred a sweet, strong wine to a lighter, dry one; there may be some truth in this. It is no less true, though, that pipes of fortified port would have arrived in a reliably stable condition on the Bristol quayside, protected by their brandy from the hazards of the journey, whereas pipes of Douro table wine would, on occasion, have leaked, oxidized and turned acetic. Sales materials in the age when wines were shipped in casks constantly stress 'freshness'; the newest wines were the best.

The fortunes of fortified wine have undergone a steady decline during the 20th century: they once represented a substantial proportion of internationally traded wines, but now unfortified table wines are vastly more important. This is to some extent a question of taste: in the age of the car and the gym, not everyone wants to sip wines which contain as much as 20 per cent alcohol. More important, though, is the fact that most table wines can now be relied upon, in large part because of bottling at source, to be consistent and fault-free (if not always of excellent quality). Fortified wines have lost, during the 20th century, their unique selling point: a near-monopoly on reliability and consistency.

WHAT'S IN A NAME?

In my attic, I have a small label collection which dates back to the period in which I first became interested in wine: 1973–76. The most treasured label reads, simply enough: Châteauneuf-du-Pape, Grand Vin de Bourgogne.

'The penalty of virtue,' wrote Raymond Postgate in *A Plain Man's Guide to Wine* (Michael Joseph, 1951), 'is to be imitated. Some of the finest and most famous red wines in the world have the misfortune to have easily remembered names. Therefore Volnay, Pommard and Beaune are among the most frequently forged names in the world. He is a rash man who buys a bottle with nothing but one of those bare names on the label; he would be lucky, between the wars at any rate, to be served nothing worse than a Rumanian or Algerian red.' Even Postgate, having cautioned the reader against fraudulent burgundy, then goes on to describe the flavour of the real thing as being, by comparison with Bordeaux, 'fuller, sweeter and heavier'. This is a comparison no drinker or producer of red burgundy today would recognize. Authentic red burgundy is, compared with Bordeaux, an aerial wine, a wine of grace and perfume, its power often concealed within the lightest of lineaments. A red burgundy which is full, sweet and heavy is a fake.

It was no accident that two-thirds of all internationally traded wine in the 1950s crossed the Mediterranean between Alger and Oran and Sète's Quai d'Alger. This was the climax to a trade which began in the 19th century, during the phylloxera crisis. In 1938, Algeria (then part of France) had 400,000 hectares under vine. The red wine of France's North African colonies probably found its way into most of the mainland's reds, especially those thought too light for the market due to climatic inclemency or overcropping. It was routinely blended, for example, into inexpensive Bordeaux during the first two decades of the 20th century; merchants such as the Gilbeys felt the wines were much better for the addition.

Regional names like Chablis, Hermitage and Burgundy itself were widely used as stylistic descriptors in most wine-producing countries regardless of the origin of the wine; some, indeed, still are. Maurice Healy fulminated against advertisements in the London Underground during the 1930s which employed a quotation from George Meredith praising the splendours of great burgundy in order to sell 'Australian Burgundy'. Those who worked in the bottling halls of wine merchants, even as late as the 1970s, were used to seeing single consignments of bulk wine arrive and leave under, say, three different labels of origin and with four different vintages. Put simply, for most of the 20th century, the further a wine travelled from its cellar of origin, the more likely it was to be inauthentic.

This was not merely human deviousness. The three great cataclysms of powdery mildew, downy mildew and phylloxera at the end of the 19th century profoundly disrupted the world's wine trade; parched markets were supplied with wine from any available source, which was sold under the names most familiar to the purchasers (who in any case had never had any option but to take authenticity on trust). Consumers have always preferred good wine to bad, so if cheap Bordeaux could be improved by the addition of 20 per cent Tlemcen (an Algerian appellation), why not? Nonetheless a consensus grew that these abuses needed to be addressed. France's first legal definition of wine dates from 1889 (the Loi Grippe, which declares that wine 'is the product only of the fermentation of fresh grapes'); German wine law was first formulated in 1892 and revised

Authentic red burgundy is, compared with Bordeaux, an aerial wine, a wine of grace and perfume.

in 1909; Italy's first wine law came into being in 1904. The initial legislative impulse was simply to ensure that wine was wholesome, made only from grapes, and (beginning in France in 1905) that it came from where it claimed to come from.

This system of 'appellations' predated *Appellations d'Origine Contrôlée* (AOCs) by 30 years; Bordeaux, for example, was defined in 1911. As Australian wine authorities discovered in attempting to define the boundaries of Coonawarra in the 1990s, though, this can be an extremely controversial matter.

△ Over 2,800 bottles – the traditional straw-jacketed *fiaschi* – make up the spectacular centrepiece of this early 1930s Chianti festival.

Champagne was a region where such legislative controls were badly needed. Even reputable Champagne houses bought grapes from Chablis; less scrupulous producers used Picpoul grapes grown in the Midi to make their 'Champagne', and local growers often struggled as a consequence despite the high prices for which such 'Champagne' was sold. An appellation was required, and in February 1911, the authorities took the view that the wines of the Aube region, 110 kilometres from Epernay, should be excluded from this. Thirty-six local mayors immediately resigned; the growers marched on Bar-sur-Aube, and an effigy of the prime minister was burned. In April, the government backed down, allowing wine from the Aube once again to be called Champagne. This in turn led to a mob marching on Epernay, where a squadron of cavalry blocked their route;

the demonstrators made for Aÿ, and by the end of the day 41 buildings or warehouses had been ransacked. There was new, restrictive legislation in place again by 1914, with the Aube now classified not as Champagne proper but as a 'Second Zone'. Eventually, in 1927, the Aube was restored to full membership of the Champagne club.

Needless to say, merely delimiting the boundaries of a region was not enough, in itself, to prevent sub-standard wine being produced there. After phylloxera, many French vineyards, for example, were planted with 'safe', hybrid vines which produced large quantities of mediocre wine. Châteauneuf-du-Pape has always been one of those 'easily remembered names' to which Postgate alluded, and it was in 1923 that its growers formed a kind of self-help group to improve the quality of genuine

Châteauneuf, under the leadership of Baron Le Roy de Boiseaumarie. The new Châteauneuf regulations went much further than mere geographical delimitation: grape varieties were specified (even if the list stretched, famously, to no fewer than 13 varieties); training systems, pruning requirements and minimum alcoholic strength were also regulated. There was to be no more Châteauneuf *rosé*.

The Châteauneuf regulations became a model for France's entire AOC system when, faced with continuing over-production and fraud, it came into being in the mid-1930s. Not only was the geographical area for a particular wine delimited, but so, too, were its grape varieties, yields, alcoholic strength, and even certain aspects of viticulture and vinification. The AOC system remained the backbone of French wine law until the 1950s, when the category of *Vin Délimité de Qualité Supérieure* (VDQS) was added: this was a scheme for 'apprentice' AOCs. More fundamental changes came in 1973 when the *vin de pays* category was born, as a ladder of incentive for non-AOC wine producers to use to haul themselves out of the mire of *vins de table*. Greater flexibility in choice of grape variety was permitted to producers of these higher-yielding 'country wines' than to AOC producers, and labels could state those varieties. This was forbidden to producers of AOC wines, since the idea that a wine tasted of its grape varieties rather than its place of origin ran counter to *terroir*-based AOC philosophy.

In the early days of *vin de pays*, this acknowledgement of variety represented a relatively minor difference between the two categories. However, the varietal wines of countries like the United States, Australia, New Zealand, South Africa, Chile and Argentina have achieved spectacular success in many of France's traditional export markets during the 1980s and 1990s. Younger consumers in particular find purchase choices based on grape variety more meaningful and comprehensible than purchase by region of origin, and this has helped varietal *vins de pays* to compete successfully with theoretically 'superior' AOC wines (and even helped to eclipse the notion of *terroir* itself). Nearly 100 regional *vins de pays*

names exist, promising the consumer some sense of local character, yet most of these remain unused or of strictly local interest. Instead it is the near-meaningless departmental or regional *vins de pays* names such as Vin de Pays d'Oc or Vin de Pays de l'Hérault which are ubiquitous,

For most of the 20th century, France's AOC system has served both wine consumers and producers well.

together with international grape variety names such as Chardonnay, Cabernet Sauvignon or Merlot. To call them France's New World wines is to state the obvious: they are varietal wines whose character and style are conditioned by the aspirations and abilities of the winemaker.

For most of the 20th century, France's AOC system has served both wine consumers and producers well, and for this reason it has been widely imitated by the wine legislators of other European countries such as Italy, Spain and Portugal. It helped consumers since it put a stop to fraudulent French wines and pointed most of the honest winemakers in the general direction of quality. (It could never, alas, guarantee quality, not even in those cases where appellation regulations require a tasting panel to approve all wine before sale. Local politics always take precedence over questions of quality; local palates are not international palates; and wine law is, in any case, impossible to police efficiently.) It served producers well since appellations gave individual small growers a 'brand' to sell under, and therefore enabled

Varietals whose character and style are conditioned by the aspirations and abilities of the winemaker.

them to compete on roughly equal terms with large merchants and bottlers. The fact that tens of thousands of obscure and modestly-resourced wine-farmers across Europe have been able to export and sell their wines throughout the world during most of the 20th century is a remarkable triumph over the customary laws of the marketplace. Without AOC and its equivalents, this would not have happened.

◁ In the early 20th century Australian 'Empire' wines were shipped in large casks to far-flung destinations.

▷ The French port of Pauillac, now used mainly by fishing boats, was a point of exchange for exports and imports of wine at the start of the 20th century.

◁ Movement of wine in barrel from docks to the wine merchant's vaults was a common practice until the 1960s.

▷ The Bordelais introduced the 225-litre (50-gallon) oak *barrique* or *barrica* when they left phylloxera-ridden France to build wineries in Spain in the late 19th century.

▷ The 'barco rabelo' was the most practical way to bring young ports from the quintas in the Douro Valley to the port lodges in Vila Nova de Gaia until 1953, when the river was dammed.

▽ Christmas, 1946: casks of table wine, sherry and port await customs inspection at London Docks.

△ Kym Milne MW, Australian oenologist, consultant and flying winemaker, operates in a dozen countries.

During the last two decades of the 20th century, though, the limitations of the system have become apparent. Many of Italy's finest wines began to be made outside the framework provided by the country's DOC (*Denominazione di Origine Controllata*) system since its laws, in codifying tradition, sanctioned practices which held quality in check (poor choice of grape varieties, for example, or over-long barrel ageing). There is a growing sense within the international wine community that European wine law is overly proscriptive, that what may have been a good solution to the problems of the first half of the 20th century no longer addresses the requirements of modern consumers. Yet many of those who work within the system are fiercely supportive of it, since they know that their own survival depends on it, and since it expresses the philosophy of 500 years or more of European winemaking. Europe's most celebrated appellations will unquestionably survive, undergoing necessary revisions from time to time to improve quality and intensify the focus on *terroir*. Europe's less well-known appellations, by contrast, face an uncertain future. The choice will be between slow shrinkage, catering to an increasingly local market, or a switch away from the difficult pursuit of *terroir* to produce the simpler, fruit-dominated, branded varietal wines which will monopolize inexpensive international wine sales in the first part of the 21st century.

Geographical delimitation of growing areas is well under way in the United States and in southern hemisphere wine-growing countries, but choice of grape varieties, yield and production methods are always regarded there as matters for the individual producer. Given these freedoms, given the fact that an intimate understanding of site takes many decades to acquire, and given the highly competitive, 'brand-first' philosophy of most producers in these countries, such geographical delimitations seem likely to remain only modestly meaningful for the first half of the 21st century.

MOVING PEOPLE

Kym Milne MW is an Australian based in Britain, who supervises winemakers and makes wine himself around the world – most of his clients are supermarkets in the United Kingdom. Here is his 1999 travel schedule:

January: lecturing, United Kingdom.
February: blending, Italy and California.
March: blending, Hungary; consulting, Sardinia.
April: consulting, Spain; blending, South Africa.
May: Wine Trade Fair, United Kingdom.
June: Vinexpo, France.
July: planning vintage, Italy; blending, New Zealand.
August: planning vintage, Hungary; winemaking, California.
September: winemaking, Italy.
October: wine-judging, Australia; blending, Italy.
November: planning vintage, South Africa; blending, Hungary and Italy.
December: blending, California; Christmas in New Zealand/Australia.

Air travel may be of little or no significance in terms of moving wine from country to country, but it has been hugely significant in improving the quality of that wine. It has made human expertise itself mobile. There was, at the beginning of the 20th century, relatively restricted contact between those who made wine and those who sold it. The winemaker followed ancestral methods, learned from father and grandfather; quality (or the lack of it) depended on nature's whim. Letters passed between agents and brokers, detailing the niceties of supply and demand; casks of wine crossed seas and frontiers as a consequence. The first sniff that the selling community generally had of a new vintage would have been on the quayside.

During the 1920s and '30s, the more adventurous merchants began to journey to vineyards and meet growers; neither, though, presumed to interfere much in the work of the other. Charles Walter Berry's *In Search of Wine* (Sedgwick and Jackson, 1987), the lengthy jottings of a wine merchant taken during a 1934 journey around France's vineyard areas, shows its author to have been an assiduous taster and gourmet, but in matters of viticulture and vinification little more than a well-informed and curious tourist.

Travel swiftly became easier during the 1960s and '70s, as did telephone communication. This

◁ Angela Muir MW, who pioneered the tailoring of mostly Eastern European wines to suit British tastes and pockets.

enabled wine merchants to discover and purchase from small growers without the intermediary of an agent, should they wish; it also meant that the purchasing community began to understand the principles of wine production more intimately than had ever been possible before. It brought the growers to meet

◁ Michel Rolland, one of a new breed of consultants, supervises the entire winemaking process from vineyard to bottling line.

△ Robert Parker, the world's most influential wine critic, devised the controversial 100-point scale, based on the American system where 50 = 0.

the eventual consumers of their wines, too, so allowing them to gauge the reaction of non-local drinkers to their products.

In 1987, a British mail-order wine merchant called Tony Laithwaite took this purchasing interactivity a step further. He and others were already making stylistic requests to wine producers; his next idea was to bring over Australian or Australian-trained winemakers, under-employed during winter in the southern hemisphere, to make wine in southern French cooperatives using local grapes vinified by Australian techniques. The results proved very popular with Laithwaite's customers and, provided the arrangements were made sensitively enough not to bruise local pride, everyone benefited from such joint-venture approaches to wine production.

Lees handling and the use of oak products for richness of flavour proved popular with consumers.

'Flying Winemakers' was the name chosen by Laithwaite to christen the series of wines commissioned in this way, and his example was quickly followed by others; by the end of the 1990s, it was not unusual for ten per cent or more of British supermarket wine offerings to have been created by itinerant, non-resident winemakers working with selected local fruit. The techniques used were preponderantly Australian, with an emphasis on hygiene, the use of enzymes, and adjustment of alcohol and acid balances to obtain clean fruit flavours in varietal wines. Lees handling and the use of oak products for richness of flavour proved popular with consumers, too.

This exchange of ideas was not unidirectional, though; the northern hemisphere had a winter, too. Bordeaux's Jacques and François Lurton were leading suppliers of such wines to British supermarkets during the 1990s, while for more expensive and ambitious wines the Pomerol-based consultant Michel Rolland became a figure of international importance during the same period.

These winemaking journeys had an enormous and sometimes controversial influence on the stylistic evolution of wine during the late 20th century. Critics alleged that they imposed a stylistic homogeneity on wine at all levels, exaggerating the importance of the winemaker and eroding any sense of *terroir* in such wines. Indeed, in vulnerable and underdeveloped winemaking communities such as those of Eastern Europe they may even extinguish long-standing winemaking traditions altogether.

This seems, on balance, a needlessly pessimistic view. Flying winemakers such as Kym Milne MW, Hugh Ryman and Jacques Lurton have helped many winemaking communities evolve and develop a basic oenological literacy far faster than they would otherwise have done. They have won valuable foreign sales, too, with attendant investment implications. Even stylistically, they have in general broadened the horizon of possibilities.

In early 1999, for example, a tasting of the wine range of the Argentinian producer Trapiche revealed at least three different stylistic approaches: traditional local styles (sturdy wines given long wood ageing); Australian-influenced styles made in collaboration with Peter Bright and his winemakers (fruity wines with brisk acid balance and palpable oak influence); and French-influenced styles made in collaboration with Michel Rolland (ripe, softly balanced wines without added acidity and with discreet use of oak). It seems likely that, out of this play of possibilities, a more settled sense of stylistic individuality will eventually emerge with time, in much the same way as the true viticultural potential of individual sites also needs many growing seasons to reveal itself.

DROPPING THE VEIL

Winemakers and wine merchants are not the only ones who can fly; so, too, can wine journalists and consumers themselves.

Wine's unique property of lending a flavour to tiny nuances of geography makes it perhaps the most complicated agricultural product known to man. Fine wines have always been consumed by the wealthy and the educated, and latterly by those living far from the exact site in which such wines are produced; its conviviality makes it an object of great affection among consumers. Put all these factors together, and you have a rich field of material for poets, prose writers and journalists to cultivate. Wine writing has found a lively market among the reading public from Roman times onward. Just as the number of those drinking and enjoying wine has greatly increased over the course of the 20th century, so has the number of those writing about it. Indeed, because of its complications, the two communities are closely interlinked: wine needs explanation in a way that meat or cabbage does not. The opportunities provided by air travel have enabled wine writers and journalists to raise the public awareness of wine's intricacies enormously, and this in turn has stimulated wine tourism and wine purchase directly from vineyards. It has also affected the quality of wine itself.

During the first half of the century, writers in English on wine tended to fall into one of two groups. The first was a set of amateurs and connoisseurs who reminisced about the wines they had drunk during long and comfortable lives spent in other activities such as academia (George Saintsbury) or the law (Maurice Healy). The second group was composed of professional writers who felt they could be of most use to the 'ordinary' reader by trying to explain wine's complexities (such as André Simon, Raymond Postgate and Rupert Croft-Cooke). It was this latter role which was undertaken by the century's two greatest wine writers, Hugh Johnson and Jancis Robinson MW, both of whom documented with great accuracy, intricacy and intelligence the dramatic changes which the wine world was undergoing during the century's final three decades. This, if you like, was the century's 'classical' wine writing. It informed; it inspired; it incited the reader to undertake journeys of discovery armed with succinctly formulated background knowledge. It did not, though, generally undertake to change the wine world, or to pronounce objectively about matters of taste.

Wine's unique property of lending a flavour to tiny nuances of geography makes it perhaps the most complicated agricultural product known to man.

During the last two decades of the century this restrained and anti-polemical approach to wine writing was superseded by a more engaged, consumerist approach practised with most spectacular success by Robert M Parker. Parker, who styles himself a wine critic rather than a wine writer, claims that the objective, professional assessment of wine quality is possible. In his books and his newsletter *The Wine Advocate*, Parker passes verdicts on the wines he tastes, describing their flavours in systematic analogical language and awarding them points out of 100.

Parker's approach has proved hugely popular with wine consumers. He does not want for rivals either within America (where writers for the influential magazine *Wine Spectator* and those producing rival newsletters all adopt the same approach) or in Europe (Britain's Clive Coates MW and France's Michel Bettane and Thierry Desseauve are all taster-assessors in the Parker mould, albeit less trenchant and more diplomatic in their opinions). Parker, though, is unquestionably the dominant critical force in the wine world. At a minor level, newspaper wine columns in every wine-drinking country around the world are increasingly filled with shopping-list assessments of everyday wines. It is as if the era of explanation has ended and the era of assessment superseded it absolutely.

Most of this writing, while it helps move certain parcels of stock swiftly and is thus useful to retailers and producers (who support it with extensive sampling programmes), leaves the wine

Critics allege that the financial implications of Parker's verdicts are so significant that no European fine-wine producer can afford to ignore them, making him a stylistic dictator.

world fundamentally unchanged. Most tasters are gratifyingly inconsistent in the wines they back, and the inexpensive wines celebrated in their columns are in any case ephemeral. Parker's writing, though, has had major consequences for Europe's fine-wine producers; indeed his judgements made the market for the world's largest pool of fine wine, red Bordeaux, during the last 15 years of the 20th century.

Critics allege that the financial implications of his verdicts are so significant that no European fine-wine producer can afford to ignore them, making him a stylistic dictator. His tastes are perceived to be for deeply coloured, richly flavoured wines of overwhelming intensity but unsubtle character: low-acid, 'inky-monster' reds and densely fruited, super-succulent whites. Parker, in other words, is slowly turning the fine-wine world into a caricature of what it should be, sowing an inflationary trail for the winner wines and leaving the losers impoverished and misunderstood. Since many of the wines assessed by Parker are still years away from maturity, history will be his final judge. The excitement and market-making which Parker's work has generated, though, has brought publicity and prosperity to the fine-wine community as a whole; few would dispute that the overall quality of Bordeaux's greatest wines is higher at the end of the 20th century than it was at any time during it, and Burgundy, the Rhône Valley, Piemonte and Tuscany are also all flourishing, thanks in part to the form-making provided by his regular assessments.

Parker has consistently campaigned against routine technological interventions in the winemaking process such as clumsy acid adjustments, heavy-handed chaptalization, and the unnecessary fining and filtration of already stable young wines; his emphasis on the necessity of ensuring adequate ripeness in winemaking fruit has improved many under-performing European wines immeasurably. He has also waged a long campaign for lower yields in fine-wine production, and is a great believer in, and supporter of, the expression of *terroir* rather than intrusive winemaking in fine wine (though some believe that his criticism has had the opposite effect, for example, in Bordeaux). No palate is infallible, but among wine producers and consumers alike Parker has many more admirers than detractors.

The flood of wine writing of all sorts over the last two decades of the century has had the beneficial effect of demystifying wine production, and this in turn has led to a boom in wine tourism. For some regions (such as Bulgaria or Romania), this is only of theoretical benefit. For other areas, by contrast, like much of California and Oregon and populous parts of France, Spain and Italy, direct sales to visitors are extremely important; this, indeed, is the most profitable method of selling wine. The personal involvement felt by those purchasing wine directly from a vineyard inspires loyalty, too.

Ironically, however, the more sought-after a wine is, the less likely it is to be sold direct to callers (top Burgundy domaines and the châteaux of Bordeaux's classed growths never sell wine directly to visitors). For such wines, the only sales problem is that of allocation. Producers need to ensure that their wine is drunk around the world by those who will most appreciate it, thereby assuring its future price-stability and growth. European producers in this happy situation generally sell either through a long-established market system such as the Bordeaux *place* (an informal stock market run by *négociants* and brokers) or through a network of local agents in foreign markets. In the USA and in some southern hemisphere markets, such wines can be satisfactorily allocated by use of a mailing list for direct mail-order sales.

THE RISE OF THE DESERT VINEYARD

As we saw at the beginning of this essay, many of the 'new' winemaking areas whose wines have had such international impact during the last three decades of the 20th century are not new at all. What has brought them to the prominence they now enjoy is vastly improved viticulture, winemaking and packaging skills combined with easy, low-cost transport. The proximity of producer and consumer, hugely important in 1900, is almost irrelevant in 2000. In a growing world wine market, all have found their place, and an unprecedented choice is now available to consumers in wine shops and merchants' lists. A happy prospect, then?

Supposing that the world wine market does indeed keep growing, few wine growers need fear for for their children's livelihoods. If the market remains static, though, the scene takes on a cloudier aspect.

Many of the smaller wine-growers of Europe do, in fact, face a bleak future, and in particular those trying to make a living on the fringes of well-known areas or in areas with a marginal wine-growing climate. Most inexpensive wines from Australia, Chile, Argentina, South Africa and the United States are made from irrigated fruit grown in semi-desert or desert conditions. Vines could not naturally survive in such environments. Once irrigation water is available, though, these become some of the least problematic wine-growing sites in the world, well-adapted to large-scale, low-cost, highly mechanized production methods. The consistency and reliability of their fruit, moreover, makes them perfectly suited to the production of branded wines. Brands can be promoted and marketed in a way that individual growers' wines, or even entire appellations, cannot; once successful, they provide maximum profitability for shareholders and investors, who are thus encouraged to reinvest and build the brand further.

The characteristic inconsistency of many of Europe's wines is based on unpredictable summer and early autumn weather. It exasperates a sizeable proportion of consumers, who turn with gratitude to consistent, standardized wine brands from Australia or California. Tastes are changing, too: an older generation may have enjoyed the piercing acidity and neutral fruit of a Muscadet,

the light, curranty vividness of a Beaujolais-Villages or the cherry-stone freshness of a good Valpolicella, but such cool-climate wines may well taste over-slender and tartly dry to consumers who cut their wine teeth on bottles of Lindeman's Bin 65 Chardonnay or Gallo Zinfandel. It seems likely that branded wines made from the

The proximity of producer and consumer, hugely important in 1900, is almost irrelevant in 2000.

'industrial' fruit of irrigated, hot-climate, desert vineyards will increasingly dominate inexpensive wine sales, and that growers in northern Europe's less successful or less prestigious vineyard areas will suffer as a consequence.

The other area in which major change seems likely is in the way in which wine is bought. Its weight and bulk means that it is less well-suited than most products to being bought in a 'live' retail environment; bottle shops may have a future where adjacent parking is made available, but classic British high-street wine merchant or off-licence premises seem unlikely to survive far into the next century.

The Internet, by contrast, lends itself well to wine sales just as it does to book sales. Indeed, supposing that the considerable bureaucratic difficulties which at present prevent the free movement of wine from one country to another (and even, in the USA, from one state to another) were removed, then the Internet seems perfectly tailored for direct wine purchase. It may even

It exasperates a sizeable proportion of consumers, who turn with gratitude to consistent, standardized wine brands from Australia or California.

help preserve the livelihoods of some small growers who are likely to find access to markets through conventional routes difficult in the years ahead. Governments, however, make considerable tax revenues from alcoholic products like wine, and there are politicians who, in spite of the evidence of at least 4,000 years of healthful wine drinking, still regard it as a dangerous drug. The truly free movement of wine from one country to another will not come quickly.

New technology has revolutionized winemaking practices all over the world. Winemakers can now access a body of knowledge and a palette of techniques that offer creative possibilities once undreamt of. The results are fascinating.

Wine, Science & Technology

James Halliday

Although the impact of technological innovation – in the vineyard as well as the winery – has been hard to underestimate, it is important to recognize from the outset that there isn't one wine industry, but two. The first is concerned with the making and sale of beverage wine;

The first is concerned with the making and sale of beverage wine; the primary consideration for the customer here will be the retail price.

the primary consideration for the customer here will be the retail price. Typically such wine will account for over 90 per cent of a given retail market. The second is the fine (or premium or super-premium) wine industry. Here the product's cachet or breeding, style and quality (actual or perceived) will be the primary determinants of the consumer's decision to purchase.

Technology has been and will continue to be crucial to the development of both sectors, but the relevance of particular aspects will vary greatly between sectors. Confusion about its role is widespread, and is frequently at the heart of emotional attacks on its use. At the macro level, technology has transformed the very nature of beverage wine, or *vin ordinaire*, as it used to be called. The extent and degree of its impact accelerated exponentially in the last two decades of the 20th century. For better or worse, much of the responsibility has been laid at the door of New World winemakers and their winemaking techniques.

The changes will have attracted scant attention from the average consumer of such wine, but have been crucial in influencing the decisions of importers, distributors, wholesalers and retailers in countries such as the United Kingdom and Sweden. The impact on the domestic markets of Italy, France, Spain and Argentina has been less marked, but with the increasing globalization of the trade in wine of all kinds, change will inevitably come.

INFORMATION: A DECISIVE TOOL

It is tempting to say that technology has played a less important role in the making of the great wines, but it isn't so simple. For a start, another important distinction has to be made between the use of technology to provide information, and its use to create or influence the quality or a style of a wine. The more prestigious the producer, the more likely it is

to employ sophisticated weather stations in its vineyards, and a high-technology laboratory in its winery. But such gadgetry doesn't dictate or prescribe a response, it simply provides the basis for an informed choice.

The scene for the information century began to take shape around 1860 when Louis Pasteur correctly identified the steps in the biochemical process of fermentation, and no less importantly, the ravages of post-fermentation oxidation. In the early years of the 20th century, research scientists were able to observe and explain all the steps in the process of fermentation, and in particular the causative role of yeast.

Pasteur bypassed any study into what we now know as the malolactic fermentation, probably because he was unaware of its existence or significance. The first detailed study of this so-called secondary fermentation (which normally occurs in whole or in part after the end of the primary fermentation) was carried out by Professor Ribereau-Gayon

in the 1930s. Relatively little publicity was given to his work, and in Australia Dr John Fornachon carried out similar research in 1943. Alan Hickinbotham, another Australian, published research in 1948 showing the link between the pH of wine and the malolactic fermentation. Up to this point there was little understanding, in Australia or Europe, of the importance of pH and the linked level of acidity.

The malolactic fermentation (MLF) involves the bacterial conversion of malic acid (a stronger acid) into lactic acid (softer and weaker).

The malolactic fermentation (MLF) involves the bacterial conversion of malic acid (a stronger acid) into lactic acid (softer and weaker); carbon dioxide (CO_2) is also created and released as part of the process, just as it is during the primary fermentation. It is accompanied by a rise in the pH, which (alongside the level of alcohol), is

△ Labour-intensive cultivation in Champagne, where even today machines are banned at harvest time and al picking is by hand.

△ Young wines being racked from large, old casks. Most houses now use stainless-steel tanks, though some favour oak barrels to keep batches separate for use in complex blends.

the most important chemical measure of a wine. The pH is a logarithmic scale reflecting the amount of active acid present in a wine, and has many implications for both the wine's sensory character and its susceptibility to bacterial attack.

Almost all red wines undergo MLF; in an uncontrolled environment it is likely to commence in the autumn of the harvest year, then be brought to a halt by the winter cold,

MLF gave rise to the widely held French belief that the wines in the cellar responded in sympathy or unison with the spring bud-burst of the vines.

and recommence (and finish) the following spring. (It proceeds best at a wine temperature of 20°C (68°F), ceasing below 15°C (59°F).)

MLF gave rise to the widely held French belief that the wines in the cellar responded in sympathy or unison with the spring bud-burst of the vines. The observation was accurate, if the explanation was not.

It is a wholly desirable change in red wine, producing the essential element of softness in the taste profile. In cold climates, the pH will be lower at the start of the MLF, but may rise dramatically if the malic acid level of the wine was high. In warmer climates, the pre-fermentation pH is likely to be higher, but the dominant grape acid will be tartaric (unaffected by the MLF) and the rise in pH will be less marked. While winemakers in earlier eras trusted to chance and time to effect these transformations, the modern winemaker can turn our understanding of them to his advantage. He or she will know the precise composition of the acid components in the wine, and through this knowledge and prior experience, will adjust the acidity (usually by the addition of tartaric acid) during the primary fermentation. Provided it is done during this stage, and provided the pre-existing composition of the must was in reasonably good balance, I strongly assert that an expert taster cannot detect the difference between naturally occurring (tartaric) acid and added (tartaric) acid.

However, if the grapes were overripe or had a pH of 3.8 or above when they were picked, and heavy or late additions of acid are made, you will be able to taste the added acid character or, more probably, the underlying lack of quality in the base wine.

Most winemakers would seek to have a pH of between 3.4 and 3.6 for their red wines at the time of bottling. Below 3.4 there will be a tendency for the wine to be hard in the mouth; over 3.6 the wine will be more susceptible to bacterial spoilage and to age prematurely. A give-away of high pH in a young wine is a dull, slightly blackish edge to the colour; a low pH wine will normally be bright with purple-red hues.

With white and sparkling wine the incidence and the desirability of the MLF becomes much more controversial. I have already indicated the impact of temperature; sulphur dioxide (SO_2) has an equally great, if not greater, impact. Used in conjunction with temperature control and sterile filtration, it allows the maker to inhibit, in whole or in part, the MLF.

With aromatic wines such as Riesling or Gewürztraminer, and other early-bottled, steel-fermented wines such as Australian Semillon, total inhibition of the MLF is standard practice. The bright fresh acidity and low pH (3.0 to 3.2) are essential attributes of the wine and its capacity to age.

A POTENT INGREDIENT

It is with Chardonnay that the fun starts: MLF makes the texture of the wine softer and more complex, and alters the aroma and flavour by introducing nutty/creamy characters. Unless the maker busily re-introduces the acidity removed by the MLF, it will also reduce the acidity. In cold climates, that reduction will be part of the reason for encouraging the MLF in the first

place, and there will be no question of readjusting the acidity upward. But where MLF has been used against a background of initially low acidity, adjustment will be necessary.

The other consequence will be a reduction in the primary varietal fruit character of both the bouquet and palate. It is here that attitudes and practices vary significantly from one country to another. If, as in Burgundy, you start with flavour which is very concentrated and powerful, and acidity which is naturally high, the MLF will be

It is a prime example of the misuse of technology, of apeing the practices of Burgundy without understanding the underlying reasons for its use.

beneficial. I liken it to a sculptor with a mass of wet clay. If it is a large mass relative to the finished sculpture, the artist can hack away large pieces of clay without imperilling the shape of the finished work. If, however, there is only a small mass to start with, extreme care will have to be taken to conserve as much as possible of the raw clay; if not, there will be holes in the finished work, or it will be unable to support itself. Thus in certain parts of the world (both old and new) where Chardonnay has been a relatively recent introduction, the MLF has been encouraged without due consideration of the quality and characteristics of the base wine.

It is a prime example of the misuse of technology, of apeing the practices of Burgundy without understanding the underlying reasons for its use. It is a recipe for the production of wines boringly similar to each other, 'carbon copy spit-outs', as a Californian winemaker once described them to me.

Both the scientific and practical understanding of the mechanisms of the primary and secondary fermentations have provided the general backdrop to the progress of winemaking technique in the 20th century; almost all the other changes and advances are of lesser significance, however intense the level of debate may be as the new century opens. Somewhat arbitrarily, I will turn first to the use of oak. It is fashionable to suggest that up until the 1960s (or thereabouts) oak was seen purely as a maturation vehicle. In Italy and Germany it happened to be in the form of very large casks or vats; in France and Spain, small barrels ranging from *barriques* (225 litres) to *puncheons* (500 litres). It is true that the large vats had little or no impact on flavour, and that the evolution of the wine would be very slow; tartrate build-up on the inside of the casks would present a near-impermeable barrier; precipitation of solids rather than controlled oxidation would be the most significant change. But the impact of the flavour of new-oak barrels has long been known. The attitude to it varied enormously: in Jerez and Oporto the barrel is likely to have been 'seasoned' by the fermentation of a cheap white wine before being introduced into the main winemaking programme, but not so in Bordeaux or Burgundy. Here new barrels were regularly introduced, but not necessarily as part of the sort of structured programme taken for granted in the 1990s.

When Robert Mondavi made his pilgrimages to France in the 1960s in an effort to learn more about the choice of oak type and its use, he learnt far less than he had hoped. The winemakers he talked to regarded his questions

▽ Foot-treading newly harvested grapes in Portugal in 1951. Wines made in 'up-country' *quintas* are still trod in concrete *lagares*: the process is highly effective in extracting colour and tannin from the skins.

as strange: it was not their function to know whether the oak came from the forest of Tronçais, Nevers or Allier, even less what degree of toast was used in its making.

These were questions for the cooperage which had supplied the winery with oak for decades, and which knew what characteristics of the oak were required. Similarly, when Edmund Penning-Rowsell wrote his seminal guide to *The Wines of Bordeaux*, first published by Penguin in 1969, he observed 'only the top growths can afford these days to have entirely new casks every time, for they cost about £14 apiece. To spend nearly £10,000 a year on new casks as they do at Mouton, even for a bad vintage, is a formidable outlay. They must certainly make some difference to the style of the wine, for young oak does give a flavour quite distinct from the rather disagreeable taste of a wine which is "casky".' These comments to one side, Penning-Rowsell seldom makes any note of the use of new oak (or otherwise).

FLAVOUR OF FRUIT – OR OF OAK?

The progression of knowledge since that time has been remarkable. In the 1970s, many New World – particularly Californian – winemakers chose Limousin oak, much to the puzzlement of the French, who regarded it (rightly) as a coarse-grained oak suitable for Cognac, but not for quality table wine. Few use it these days; instead Nevers, Allier and Tronçais (from the centre of France) and Vosges are the favoured oaks.

Most recently of all, there has been a trend to specifying 'tight-grain' oak as the foremost requirement, rather than one forest or another. But prior to that, increasing knowledge of the importance of the level of toasting (or firing) during the making process led to the specification of low, medium or high toast, or even shades in between. Similarly, knowledge of the importance of ageing the staves has led to the distinction between kiln-dried and air-dried oak, and between two-year and three-year (or longer) air-drying.

Cynics tend to say that French coopers will be happy to supply whatever is ordered, secure in the knowledge that the customer has little

hope of recognizing the difference between one forest or another, let alone the degree of 'toast' or the method of stave preparation. There is an element of truth in this; it is better to place one's faith in the integrity of the cooper and on building a long-term relationship.

While Rioja has long embraced American oak (and busily egg-white fined most of its flavour out of the wine every year), it took Australian use of the oak to persuade American makers it was worthy of consideration. In the late 1940s and early '50s American oak was imported in bulk into Australia, and air-dried for

△ Oak chips and oak cubes allow winemakers to infuse the wine with oaky flavours without going to the trouble and expense of using good-quality oak barrels.

While Rioja has long embraced American oak it took Australian use of the oak to persuade American makers it was worthy of consideration.

up to five years before it was made into barrels using traditional making and firing methods. This gave a result dramatically superior to the machine-sawn, steam-bent barrels manufactured for the bourbon makers and which had given

American oak such a bad reputation. Now that French coopers have set up business in California to make American oak barrels, the situation has changed radically.

It hardly needs be said that these are matters for the producers of super-premium wines, and that at the beverage end of the scale oak flavour rarely, if ever, comes from barrels. Rather it comes in the form of oak cubes or oak chips

Enthusiasm and fervour are no substitutes for experience and sensitivity; the wine should be built around the fruit flavour of the grape, and not oak.

(legal in most countries) or possibly as powder or liquid essence (correspondingly illegal). To add spice, the cubes or chips are usually strongly toasted. The skill comes in measuring the level of oak extract needed and ensuring it is introduced in the primary fermentation. The aroma and initial palate flavour of such oak can be attractive, but the finish is often disastrous: coarse, bitter phenolics will obliterate typically modest fruit flavour. In other words, it has to be used with extreme discretion.

The over-arching question on oak remains: how much is good, and how much is too much. I suspect the answer is akin to that of consumers who talk dry and drink sweet; it is fashionable to decry the excessive use of oak, yet given a generously oaked Chardonnay or a Shiraz with no information about its provenance, it is inherently unlikely the average consumer will make any comment about the oak level, let alone reject or criticize the wine on this score. But expert tasters will. It all comes back to the skill of the winemaker, and the extent of his or her experience in handling oak. Anyone who was exposed to the Italian *barrique* phenomenon in the early 1980s will know what a parody can result. Enthusiasm and fervour are no substitutes for experience and sensitivity; the taste of wine should be built around the fruit flavours of the grape, and not oak.

Much the same issues arise across the broad spectrum of technology. German experiments before and after the Second World War in conserving fresh grape juice for prolonged periods by saturating it with CO_2 under pressure in stainless-steel tanks indirectly led to the computer-controlled, dimple-plate-jacketed stainless-steel fermenters of today; the winemaker can program the whole process of fermentation a month before vintage and thereafter sit in an office watching computer-generated printouts. Similarly, centrifuges, rotary drum vacuum filters, fine micron cartridge filters, earth filters and so forth can be used at will, the results promising minimal negative impact but having very positive implications for the ultimate quality of beverage wine. These are highly efficient, semi-industrial processes that can protect and enhance the modest colour, aroma and flavour of the product.

The same tools, the same methods, can be used in making super-premium wine. Here most winemakers would say that their task is to decide whether or not to use a given technological tool. Such winemakers would be expected to have a clear understanding of the result the technology is intended to produce and its impact on the style of the wine, and, above all else, to avoid derivative use ('the Burgundians use it, so we should too') of any tool or technique at all.

The best example of all is filtration. At one end of the spectrum Professor Emile Peynaud, the pre-eminent French oenologist, says 'the more a wine is clarified, the finer the filtration, the smoother and more supple the wine will taste. Filtration properly carried out does not strip or attenuate a wine; it clears it of internal impurities and improves it. To deny this is to say that a wine's quality is due above all to foreign substances in solution.'

At the other end critics such as Robert Parker (who has never in fact made wine) denounce its use as automatically and inevitably detrimental to a wine, even to the extent that he can determine before tasting the wine how many points he will deduct from the score he would otherwise have awarded.

Reality lies somewhere in the middle. If a wine has a bacterial population, is cloudy, or has residual sugar, the argument in favour of filtration is almost irresistible. But if it is star-bright and stable, there is no reason to subject it to a treatment which, if not expertly handled, may indeed oxidize or otherwise harm the wine, and which takes time and costs money.

A similar argument can be and is raised in relation to the use of cultured yeast. It is of course highly fashionable these days to proclaim the use of wild or indigenous yeast, often in combination with the denial of the use of filtration. The whole issue abounds with misconceptions, half-truths and complete fallacies. First, what is meant by wild yeast? Is it simply the yeasts which adhere to the skin of the grape in the vineyard? If so, such yeasts all expire when the fermentation has produced around two and a half to three degrees of alcohol. Thereafter different yeasts, probably winery residents and very likely descendants of commercial yeasts or isolates used years previously in the winery, will take over the job of fermenting the remaining sugar.

If there is a real benefit from the use of 'wild' or 'indigenous' yeasts (other than no cost) it will lie with the slower rate of fermentation. For small wineries without the means of cooling white wine fermentation in barrel, this becomes a significant advantage, for it also means the peak temperature will be lower.

FASHION AND FALLACY

The downsides of using wild yeasts are twofold. First, there is a significantly increased risk of 'stuck' fermentation with white wines; in other words, the last few grammes per litre of sugar are not converted to alcohol, leaving the wine with undesirable sweetness. Second, unpredictable levels of sulphide and/or volatile acidity may be produced by indigenous yeasts which have mutated between one vintage and the next.

The winemaker who carefully chooses a specific cultured yeast which he or she knows is particularly suited to the grape variety and the desired wine style is legitimately able to ask 'why should we throw away the knowledge gained through decades of painstaking research and instead opt for a game of Russian Roulette?' Moreover, I am convinced that the influence of

yeast on wine is largely transient (unless it has caused the formation of sulphides or volatile acidity). Any winemaker knows about the wonderful aromas produced by white wines during fermentation, and the less penetrating but more exotic aromas of red wine. These

△ The outer bark of the cork oak is harvested from mature trees once a decade and undergoes a long crying and treating process before being cut.

Why should we throw away the knowledge... and instead opt for a game of Russian Roulette?

characters may persist (in diminishing amounts) in the maturation phase in tank or cask, and be very evident in stainless-steel-fermented, early-bottled wines. However, after a year or so in bottle the 'yeasty' influence on a white wine

◁ A successful graft in this Californian vineyard will allow the Sauvignon Blanc rootstock to bear Cabernet Sauvignon grapes.

▷ Immense vine-straddling tractors have mechanized pruning, hedging and harvesting at large estates, but their use remains controversial.

2720

◁ Masks protect winery workers at Rutherford Hill winery in Napa Valley from sulphur as they fumigate the barrels to prevent bacterial infection.

▷ Stainless-steel tanks at the pioneering Orlando winery in South Australia, whose wide-ranging output is headed by the huge-selling Jacob's Creek.

△ Cleaning the press at one of Concha y Toro's many *bodegas* in Chile. This house also runs a joint venture with France's Mouton-Rothschild.

▷ Some Champagne houses still use manual *remuage* for their *cuvées de prestige*, but here at Domaine Chandon in California, fully automated *gyro-palettes* do the same job; computers record every manoeuvre.

disappears. Much the same happens with red wines, as often before bottling as after. As I have said, the notion that technology can deprive a wine of its personality is, to put it mildly, suspect. If the combination of site, climate and variety is inherently capable of producing a wine of real quality and character, technology (properly used) can only assist in revealing and protecting that character. The

It became fashionable to proclaim that great wine is made in the vineyard, and to view the role of the winemaker as a quality-control officer.

longer the wine is aged, the more that character will develop: 'technological' wines of common provenance may look similar in their youth, but over time their character will emerge.

Witness the revolution that has taken place in the wines of Burgundy and Chablis over the past 30 years. The traditional taster's description of Chablis (coined by English writers) was of a wine smelling of gunflint and with a taste reminiscent of sucking river pebbles. My own slightly more emotive descriptions of old 'artisan' white burgundies are (variously) scorched rat, dead rat and skunky old socks. In each instance (Chablis and burgundy) the primary cause was the excessive use of SO_2 combined with the warm fermentation of largely unclarified juice.

The amount of SO_2 used in making white burgundy and Chablis today is but a fraction of the levels used in the 1960s and earlier. It is no longer as easy as it once was to pick a young first-growth white burgundy from a top-end California or Australian Chardonnay in a blind tasting. However, any difficulty will disappear as the wines mature over a five- to ten-year period. The same changes, incidentally have transformed white Bordeaux and Sauternes.

Then there is the issue of clonal selection; if ever there were an example of the misuse of technology, this is it. Just as, at around the start of the 20th century, the Germans embarked on a disastrous programme of cross-breeding *vinifera* varieties to produce higher-yielding,

earlier-ripening vines, viticulturists around the world selected clones on the basis of higher yield rather than better quality. Similarly, rootstocks were selected for the vigour they imparted or, in the case of the foolhardy foray by Californian viticulturists into AXR-1 rootstocks (notoriously non-resistant to phylloxera), for ease of grafting.

To compound the problem, sensory analysis of the grapes produced from these new varieties, clones or rootstocks, was either not undertaken at all, or done on micro-vinifications (experimental vinifications of small batches) by poorly paid researchers who typically had little or no exposure to the great wines of the world. There was, in effect, a glass wall between the viticultural researchers and the winemakers.

By the start of the 1980s the problem was all too obvious, and researchers such as Professor Raymond Bernard of the University of Dijon began to wind back the hands of time, searching for clones which produced smaller berries, smaller bunches, lower yields and higher quality. It was also around this time that it became fashionable to proclaim that great wine is made in the vineyard, and to view the role of the winemaker as a quality-control officer. The incursion of the winemaker into the vineyard was a New World invention; in the Old World it had been the practice since the dawn of oenological time. Only in the 20th century did the wheels fall off the track in the Old World with misguided clonal and rootstock selection.

THE ROOTSTOCK DEBATE

In the resulting confusion, many *vignerons* came to the view that a blend of clones is preferable to a single clone. It is not always clear whether this is a risk management/financial preference, or an organoleptic one. About ten years ago Professor Bernard brought a series of Pinot Noirs to Australia; they were all made in the same way at the same cooperative winery from different clones grown on a single vineyard. The differences in quality and character were marked, but a clonal mix of the lesser wines – or all the wines – was not as good as a mix of the best clones or the best single clone. It seems an obvious point to make but it is a significant one: a clonal mix will not automatically produce a better wine.

At this level, only an extremely biased selection of new and unusual clones could possibly affect local character, or regional typicity, and even then you have to decide whether or not that character had intrinsic quality that was worthy of protection in the first place.

Where does all this leave us as we review the last century and launch into the next? First, there is a great deal of work to be done in the vineyard – and there's a monster lurking in the corner: the argument about genetic modification (GM) hasn't even begun. Here my hope is that healthy argument and discussion won't be stifled at birth.

At one extreme the organic and biodynamic grape-growers will point to the undoubtedly impressive achievements some have made, and no one in their right mind could do anything but praise those achievements and therefore the rationale. At the other extreme will be the proponents of GM.

The major thrust of GM research into vines has been to find ways to build in resistance to botrytis and the mildews, downy and powdery. There are also certain phytoplasmic and viral diseases of the vine for which there is no known chemical cure and which might be combated by altered genetics. The curious thing is that each approach has a common aim: the reduction of chemical inputs into the vineyard.

Cynical observers suggest it is important that the French make the GM breakthrough and start to licence the know-how. Those cynics suggest that successful New World pioneering might be met by the argument that the grape will have lost its varietal pedigree and will not be recognized as being Chardonnay, Cabernet Sauvignon or whatever the case may be.

THE SCIENCE OF RIPENESS

At a less technical – and less controversial – level, research continues into the precise mechanisms involved in the ripening of grapes, with a clear distinction being drawn between chemical and physiological ripeness. No longer do viticulturists use the crude measures of tonnes per acre or hectolitres per hectare, or even yield per vine, but rather square centimetres of functioning leaf area per gramme of grapes, winter pruning weight per kilo of grapes, and so on and so forth.

Increasing awareness of the importance of growing physiologically ripe grapes in a controlled-yield environment has been mirrored in the development of new fermentation aids and techniques in the winery.

The most glamorous and much talked about are the reverse osmosis concentration machines which are installed in great and not-so-great châteaux across the length and breadth of Bordeaux. In bygone days, the responses to a vintage diluted by ill-timed and excessive rain included cross-blending with either the preceding or succeeding vintage if either was

...development of new fermentation aids and techniques in the winery. The most glamorous and much talked about are the reverse osmosis concentration machines...

substantially riper or more concentrated. Alternatively, or in addition, part of the juice was run off from the fermentation vats immediately after the grapes were crushed.

Saignée (blood-letting), as the process is called, has ambivalent results. It certainly concentrates the remaining must, but, having used it with Pinot Noir, I know that it reduces the middle-palate vinosity of the wine, and typically increases the pH of the remaining must.

The reverse osmosis machines seem to be the perfect answer: they remove only water, thus preserving all the flavour constituents in the must, and not changing its pH or acidity. The word 'seem' is used advisedly; intelligent use in vintages swollen by rainfall will result in a significantly better wine. The problems may come in normal to good vintages; it will be all too easy to produce Bordeaux-on-steroids, with unnaturally deep colour and extract, not to mention alcohol and acidity.

△ Newly grafted vines await planting in the nursery bed. The 'scion' of the chosen variety, with its single bud, is dovetailed onto the selected rootstock.

Such wines will almost certainly lose typicity when young; only time will tell whether it will return when the wines mature 20 or 30 years down the track. Instinctively, I doubt it, but this may be of little concern to the château proprietor seeking 95 points from the major United States commentators, thereby ensuring a highly lucrative *en primeur* campaign.

Similar considerations apply to the use of cryo-extraction in Sauternes. Here, freezing the must allows differential extraction of water and the consequent concentration of the resulting wine. (Reverse osmosis, it seems to me, would be equally feasible.) Once again, restrained use in the lesser vintages can only produce better wine.

Wineries which look like refineries and are locked in a worldwide battle for market share will produce stereotypical, quasi-industrial wine.

The risk is that it will lead to earlier picking before botrytis has had a chance to work its full but dangerous magic. The uncertainty lies in untimely rain which converts 'noble rot' into ignoble (black or grey) rot, resulting in the loss of that part of the crop which is unpicked.

Early picking plus cryo-extraction will produce wine with the appropriate chemical composition of fully botrytised wines, but without the racy cut of botrytis. Another fermentation practice appeared in the mid-1980s, and – particularly in Burgundy – caused great controversy.

Guy Accad, Lebanese-born and trained, advocated the use of high levels of SO_2 (four to six times as high as conventional additions) in the must, aimed at delaying the onset of fermentation. Cold-soak, as it is called in the New World these days, or pre-fermentation maceration, relies on the extraction of anthocyanins (the coloured form of tannins) by the solvent action of SO_2 in an aqueous solution. Post-fermentation is designed to extract anthocyanins in an alcoholic solution, and to change their nature by polymerisation into what are called long-chain tannins.

TYPICITE AND TERROIR

The New World makers of Pinot Noir have used modified Accad methods with considerable success by using a combination of must-chilling and reduced (though still significant) levels of SO_2. Those makers are less affected by the principal controversy in Burgundy, which – as with reverse osmosis – is a loss of *typicité*. Accad's answer has always been to wait until the wines are mature, when their typicity (or their *terroir*) will express itself.

The irony is that this approach is as old as time. In the 19th century, before the appearance of cultured yeast, with traditionally high levels of SO_2 use, and before there was any question of warming (or cooling) ferments, the process of fermentation typically took a week or more to start. Moreover, Accad was merely seeking a short-term cure while his longer-term strategy – significantly reducing berry size, bunch weight and yield – could take effect. *Plus ça change*, indeed.

As for the wineries of this new century, they will reflect the business and marketing strategies of their proprietors. Wineries which look like refineries and are locked in a worldwide battle for market share will produce stereotypical, quasi-industrial wine. Here the aim will be akin to that of a brewery or distiller:

to produce a product which tastes the same day in, day out, year in, year out. At the other end of the spectrum are the wineries which produce hand-crafted wines with a high level of intellectual (and sometimes physical) input by their winemakers. There are in fact wineries (or groups under common ownership) which include both ends of the spectrum: Mondavi of California, Southcorp of Australia and, to a degree, the Mouton-Rothschild empire are notable examples.

The Mondavi group (with Woodbridge providing its 'industrial' wine) has shown how powerful synergies can be harnessed between big and small, between passion and discipline, risk and safety. It established a small winery working group at its main winery in the Napa Valley, with the aim of producing limited quantities of hand-crafted wines with no cost limitations and quality the sole criterion of success. The challenge was then thrown down to the main winery to produce wines with equal character and quality but in very much larger volume, and it has to be said the challenge was in large part answered.

Risk was very much part of the template, for Mondavi went a long way down the no-filtration path, discovering in so doing that the *brettanomyces* bacteria had a nasty habit of increasing its population in anaerobic conditions – that is, after the wine was bottled.

DEVELOPING 'PARALLEL' SYSTEMS

In Australia, Brown Brothers, a once small but now large family-owned and -run company took the Mondavi idea one step further by establishing its 'kindergarten' winery in a separate, purpose-designed winery with a crush-capacity of 250 tonnes (compared to the 10,000-plus tonne crush of the principal winery).

It features such ingenious ideas as giant aluminium airship-shaped balloons to capture the CO_2 emitted from the fermentation tanks, and then using that gas as a protective cover when handling wine which has completed its fermentation. The use of CO_2 and/or nitrogen is nigh on universal in modern wineries, large or small, when moving white wine around the winery. Its use is particularly critical when the wine is being bottled.

A final anecdote takes me back to the vineyard. In 1994, a group of winemakers from Burgundy came to Australia on a part-promotion and part-study tour. In the course of this they visited Coldstream Hills, which my wife and I had founded. They were tasting our 1993 Pinot Noir, and some of their conversation (in French) was overheard. One of the group pointed to the drip irrigation lines which run throughout the vineyard on the steep, bony mountain soils. 'Aha,' he exclaimed, 'you can taste the irrigation in the wine.'

The weather gods have never attended a viticultural school, and can be decidedly careless and unscientific in their watering of vineyards.

In fact, 1993 had a relatively wet summer, and we had not turned on the irrigation once. The weather gods have never attended a viticultural school, and can be decidedly careless and unscientific in their watering of vineyards. In 1993 the continuous supplies of god-given water increased berry size and bunch weight, and hence the Pinot Noir did indeed lack the intensity of the best vintages.

Those best vintages are years in which we have control over the amount of water, making sure it is just enough to keep the vine functioning efficiently up until *veraison*, but not enough to prompt growing tips on the canes and, least of all, to increase the size of the crop. Regulated deficit irrigation, or RDI, is very much part of contemporary viticulture.

The bottom line is that winemakers should put themselves in a position where they have a choice. The greatest range of choice will come in the first instance from a sound technological base. Thereafter true decisions, taken voluntarily rather than involuntarily, can be made, including ultra-artisan, non-interventionist techniques. When Giotto – one of the most famous Renaissance painters – was asked to prove he could decorate the roof of a cathedral, he provided a perfectly drawn freehand circle, and nothing else.

Winery owners and merchants were historically the 'big names',

but powerful new influences have fought their way to the forefront.

Winemakers, once the back-room boys, have asserted their authority,

and a wine critic's verdicts can determine a bottle's commercial future.

Movers
& Shakers

Stephen Brook

The wine world is crammed with larger-than-life personalities – winemakers, estate owners and even wine writers – but that was not the case a century ago. In 1900 the very notion of a winemaker was tenuous, and the recognizable names outside the narrow frontiers of the wine industry would have been those of major proprietors: the Antinoris or Frescobaldis in Tuscany; the grandees of Champagne; and the

The European concept of wine production revolves around the primacy of terroir.

powerful families, such as the Rothschilds, and the influential merchants, such as the Cruse and Barton clans, in Bordeaux.

Even today there is greater resistance to the concept of a winemaker in Europe than there is in the New World. The high-profile winemakers of California (Paul Draper, Helen Turley, Randall Grahm) or Australia (Brian Croser, Stephen Henschke, Paul Duval) don't have their counterparts in the Médoc. Who, one may well ask, is the winemaker at châteaux Beychevelle or Pontet-Canet? Bordeaux's influential figures tend to be *négociants* such as Christian Moueix, an entire class of château

proprietors such as the Lurton family, or impresarios such as Jean-Michel Cazes, who runs not only his own properties but also a clutch of top international estates belonging to the insurance giant AXA.

The European concept of wine production revolves around the primacy of *terroir*. Given the right patch of land, such as the gravelly undulations at Latour or the slatey scree of Wehlener Sonnenuhr, the wine can more or less be left to make itself.

In France, the methods of viticulture, harvesting, vinification and *élevage* were, until just a few decades ago, unvarying. A *chef de culture* kept an eye on the vineyards, decided when and how to prune and which treatments were necessary, and advised on the best time to harvest. And in the cellar a *maître de chai* would supervise the vinification, monitor the barrels, order the racking and fining and other cellar operations, and advise on when to bottle. But the style of the wine was determined by the varietal mix in the vineyard and by the nuances of soil and microclimate.

Nature, however, could not always be relied upon, and the men charged with nurturing the vines and wines could also err. In periods of crisis, the natural order came under greatest stress, either because of adverse climatic conditions or during periods of neglect when trade was bad. An increasingly scientific grasp of the processes of farming and vinification allowed for more effective human intervention.

DECISIVE ACTION

I like to imagine the moment when Russian-born oenologist André Tchelitscheff, lured from France in 1938 by Georges de Latour to take charge of Beaulieu Vineyards, walked in the door of the venerable Napa establishment. As he entered the Beaulieu winery, he found, even here at this most prestigious of Napa estates, a network of corrosion, rust and bacteria-infected vats.

Tchelitscheff moved decisively to demand the investment necessary to bring Beaulieu into the modern world. He knew about the importance of temperature control during the fermentation and had an instinctive understanding of malolactic fermentation. Latour agreed to his new winemaker's demands, and Tchelitscheff presided over a series of often magnificent wines until his retirement from Beaulieu in 1973. But that was not the end of his influence.

Over the next 20 years Tchelitscheff acted as a consultant to wineries throughout California and the Pacific Northwest. He had been giving technical advice to local wineries since 1947, and it is hard to think of a single figure in America who had a greater influence over the education and skill of generations of future winemakers.

There were, of course, distinguished professors at the Department of Viticulture and Oenology at the University of California at Davis, notably Maynard Amerine and Albert Winkler. Their advice and discoveries were considered highly important at the time – they devised the heat summation system for measuring climatic zones suitable for grape-growing – but with hindsight much of their advice proved mistaken and their quasi-scientific work flawed.

It was at another university, that of Bordeaux, that some truly pioneering work was undertaken. Here the presiding genius was Emile Peynaud. Like Tchelitscheff, Peynaud was a consultant,

◁ André Tchelitscheff, the Russian-born winemaker, launched the revival of the Californian fine wine industry after the vandalism of Prohibition.

advising countless Bordeaux properties on how to improve their winemaking. His most notable achievement was to master the nature and importance of malolactic fermentation, but in other respects, too, he was the father of modern vinification techniques, urging the need for ripe and healthy fruit in the vineyard and gentler handling of the grapes and wines in the winery. He also advised estates to be as selective as possible in both vineyard and *chai*, to ensure

Renowned as a taster, Peynaud was keen to pass on those skills to his pupils, and his influence on winemaking standards in Bordeaux was incalculable.

that only the best of the crop was bottled under the château name, while the remainder was consigned to a second label or dispatched to wholesalers. Renowned as a taster, Peynaud was keen to pass on those skills to his many pupils, and his influence on winemaking standards in the Bordeaux region was incalculable.

The University of Bordeaux continues to be a world-class centre of research. Here Denis Dubourdieu has explored the nuances of skin contact and lees-stirring (*bâtonnage*) for white wines. Meanwhile, further south, in the sleepy Madiran wine region, Patrick Ducournau of Chapelle Lenclos has invented the controversial technique of micro-oxygenation, which allows a wine to be aerated while remaining on its fine lees, the theory being that the lees continue to nourish the wine, while the oxygenation takes the place of routine racking

Oenologists and winemakers are like actors: on stage and often public figures. Viticulturalists are more like production staff, crucial to the success of any performance.

off the lees. Its short-term effects, especially with tannic wines that can be unpalatable in their youth, have been impressive, and the technique has been adopted by many wineries worldwide, but no one is sure what, if any, long-term consequences there will be on wines thus treated.

The true successors to Peynaud are the growing band of wine consultants. In Bordeaux, Professor Dubourdieu is a formidable example among white wine specialists, while the leading red wine consultant – who seems to have been employed in just about every wine region of the world – is Michel Rolland. Their role is controversial. They have been accused, as have the 'flying winemakers', of imposing a set style on whichever wine they touch. It is true that Rolland has certain stipulations, such as the need for phenolically ripe fruit before harvesting, and his preference for allowing the malolactic fermentation to take place in barrel rather than tank. But it would be unjust to accuse him of standardization, although inevitably he expresses his own stylistic preferences. I recall blind-tasting a young Margaux wine and noting that its voluptuous fruit quality was atypical of the region. The wine turned out to be Château Kirwan, and Rolland its consultant. Rolland, who insists that he adapts his advice to local circumstances and conditions, would argue that while his stylistic signature may be apparent when the wine is very young, with age the subtleties of *terroir* will emerge more strongly.

The consultant oenologist has also become a major force in Italy, and has raised standards at estates across the nation. The leading names include Vittorio Fiore, Maurizio Castelli and Franco Bernabei, while in Portugal the craft is represented by David Baverstock and João Portugal Ramos. Having accompanied some of these gentlemen on their rounds, I can vouch for the fact that the wines they supervise remain utterly distinct.

Oenologists and winemakers are like actors: on stage and often public figures. Viticulturalists are more like production staff, crucial to the success of any performance, but largely invisible manipulators of the props and scenery. Yet no one would deny the central importance of those whose aim is to deliver to the wineries the best grapes possible in the face of climatic uncertainty. As the back-room boys of the wine world, their contributions are often underestimated. Raymond Bernard has done wonders to improve the selection of clones and rootstocks available to Burgundian growers with integrity, while Claude Bourguignon has had a comparable influence in alerting those same growers to the disastrous impact on the soil of decades of fertilizers and chemical treatments.

TRAINING AND MANIPULATION

Once vines are in the ground, all manner of questions arise as to how they should be trained and treated. In Austria Dr Lenz Moser III devised a method of training widely spaced vines high above the ground, a labour-saving system adopted as far away as Bergerac as well as throughout his native land. Many question whether his system gives outstanding fruit quality, and similar doubts have been raised about another system, the Scott Henry, created by the grower of that name in southern Oregon.

In recent times the aim of viticulturalists has been to increase yields and maximize maturation without, it is claimed, any diminution of quality. To achieve these goals, they have been experimenting with canopy management, manipulating the growth of foliage to ensure that just the right amount of sunshine reaches the bunches.

In France, Professor Alain Carbonneau devised the Lyre system of training vines, which has been enthusiastically adopted by some producers of generic burgundy, notably Antonin Rodet, in an attempt to grow sufficiently large quantities of grapes without compromising their quality.

In Australia, the crusading Dr Richard Smart, author of innumerable books and articles on viticulture, devised trellising systems that were put into effect in regions as diverse as Napa Valley, New Zealand and Argentina. If Smart's own advocacy is to be believed, his Smart-Dyson trellising system combines fecundity with quality plus suitability for mechanical pruning and harvesting. His critics doubt that his control over maturation and yields is as complete as he would have his clients believe, but his ideas have nonetheless had a formidably beneficial effect on viticulture, aimed at large-volume production without sacrifice of quality.

ESTATE OWNERS

If the viticulturalists are the behind-the-scenes manipulators of the wine industry, the major estate owners have been very much front-of-house. Some of their forbears were prominent in the 19th century too. Thus in the 1870s, Baron Bettino Ricasoli was largely responsible for defining the style of modern Chianti. A similar role was played in the 20th century by the likes of Baron Le Roy, who created the 'formula' for Châteauneuf-du-Pape that persists to this day.

Most proprietors, especially of large aristocratic estates, were absentee landlords, content to allow their stewards or *régisseurs* to run their properties. Not so Baron Philippe de Rothschild who, when he took over the running of Château Mouton-Rothschild in 1922, astonished his family by living at the property, which in those days lacked creature comforts.

Baron Philippe brought showmanship to the wine business. His decision to château-bottle the entire 1924 vintage, his commissioning of a new *chai* from the architect Charles Siclis and original wine labels from leading artists for each new vintage, the creation of a superb wine

museum – these initiatives were partly directed at securing the promotion of Mouton to first growth status, an ambition finally realized in 1973. He was a shrewd businessman, devising the name of Mouton-Cadet to spearhead a large *négociant* business, which sold millions of bottles of often overpriced Bordeaux of modest quality. He was courageous too. Many an eyebrow must have been raised in Bordeaux when in 1978 he and Robert Mondavi cooked up their splendid joint venture, Opus One, in Napa Valley. After Baron Philippe's death in 1988, his daughter Philippine resolutely stepped into her father's shoes, promoting her wines with the same flair he had always shown.

If Baron Philippe strove for acceptance by the world's most exclusive wine club, the giants of the Italian wine industry took a more cavalier view of local traditions. Dr Piero Antinori is the latest head of a family involved in the wine business since 1385. Under the Marchese's direction, this venerable business has expanded and the family now owns about 1,300 hectares, 1,000 of them in Tuscany, producing some one million cases a year. He has also made a valiant, if not wholly successful attempt to produce Sangovese wines from his Atlas Peak estate in Napa Valley. In Tuscany, Antinori, urged on by his oenologist Giacomo Tachis, was a pioneer of what became known as 'Super Tuscan' wines, producing high-quality wines outside the formal structures of the complex and ossified Italian DOC regulations.

If Baron Philippe strove for acceptance by the world's most exclusive wine club, the giants of the Italian industry took a more cavalier view.

Antinori's Tachis' Tignanello became the standard-bearer for luxurious *barrique*-aged Sangiovese-based red, although other wines in the same mould can rival its quality. Antinori was also one of the first Tuscan producers to launch a Bordeaux-style wine, Solaia, although his cousin beat him to it with the celebrated Sassicaia. While open to outside influences, Antinori remains resolutely Italian, expanding his range of first-rate wines with acquisitions

◁ Georges Duboeuf, tireless enthusiast for the charms of Beaujolais, is now responsible for making ten per cent of its production.

▷ The late Baron Philippe de Rothschild, a remarkable man of many talents, spent 51 years fighting to have his beloved Mouton promoted to the ranks of the first growths. In 1973 he succeeded.

◁ Emile Peynaud of Bordeaux applies scientific principles to oenology, but never relinquishes the idea that wine's primary purpose is to give sensual pleasure.

▷ In the 1970s, Angelo Gaja shocked his Piemontese neighbours by ageing his wines in French oak barrels. Today, many do this, but few as skilfully as Gaja himself.

◁ Miguel Torres of Catalonia brought the international grape varieties to Spain, and at the same time has revived the reputation of Catalonia's indigenous grapes.

▷ Bernhard Breuer led the fight to restore the image of Rheingau Riesling as Germany's answer to Chablis: the perfect white wine with food.

◁ Without the inspiration and ambition of Alain Brumont, the southwestern French district might still be a backwater rather than one of France's most exciting wine-producing regions.

▷ Vintage port is created in the vineyard and blending room. Few showed as much knowledge and skill in both disciplines as Bruce Guimaraens of Fonseca.

of new estates in Chianti and the esteemed Piemonte house of Prunotto. Piero Antinori has been tireless in promoting his wines worldwide. Now in his sixties, he could retire to his *palazzo* in Florence and let his three daughters run the business. But he is still looking ahead, casting his gaze over southern Italy, which he believes will be making wines of high quality in the 21st century. Tuscany remains a region of large aristocratic estates,

△ Robert Mondavi, by sharing his research and ideas with his fellow Californians, was largely responsible for the elevation of California wines into the ranks of the world's best.

▷ Even those who do not admire his wines admit that Ernest Gallo created a phenomenally successful business from the most modest beginnings.

but not Piemonte, with its multiplicity of smallholdings. Despite the great prestige of Barolo and Barbaresco, many of the wines were harsh and rustic, spoiled by excessive extraction and prolonged ageing in large old casks.

It took one man, Angelo Gaja, to transform Barbaresco and Barolo into wines that were acceptable on an international market yet retained the unique typicity of the region. His revolution was complete: gentler fermentation, the use of *barriques*, smart packaging and high prices stamped him as a modern marketeer, but no one could deny the stupendous quality of his single-vineyard Barbarescos. Where he led, many followed, and the staggering amelioration in quality of Piemonte wines since the late 1980s is due largely to his example. The Gaja range includes fine Chardonnay and Cabernet Sauvignon, but the mainstay of his production remains the highly individual Piemonte wines made from Nebbiolo, Barbera and Dolcetto.

In Catalonia, Miguel Torres performed a similar balancing act between the preservation of tradition and a zeal for innovation. But this is a much larger operation than that of Gaja, and has for many decades been highly commercial – in the best sense. Torres wines are exported the world over, from zesty whites made with local varieties to toothsome Grenache-based blends, to the long-lived Black Label Cabernet Sauvignon, now known by its vineyard name of Mas La Plana.

During the decades when Spain was known for overblown rustic reds and tired pallid Riojas, Miguel Torres always showed what could be done if an intelligent approach was adopted to replace dogged adherence to weary 'tradition'. From the 1960s he overhauled the family firm, completely renovating the vineyards by doubling the vine density and employing previously untried trellising systems, and installing modern vinification and barrel-ageing facilities at his winery in Penedès.

Meanwhile, at the other end of Spain, in Jerez, another powerful figure was working to the detriment of the wine industry. In the 1960s, José Maria Ruiz-Mateos began buying up sherry *bodegas*, which he grouped under the name Rumasa. By 1977 he was the largest *bodega*-owner in the region and controlled one third of the sherry industry, but his price-cutting had disastrous consequences for the overall quality and image of sherry. In 1983, Rumasa, on the brink of collapse, was nationalized and then broken down and privatized. But the damage had been done, and sherry has never fully recovered, despite the undoubtedly brilliant quality of wines from the leading *bodegas*.

POWERFUL FORCES

In the United States the undisputed giant of the wine industry is surely Ernest Gallo. Given the average (often below-average) quality of much of his company's wine, and strategic marketing of products such as Thunderbird to ethnic minorities, it is hard to discern the Gallo family in heroic terms. Nonetheless, the achievement of Ernest and his brother Julio in steadily transforming the company from modest beginnings in California's Central Valley into a firm that at one time produced more wine than the whole of Australia can hardly be ignored.

The Gallo company is renowned for proceeding mercilessly against anyone who, however innocently, adopts the family name – including, at one point, their own estranged brother who tried to launch himself as a cheesemaker. Yet despite its vast power and its iron grip, with so many subsidiary labels on the lower ends of the American wine market, Gallo has never become complacent. In the 1980s they began acquiring large tracts of land in Sonoma and, with the help of the brothers' grandchildren, charged into the premium wine market with the Gallo Sonoma range.

If the Gallos have a chequered record, there is no blot on the reputation of Robert Mondavi. A family estrangement in the 1960s persuaded Robert to set up his own winery in Napa Valley, and from the outset he produced wines of remarkable quality. In the beneficent climate of Napa it doesn't take a genius to produce good wine, but it does take remarkable gifts to produce fine wines in enormous quantities, which is exactly what Bob Mondavi has done. His achievements are numerous. He exhaustively

researched the properties and nuances of French oak before deciding how his own wines should be matured; he created singlehandedly an oaked style of Sauvignon Blanc that he named Fumé Blanc and which is still going strong; he was one of the first California producers to make fine Pinot Noir on a regular basis and he boldly went into partnership with Baron Philippe de Rothschild to create a Bordeaux-style Napa Cabernet in Opus One. From the outset, his winery tours and educational projects have helped Americans to understand what fine wine is all about, and he has never ceased to travel the world, promoting the glory of wine as a cultural asset and combating the neo-Prohibitionists rampant in the United States.

But it does take remarkable gifts to produce fine wines in enormous quantities, which is exactly what Bob Mondavi has done.

Mondavi is reluctant to disclose its production figures, which are estimated to be at least 650,000 cases, not counting the six million cases produced in the Lodi region by the Mondavi-Woodbridge winery under a separate label. Despite this vast output, all this wine is of sound quality, and at the top reserve levels can

△ How to create a cult: an evocative name, elegant packaging and great wine; the result: David Hohnen's Cloudy Bay Sauvignon Blanc.

▷ Michael Broadbent MW: writer, taster, auctioneer and critic, is hailed internationally as an expert in fine and rare wines.

determination. The French have a nice word for such individuals: *locomotives* – mighty engines that tug in their wake a string of lesser producers. Angelo Gaja is a case in point in Piedmont, but there are many other examples. Not every great winemaker is necessarily a *locomotive*. Henri Krug, Miguel Valdespino, Olivier Humbrecht, Jean-Marie Raveneau, Dominique Lafon, Giuseppe Quintarelli, Gérard Chave, Paul Draper, FX Pichler, Charles Rousseau – are all consummate winemakers but do not see any need to challenge the status quo. A *locomotive* is dynamic, an originator.

VISION AND DETERMINATION

Madiran in southwest France seemed in decline until Alain Brumont, a local grower, visited Bordeaux and realized how his own region lagged behind in terms of winemaking skills. His insistence on lower yields and the use of small oak barrels was met by incomprehension and even wrath from many of his neighbours. But his single-mindedness paid off, and the wines Brumont produces from his two properties at Montus and Bouscassé are among the great wines of France.

Other notable French *locomotives* are Marcel Guigal, who brought true greatness to Côte Rôtie; Henri Ramonteu, who revived Jurançon as one of the world's most enchanting sweet wines; and the young Bruno Bilancini, who has restored Monbazillac to its former glory. In Bordeaux, much of the credit for the revival of white Graves, and in particular the creation of the Pessac-Léognan appellation, goes to the indefatigable André Lurton.

In the mid-1990s, I spent two days at the cellars of Georges Duboeuf at the invitation of his British importer. We tasted our way through literally hundreds of samples, mostly Beaujolais, so that the importer could make his selection for the British market. The visit clarified the extent of Duboeuf's understanding of his native region. Beaujolais has long been popular, but can also be a wine subject to cynical manipulation. Duboeuf's integrity has ensured that the wine world has access to a full range of authentic generic and *cru* wines from Beaujolais, both

compete with just about any other winery in California. The likes of Piero Antinori and Robert Mondavi are big players in their native countries, but there are also local heroes. Many small regions, slumbering in complacency and sometimes mediocrity, have been galvanized by the emergence of a single producer of vision and

blends and single-vineyard bottlings. Indeed, ten per cent of all Beaujolais is now marketed by Georges Duboeuf, and his *Hameau de Vin* at Romanèche-Thorins deftly combines educational centre, tourist attraction and retail outlet.

In Pouilly in the Loire, Didier Dagueneau began talking to some old-timers and realized that in the past Pouilly-Fumé had been taken more seriously as a fine white wine. By the 1980s it was being universally vinified in stainless-steel tanks and consumed young, when the fresh Sauvignon Blanc fruit was at its most vibrant. Dagueneau decided to take Sauvignon more seriously, reducing yields and vinifying the wine, in top vintages, in a sizeable proportion of new oak. Some of his wines have proved both outstanding and long-lived; others have been less successful. But he transformed the image of Loire Sauvignon from an easy-drinking white to a variety that was at least potentially capable of producing great and complex wine.

Alois Kracher in Austria has set new standards for intense botrytis wines, and his example, and indeed his commercial success, have persuaded many fellow growers to follow in his footsteps.

In Tokaj in Hungary, István Szepsy is working without compromise to recreate the style of wine that once made it so highly valued among the royal courts of Europe. In Germany, Bernhard Breuer and the late Graf Matuschka-Greiffenclau founded the *Charta Association*, recreating Riesling from the Rheingau as an off-dry wine that was as exemplary a match for certain foods as Premier Cru Chablis.

In Italy's the Veneto, Roberto Anselmi went to battle with the mediocre style of Soave promoted by the all-powerful cooperative, and showed that the region could make exceptional white and sweet wines. These people, and others there is not space to mention, were not just good winemakers, they refashioned, and in many cases revived, classic winemaking styles, and saved their regions from a decline into mediocrity, often incurring extraordinary hostility from vested interests as they did so.

In countries such as Australia, where there is less emphasis on regional styles than there is in Europe, the major figures have been master blenders rather than *locomotives*. Max Schubert

◁ André Simon, originally a Champagne salesman, became the world's most erudite wine historian and *bon vivant.*

◁ Hugh Johnson: the first populariser of wine, is the world's favourite wine writer whose refreshing, authoritative work has sold millions of copies in over a dozen languages.

in charge of winemaking at Penfolds in the 1950s, realized how far the company's wines fell short of the profound, long-lived *barrique*-aged wines of Bordeaux. Cabernet Sauvignon was a rarity in Australia in those days, but there was ample old Shiraz, and these vines, sourced from different locations, became the basis of Grange

Hermitage, Australia's mightiest and most long-lived red wine. And in the absence of good French oak Schubert made do with good new American oak. Subsequently an entirely new style of wine, echoed in countless examples of South Australian Shiraz, was born.

The most influential figures in Australian winemaking are the men who have continued where Max Schubert and his contemporaries left off.

Despite the phenomenal skills of regional winemakers such as Andrew Pirie in Tasmania, Bailey Carrodus in Yarra, Jeff Grossett in Clare Valley, and David Hohnen and Kevin Judd of Cloudy Bay in Marlborough, New Zealand, the most influential figures in Australian winemaking are the men who have continued where Max Schubert and his contemporaries left off. Philip Shaw has overseen the expansion of the highly successful Rosemount winery, and John Duval has kept the quality of Penfolds wines astonishingly high.

THE COMMUNICATORS

As the 20th century progressed, the growing importance of communications and marketing has seen the invention of a new creature: the wine journalist or critic. In the early part of this century, the wine writer was a gentleman amateur, musing over rewarding evenings enlivened by ancient vintages. This kind of writing could be highly professional, as the lasting legacy of André Simon confirms. The London agent for Pommery, he also wrote histories of the wine trade, lectured extensively, and founded the Wine and Food Society.

In the mid-century the most enterprising wine merchants doubled as ardent promoters of wine: men such as Alexis Lichine and Frank Schoonmaker, who brought the finest wines of France, Germany and California to the attention of the American market. In England, Ronald Avery and Harry Waugh did much to raise public appreciation of fine wines. The modern wine writer, by contrast, is not writing for a closed circle of connoisseurs, but for a

readership hungry for knowledge and education. Hugh Johnson was one of the first writers to combine a wide knowledge with an elegant literary style that enabled him to impart information without patronizing his readers. His *World Atlas of Wine* (Mitchell Beazley, 1971) was a pioneering book, combining definitive research with stylish exposition. Specialists in specific regions – such as Edmund Penning-Rowsell on Bordeaux and Anthony Hanson on Burgundy – have produced definitive studies of the world's most important wine regions.

In Britain, Johnson's pre-eminence has been complemented by Jancis Robinson, whose achievement is quite different. She has brought an almost scientific discipline to her books – again, without intimidating the reader – infusing with great authority her studies of grape varieties, of the life span of classic wines, and of the medical problems associated with alcohol consumption. Her erudition has been encapsulated more recently in the majestic *Oxford Companion to Wine* (Oxford University Press, 1994).

An entirely different approach has been adopted by another British wine writer, Oz Clarke, the unquenchable enthusiast and great communicator. His zest and occasional over-exuberance should not disguise his own immense knowledge. Never shy about voicing criticism of regions with an inflated idea of their own importance, his broadsides are generally based on solid foundations.

Australia has revelled in having Len Evans as a kind of frontman for the industry: winemaker, wine judge, restaurateur, communicator and wit. In America, an entirely different school of wine writing has emerged. If readers turn to established British writers for information, for history, for considered judgement, they turn to their American counterparts for wine assessment. American consumers have grown up in a world where wine knowledge has not, for the most part, been ingrained in the culture. Except in major cities, most of the wines available are Californian, and the lack of availability of the wide range of wines the British consumer has come to take for granted means that judgments are insecure.

How welcome then have been publications such as Marvin Shanken's the *Wine Spectator* and

Robert Parker's *The Wine Advocate*! Shanken's team of journalists and the prodigiously industrious Parker have had the simple idea of scoring wines as though they were college essays, this being the law-school-educated Parker's original frame of reference.

Publications by British writers and tasters such as Michael Broadbent MW and Clive Coates MW used a more rudimentary scoring system, as do journals such as *Decanter* and guides such as France's *Le Guide Hachette*. In Italy, Luigi Veronelli and in France, Michel Bettane have also developed well-deserved reputations as formidable tasters and assessors of wine.

But the American 100-point system gave the kind of definitive judgement that Americans and other consumers were thirsting for. The enormous sums demanded by the Bordelais, in particular for their wines *en primeur*, compounded the need for authoritative advice. When forking out $500 or more for an untasted wine still in barrel, it was comforting to know that Robert Parker or James Suckling rated it highly. Still, the system has come under justified attack. It offers certainty in an area where certainty cannot exist. Wine is a living thing, constantly changing in the bottle, and varying according to temperature and the context in which it is consumed.

Moreover, the critics' ratings have been abused by some of the wine trade, who shamelessly use them, rather than their own opinions, to sell or auction expensive wines. A tyranny has developed whereby a wine scoring 90-plus points walks off the shelves, while one rated a mere 85 is doomed to relegation in the bin-end section.

In an oenological spin on Heisenberg's Uncertainty Principle, the observer has come to affect that which is observed. A shrewd understanding of the characteristics that tend to meet Robert Parker's favour has led some producers, especially in France and California, to calibrate their winemaking styles to ensure a high score. For points, in this world, mean prizes – substantial orders from the trade and the kind of reputation that can lead to inflated prices for future vintages. This may not be the critic's fault, and I believe Robert Parker is right

to protest that his taste is more complex and refined than his critics give him credit for, but nonetheless the concentration of influence has distorted the wine world and led to growing standardization of certain red wines as well as grossly inflated prices for the most acclaimed and fashionable bottles.

With the growth in value of fine wine, a new breed of collector has come into existence. In former times, wine was bought and laid-down for consumption by individual households, but now many wines are 'collected' for simple investment (a risky business) or as a commercial enterprise. The most notable collectors are probably Hardy Rodenstock of Germany, and a handful of surgeons in the United States including Marvin Overton. Rodenstock's uncanny knack of laying his hands on bottles of astonishing rarity (such as some of those branded with Thomas Jefferson's initials in the 1790s) and his reluctance to reveal his sources have led to accusations – unproven – of skulduggery.

Some collectors enjoy organizing tastings – often vertical tastings of wines from the same estate through numerous vintages – which are tributes to their generosity and connoisseurship. Others, such as physicist Bipin Desai, sell tickets to such tastings and turn them into social/gastronomic events. Whether this kind of veneration applied to bottles of wine is a positive trend or not is open to question.

A tyranny has developed whereby a wine scoring 90-plus points walks off the shelves, while one rated a mere 85 is doomed to relegation in the bin-end section.

The trend has been encouraged by the auction houses. The pioneer of modern international wine-selling is Michael Broadbent MW, but a new generation of Internet auctioneers, such as the American Ursula Hermacinski, is snapping at his heels.

This constitutes an impressive roll-call of major personalities, but none would have come to much without the enterprise of the unsung hero of the century, the consumer.

FRANCE

Bordeaux still teases aficionados with its diversity of output: countless practical, economic and social variables conspire with the capricious maritime climate to maintain the wines' elusive fascination. But history has not been easy on the world's favourite wine region.

Bordeaux

Michael Broadbent MW

The name 'Bordeaux' conjures up tradition, dependability, continuity and class; nearly 1,000 years of trade, for three centuries under the English crown. But there were two major blips. In the mid-19th century the vineyards were seriously affected by oidium. No sooner had this been eradicated than a more deadly

With the outbreak of the First World War, manpower was sucked remorselessly into the Front, creating serious labour shortages.

pest appeared: phylloxera. The production of wine was seriously affected, and both the château proprietor and the Bordeaux trade languished at what should have been its most prosperous period.

So the 20th century opened with a depressed scenario. In the vineyards, though grafting vines onto American rootstocks held phylloxera in check, it was not completely eradicated. And adding to production problems was the pressure of the Bordeaux merchants. For most of the previous century – and, indeed, for half of the

last – 'Les Chartronnais', the name deriving from the *quai* alongside which the powerful merchants had their cellars, held the whip hand. The château proprietor, no matter how grand, was in thrall to these *négociants*. For example, the excellent 1899s had been taken up enthusiastically by the trade but when the equally good 1900s came along the merchants held back until châteaux proprietors were forced to offer it at bargain-basement prices.

In general, however, prosperous British wine merchants, maintaining close connections with gentlemanly importers who, in turn, bought from powerful and prosperous principals in Bordeaux, were all doing very nicely.

With the outbreak of the First World War, manpower was sucked remorselessly into the Front, creating serious labour shortages. Weather conditions deepened the gloom: 1915 was so bad that neither châteaux Latour nor Yquem were able to offer their wine for sale. One market lost forever was Russia, whose Tsars and aristocrats had a partiality for the finest Sauternes. Yet, as always during periods of shortage, some merchants, and not just in Bordeaux, did well,

1900

A classic vintage in Sauternes made rich, powerful wines.

1907

The School of Viticulture and Oenology was established at Château La Tour Blanche in Sauternes.

 Château d'Yquem in Sauternes. After centuries of ownership by the Lur-Saluces family, the world's most famous sweet wine estate succumbed to corporate takeover by LVMH in 1998.

amassing sufficient cash to invest in top properties at the end of the war. These outsiders included Cordier and Ginestet, both of whom became important merchant/proprietors.

THE GLORIOUS 1920S

Although manpower shortages and difficulties continued, the 1918 and 1919 vintages were of respectable quality. The 1920s produced an unprecedented array of great vintages and wines. Initially, as normality returned, trade improved, and the 'merchant princes' of Bordeaux and to some extent the châteaux proprietors thrived.

But it didn't last. Moreover, the fledgling American market was destroyed by Prohibition, and legitimate trade ceased to exist until the mid-1930s. 1920, the first vintage of the decade, was good for reds, and the following year was

spectacular for Sauternes. 1924 and 1926 were good, 1926 Lafite achieving its highest ever price The decade ended with 'twins', both excellent but of contrasting style: the long-lived tannic 1928s and the more charming 1929s.

One event that shook the complacent and conservative Bordelais was the sudden appearance on the scene of a young man whose flair, imagination and drive made him the single most influential figure in the history of Bordeaux. His name: Philippe de Rothschild.

Château Mouton – then known as Brane-Mouton – was bought by Baron Nathaniel in 1853. In a run-down state, it had failed to achieve first-growth status in the famous 1855 classification. Although making decent wine, Mouton was virtually ignored by the family until, at the age of 20, the young Philippe was put in charge. His first vintage was in 1924,

1920	**1921**		**1924**
A uniformly good vintage for red wines. Latour and Margaux were superb, and still can be if well stored.	An extremely hot year, and difficult for the reds; Cheval-Blanc was the star. Superb in Sauternes, enabling Yquem to make a wine of such concentration and quality that it remains the finest of the century.		Philippe de Rothschild's first vintage, commissioning Jaques Carlu to design the label.

△ The post-war trio of Bordeaux vintages measured up to the legendary pre-phylloxera 1865 and 1870; some wines took 50 years to mature and are expected to last well into this century.

The 1930s were an appalling time for trade and producer alike. The cellars of English wine merchants were full of the best wines of the 1920s. The 1934 vintage was quite good, but no money was to be made out of it. After Prohibition was repealed in 1933 it took some time for American trade to revive. As for Bordeaux, châteaux proprietors were in despair and many properties changed hands at ludicrously low prices, the most notable acquisition being that of Haut-Brion by the American banker Clarence Dillon in 1935. 1937 perked up, but by the time wines were ready for bottling, Europe was again at war. Again, growers were beset by shortages of manpower, equipment, sprays and fertilizers. Some surprisingly sound, attractive wines were made during the war: particularly the 1943s. One of the visible effects of shortages was of bottles: pale green and pale blue bottles proliferated.

In the 1940s, Bordeaux was occupied by the Germans. Although châteaux were requisitioned for troops, widespread looting did not occur; indeed, many Germans behaved honourably, paying for their supplies, no doubt influenced by a senior commandant whose family were leading Bremen wine merchants. There were more serious problems: extradition, forced labour and collaboration. And deeper tragedies too. Baron Philippe's wife died in a concentration camp, and he never forgave the Germans, refusing personal contact.

and he startled neighbours and *négociants* alike by commissioning a striking avant-garde label from a designer friend, Jacques Carlu. At the same time he proclaimed that henceforth Mouton-Rothschild would be château-bottled. In the dreary 1927 vintage he introduced a 'Carruades de Mouton', which clearly sowed the seeds of an idea – what to do with wine from a poor vintage, and how to use the label to promote a wine. After the Second World War, Philippe commissioned a fresh label design for every vintage of Mouton, each from a famous contemporary artist. It is easy to forget what a revelation these labels – now collectors' items – were.

THE DEPRESSED 1930s

The Rothschild saga continues here, for the vintages 1930, 1931 and 1932 were execrable, and coincided with the Depression. In 1934 Baron Philippe selected his best vats from these vintages and sold the wine as Mouton Cadet, the inauspicious start of the most successful branded table wine in Bordeaux's history.

THE POST-WAR PERIOD 1945–49

Almost miraculously, the immediate post-war period was blessed with three outstanding vintages: 1945, 1947 and 1949 – in Sauternes as well as for red wines. As always, quirks of nature were primarily responsible for the small concentrated 1945s, the voluptuous 1947s and the supremely fine and elegant 1949s. But not

1927	1928	1929	1935	1937
Mouton-Rothschild introduce 'Carruades de Mouton' – a solution to what to do with wine from a poor vintage.	So full and tannic that it took a half-century for Latour to lose its harsh tannins; it is drinking superbly now.	A vintage of great charm, the top wines being Cheval-Blanc and Léoville-Poyferré. Great Sauternes from Yquem and Climens.	An American banker, Clarence Dillon, buys Haut-Brion.	A tough, astringent vintage for reds, but autumn heat and *botrytis* produced magnificent Sauternes, notably Yquem.

just the weather: the vines were old, and equipment was old-fashioned, with a shortage of new-oak barrels. The cellar staff, returning from the war, were steeped in traditional methods. Moreover there were few experts around to tell them what to do! Mind you, the remedy – if remedy were needed – was soon to appear. In 1949 Jean Ribereau-Gayon became director of the *Institut d'Oenologie* at the University of Bordeaux.

Ribereau-Gayon was joined that year by Emile Peynaud, whose influence would turn out to be immense. It was Peynaud who put oenology into practice. His great tasting ability, practical experience and common sense made him an invaluable adviser to a large number of châteaux – even the greatest. He told me that his main job was to spot and rectify problems, but he also encouraged methods aimed at making the hard tannic wines more accessible, emphasizing fruit and suppleness. He soon became regarded as a 'guru' and, almost inevitably, was accused of encouraging wines to be made in a uniform style. This he denied and resented.

Wines in this post-war period were superb. If 1921 Yquem is the greatest white Bordeaux of the century, then 1945 Mouton-Rothschild and 1947 Cheval-Blanc vie to be the greatest red. The 1945 Mouton I describe as 'a Churchill of a wine': tremendous character, unmistakable; it soars above its classification, being intensely coloured, spicy, concentrated, heavenly to drink, yet with years of life. Cheval-Blanc, made in the scorching 1947 vintage, is a complete contrast, so sweet and rich it could almost be port. And in yet another style is the 1949 Mouton – a wine of exquisite finesse and fragrance. It was not only these three vintages that put Pomerol on the map; it was another larger-than-life character, Jean-Pierre Moueix. His family originated in the uplands of the Corrèze, and he purchased properties first in Saint-Emilion and, after the war, in Pomerol, also establishing himself as a distributor and taking a stake in Château Pétrus. A shrewd salesman, he virtually single-handedly gave the wines of Pomerol, hitherto mainly confined to consumers in Belgium, far wider currency. Ignoring the workings of the big-time Bordeaux *négociants*, he raised the status and price of his properties, notably Pétrus.

THE 1950s

The 1950s was a period of reconstruction and consolidation. In spring 1950, the Bordelais, atypically far-sighted and aware of the need for promotion, founded *La Commanderie de Bordeaux* which, after half a century, continues to thrive, with social wine events organized by a multitude of chapters in many countries.

There were some very good vintages: 1952 (particularly those of the right bank); 1953 almost my favourite claret vintage, wines of charm and finesse, now beginning to tire; 1955 and 1959. The latter was the first to be proclaimed 'the vintage of the century' by journalists. There were also two appalling years, 1951 and 1956.

It was Peynaud who put oenology into practice. His great tasting ability, practical experience and common sense made him an invaluable adviser.

Technological advances were yet to come. The proprietors were busily replanting, a costly and time-consuming business, and few châteaux were profitable. The *négociants*, powerful and influential, were still plying their trade. But in England, the traditional wine merchants began to crumble. While the top retailers continue to service their middle- and upper-class customers, many provincial family firms found the rising cost of stocks a hardship, and they sold out to the increasingly dominating brewers.

1945	1947	1949
A small but very concentrated year, with Mouton supreme.	A sumptuous vintage for reds Cheval-Blanc being the star. Another great year for Climens, as well as Yquem.	The most elegant of the great trio of vintages of the 1940s, notably from Mouton. Emile Peynaud starts work at the *Institut d'Oenologie* at the University of Bordeaux.

From 1952 I was directly involved in retailing and, having retained every price list, find them fascinating reading. For example, price for price, Bordeaux rated third after Burgundy and well below German wines. Top-quality Rhine and Mosel wines were the stars. In the early 1950s merchants still had stocks of pre-war vintages, even 1929s. In 1955, Harveys of Bristol listed 1949 Lafite at 24 shillings a bottle and Cos at 18 shillings and sixpence. 1952 first-growths 'for laying down' started at 24 shillings. I remember advising a friend to buy all he could of 1945 Mouton at £1 a bottle and, for everyday drinking, at 8 shillings, 1948 Cheval-Blanc. (The annual income of a family doctor at about that time would have been around £2,000.)

△ 50 years ago. The unmistakable turrets and steep-pitched roofs of Château Pichon-Longueville (now Lalande) in 1950. Since Mme de Lencquesaing took over from her father in 1978 the wines' reputation soared into the top category of Bordeaux second growths.

▷ The medieval buildings of Saint-Emilion are made from the limestone quarried from the plateau on which the town stands. A network of chambers and passages extends out under the surrounding vineyards.

1950	**1952**	**1953**	**1959**
The best reds of the decade: 1953 Lafite for sheer perfection, 1959 Mouton for opulence, and 1959 Latour for grandeur.	Alexis Lichine buys the uninhabited Château Prieur.	Lafite, the epitome of elegance, my favourite claret vintage.	Magnificent vintage of massively constituted red Bordeaux and Sauternes.

The 1950s was a good decade for Sauternes too, though few seemed to appreciate them; 1950 better than reds, 1953s charming, 1955s superb and 1959s magnificent. The price of Yquem was over twice that of the other classed growths, and higher still than first-growth Médocs.

This was the time the Americans started to renew their interest in wine, and if one man could claim more than a little responsibility, it was Alexis Lichine. Of Russian parentage and brought up in Paris, Lichine was a larger-than-life character, a man of charm and flair. After Prohibition, he worked in America with the influential Frank Schoonmaker, starting his own import business after the war. In 1952, Lichine's *Wines of France* (Cassell, 1952) was published. It was refreshingly outspoken and, not surprisingly, made him a few enemies. Although keen on Burgundy he foresaw opportunities in run-down post-war Bordeaux, and in 1952 bought the uninhabited Château Prieuré, which became his principal home until his death in 1989.

As for the market, prices remained steady. The very good 1952 and 1953 vintages were cheap, for this was still a period of austerity in Europe. Prices rose as the decade progressed. In retrospect, it was the last inexpensive period, when the English middle-classes could still take middle-classed growths for granted. Most red Bordeaux were English-bottled. Pétrus remained undiscovered. Soon all was to change.

THE 1960s

The cost of living had started edging up in the mid-1950s, but turned to inflation in the 1960s. It presaged the end of the road for the Bordeaux *négociants* and great changes in British trade channels: the structured, stratified divisions of importer/wholesaler/retailer broke down. Harveys, of which I was then a director, moved aggressively 'vertical', becoming a producer as well as importer, exporter, distributor, wholesaler and retailer. Harveys protected their source of supply by buying Delor, and in 1962 supported Pearson's purchase of Château Latour – an immensely profitable move.

Resale price maintenance was abolished in Britain in the early 1960s, and from then on supermarkets became more successful in obtaining retail licences. By the mid-1960s the wine trade became a free-for-all. Wine auctions resumed in 1966, and Bordeaux was to prove the bedrock of the saleroom.

The month of May in 1967 made Christie's reputation. On May 2nd, I catalogued over 24,000 cases of claret of the 1950s and 1960s

I remember advising a friend to buy all he could of 1945 Mouton at £1 a bottle and, for everyday drinking, at 8 shillings, 1948 Cheval-Blanc.

in various sized bottles – an unprecedented quantity to come on the open market. Quite a bit remained unsold, but nonetheless this sale in late May – and the first great 'Finest and Rarest' put wine auctions firmly on the map. This sale featured huge quantities of pre-phylloxera Lafite from Lord Rosebery's cellar. Prices were considered high at the time, though they seem ludicrously low now. The ensuing publicity enticed owners of inherited cellars to sell. By the end of the decade, I was crossing the Atlantic to conduct the first of Heublein's annual epoch-making wine auctions. In the United States as well as in London, Bordeaux wines dominated the saleroom.

In Bordeaux itself, technical developments were being introduced. Steel fermentation tanks were installed at Château Latour, which caused a bit of a stir even though the Woltner family had pioneered these a decade earlier at Château La Mission Haut-Brion.

1961	1966
A great, long-lasting vintage. 1961 Palmer is still fleshily superb.	A 'long-distance runner' of a vintage in the Graves, Saint-Emilion and Pomerol.

Typically, considering the maritime climate, vintages were dramatically different: three execrable, 1963, 1965 and 1968; three mediocre, three good and one great. 1961, another 'vintage of the century', was great for similar reasons to the 1945: nature did the pruning, this time due to poor flowering conditions, resulting in magnificent, concentrated, long-lasting wines.

1962s and 1964s I regard as twins, though not identical, the latter tainted with 'before and after the rain' tales. Heavy rain during harvesting affected mainly the north Médoc, Pauillac and Saint-Estèphe. Latour picked early

To add to Bordeaux's woes, there was a scandal. In 1974, the most distinguished of the 'merchant princes', the Cruse family, was prosecuted for fraud.

and made excellent wine. Lafite, Mouton, and Lynch-Bages were caught by the rain. In the Graves, and in Saint-Emilion and Pomerol, the 1964s produced were marvellous. For firmness allied to panache and style I favour the 1966s, the best of which I describe as 'lean long-distance runners', my favourite being Cheval-Blanc.

In Sauternes, 1962 was more successful than 1961, and 1967 far superior to 1966. 1964 was a washout. Alexandre de Lur Saluces' favourite vintage happens to be the 1967, not a mammoth Yquem but on its plateau of perfection now.

THE TURBULENT 1970S

The expansion of the market and over-heating of demand which began in the late 1960s came to an ugly head in the early 1970s. Inflation soared. The flight out of cash into property and commodities aggravated the very inflation it sought to evade. Wine was one of those hedges, Bordeaux particularly: châteaux with recognizable and internationally negotiable

names were greatly in demand, aided and abetted by a specious secondary 'investment' market. Offers from merchants in Bordeaux were made by telex demanding an instant response before the price increased yet again. It is hard now to imagine what a dangerously frenetic time this was.

The 1970 vintage, which combined abundance and high quality, unfortunately became the ideal investment vehicle. 1971, a smaller vintage, forced prices even higher. Impending disaster was heralded by the mediocre 1972s, which, unbelievably, came on the market at even higher prices. Whether this situation was initiated by over-ambitious châteaux proprietors or by greedy Bordeaux merchants is hard to say. Then the oil price hike precipitated the collapse of property values, and the value of those commodities and collectibles whose prices had spiralled. Wine was one; Bordeaux the principal scapegoat. It also hastened the demise of Les Chartronnais who, in any case, because of the high cost of holding stock, had become brokers.

Between 1973 and 1976 the recession in Bordeaux was as serious as the 1930s Depression. For two years there was no cash-flow. The market had dried up. To add to Bordeaux's woes, there was a scandal. In 1974, the most distinguished of the 'merchant princes', the Cruse family, was prosecuted for fraud. The actual fraud was pitiful and inexcusable: it involved switching the permits of ordinary red for ordinary commercial white wine. The affair was blown out of all proportion, mainly because of the high standing of the culprits, and although no fine wine was involved it greatly damaged the reputation of Bordeaux. Another direct result of the collapse of prices was a rush to unload. At Christie's in July 1974, trade stock of 500,000 bottles changed hands, mostly claret, including 2,000 cases of 1970 Mouton-Rothschild. As the wine was sold ex-cellars,

1970	**1973**	**1974**
Once thought highly promising, this vintage now looks spotty. The best wines are Latour, Cheval-Blanc, Pétrus, and Ducru-Beaucaillou.	Serious recession hits France and cash flow dries up. Mouton-Rothschild is re-classified as *premier cru*.	The Cruse family is prosecuted for fraud.

Mouton realized this was an effective way of reducing stocks and raising cash. For the first time ever, the rival Rothschild châteaux, Lafite and Mouton, combined forces in 1975 to hold a sale, offering every major vintage from 1945.

One of the lessons of this severe recession was this: if there is no market, fine wine will not be made. It was not just poor weather that resulted in a feeble 1973 and 1974; it simply did not pay châteaux proprietors to make the costly efforts in the vineyards and winery to ensure top quality. The next decade reversed the situation, amply proving that basic point.

Were there any really good wines made in the 1970s? I suppose so. A few. But the decade never lived up to its potential. Even the 1970 is patchy now. Some very good 1971s were made in Pomerol and truly excellent Sauternes. 1975 produced very tannic reds and, again, excellent Sauternes; 1976 reds were charming, as were the sweet whites; 1978 was saved by late autumn sun, but is tiring now. 1979s were prolific, tannic, but are now drying out.

On a happier note, after half a century of banging the Mouton drum, Baron Philippe's precious château was reclassified officially in 1973 as *premier cru*, confirming a position it had held in price and reputation for 50 years.

THE 1980s: BORDEAUX IN BLOOM

Although the 1980s produced as many good to excellent vintages as the 1920s, it lacked the freakish superstar reds of 1945 and 1961 and the superlative Sauternes of 1921 and 1937. Overall though a very satisfactory decade.

Weather conditions made ripe, healthy grapes, winemaking had become confident, and an international market had developed with a wide spread of wealthy buyers. More and more, the château proprietor was calling the shots, conscious of the demand for, and value of, his or her name and reputation. The prices the leading châteaux could charge enabled them to be selective, to prune more severely and to remove excess bunches to reduce the crop size.

In the spring after the vintage, they selected the best vats for the *grand vin*, the remainder, from young vines and lesser vats, becoming their second wine. This kind of selection is crucial, and became truly significant in the 1980s, resulting in many second-label wines. Some can be surprisingly expensive, even if well below *grand vin* prices, but most are excellent value.

As a brand owner, the château proprietor was in the ascendant; the *négociants* more and more became order-takers. The 'merchant princes', the Cruses, the Ginestets, the Calvets, had lost their power and influence: some went under, replaced by the newer broker/*négociants*, particularly those who had strong ties with importers in the United States and elsewhere.

More and more, the château proprietor was calling the shots, conscious of the demand for, and value of, his or her name and reputation.

Pomerol wines continued to increase in popularity (and price); the family and firm of Jean-Pierre Moueix expanded and prospered, buying other properties to tag on to their flagship Pétrus. But another star was about to emerge from an even smaller patch of vines owned by the already well-established Thienpont family of Vieux Château Certan: Le Pin.

As for the white wines, 1982 was not as satisfactory for Sauternes as it was for red Bordeaux, but 1983 was supremely successful, as was 1985, for both dry and sweet. 1986 was very satisfactory in the Médoc and Sauternes. The whites really started hitting the high spots in 1988 and 1989, both great in Sauternes, the latter vintage superb in the Graves.

1982	1989
Exceptional vintage for reds, described by some as more like California Cabernets than red Bordeaux.	Great vintage for whites and reds, and Laville Haut-Brion is one of the finest dry whites of all time.

PEYNAUD, PARKER AND SHANKEN

The 1980s consolidated the influence of oenologists, in particular Professor Peynaud. He and his successors set about advising proprietors how to make more amenable reds, less severe, with more emphasis on ripeness and fruit.

A new phenomenon emerged in the 1980s in the form of the 'wine critic'. Newspapers began to employ regular columnists, the most respected being Edmund Penning-Rowsell in *The Financial Times*. His speciality was Bordeaux. Then came the subscription 'newsletter', a medium to be completely dominated by one man, Robert M Parker Jr. A lawyer by training – here was the wine critic without equal. He provided formidable self-assurance, a fulsome descriptive vocabulary and a notorious 100-point scoring system, which from the start attracted considerable criticism, as did his seeming omnipotence.

His annual assessment of vintages and châteaux is awaited with baited breath. On the plus side he has made under-performers pull up their socks; on the minus side he has emasculated the trade. Many have lost confidence in their own judgement. Merchants, importers, retailers, even customers wait for Parker to pronounce, on the basis of which they buy – or don't. The effect on the wine producer is an increasing temptation to make a wine, opaque in appearance, with – heaven forbid – 'gobs of fruit', an over-abundance that Parker might describe as 'awesome', and is impressive, but lacks the finesse and sheer drinkability that make claret such an ideal wine for the table.

Marvin Shanken is another phenomenon. His *Wine Spectator* is another child of the 1980s which also has considerable influence; he also uses the controversial 100-point scoring system. While Parker relies on his own formidable palate, Shanken employs a panel. When evaluating the wines of Bordeaux some American tasters, I suspect, have in the back of their minds California Cabernet Sauvignon, and prefer Pomerols to the more austere Médocs.

Amongst the writer/tasters one stands out: Michel Bettane. He is a critic in the Parker mould in that his opinions are very forthright and he is feared by the under-performers. The difference is that he is French and has an encyclopaedic knowledge of the subject.

THE LAST LAP – THE 1990s

1990, not unlike 1900, had an auspicious start. The weather conditions produced high-quality red Bordeaux. 1990 was also highly successful for all white Bordeaux, and produced yet another great vintage in Sauternes. But the 1991 to 1993 vintages were dogged by ill-timed rain before and during the harvest. In April 1991, a severe frost caused great damage and decimated the potential crop. But the summer was splendid. I recall Eric de Rothschild towards the end of August telling me that if the fine weather continued Bordeaux would have a vintage of the quality of 1945 or 1961. Alas, hardly had he put

1991

Severe frost in April causes severe damage and decimates the potential crop.

down the phone when it started to rain. 1992 was the decade's worst vintage; 1994 has been underrated for reds but proved a disaster for Sauternes. 1995 saw a revival of interest trigger a lively and successful *en primeur* campaign.

Yet after a comprehensive tasting of 1995 red Bordeaux in late 1999, I was left, uneasily, with the impression that there was a common denominator: amenable character and softer tannins, aimed, consciously or otherwise, at a public eager to be pleased, and less accustomed to the necessity of laying down claret. I felt that the district differences were becoming blurred.

Is this the direction in which Bordeaux wines will proceed? I hope not. *Terroir* must surely have the upper hand, as will the unpredictability of Bordeaux's climate. Perhaps the trade and their customers will tire of uniform reds; perhaps wine writers will start to look for differences of character and, above all, for finesse rather than just fruit. Is it too much to hope that the oenologist will be persuaded to back off, to leave Pomerol to its naturally fleshier style, the Médoc to its mixture of masculine and feminine styles, both of which benefit from bottle-ageing?

Dry white Bordeaux have improved on the sulphurous wines of 50 years ago. Perhaps they have leaned too far towards the crisp and acidic, with too much Sauvignon Blanc and oak. In my opinion, Sauvignon and new oak are not comfortable bedfellows. Bordeaux whites benefit from the traditional dose of Sémillon. As for Sauternes, there is too much of a gap between the best – Yquem, then Climens and Rieussec – and most of the rest. I deplore the light minty styles, but the weather and the market conspire to make life difficult for growers.

IN CONCLUSION

Despite vicissitudes, the wines of Bordeaux are in a league of their own. Much imitated, they are in practice inimitable. During my almost

△ A familiar landmark along the Route des Château is Cos d'Estournel's pagoda-like *chai*, which overlooks Lafite. One of the stars of Saint-Estèphe, Cos regularly produces some of the Médoc's best wines.

half-century connected with wine, I have been fortunate to taste and drink wines from all over the world, but I always come home to Bordeaux.

There is nothing to match claret at table. It has the right weight, is rarely too alcoholic, and appeals to all the senses – also, in the case of the finer wines, to the intellect. Claret is refreshing, the perfect accompaniment to food, its tannin not only acting as a preservative but cleansing the palate between mouthfuls and aiding the digestion!

The dry whites now present an appealing range, for they have no equal, even if they are so often paired with the wrong food. Dare I say that Sauternes are not dessert wines? With *pâté* yes, with most cheeses yes; perhaps with a ripe nectarine. But not with *crème brûlée*, for a sweet dish turns a sweet wine dry. What is the point of emasculating rare and priceless nectar with an ill-matched pudding?

This new century will see many changes. But I remain optimistic and wish châteaux proprietors, and those who trade in this eminently tradable commodity, success. To the drinker: may the pleasure and fascination never fade.

1996	1999
Will it ever be as popular as 1995? Certainly a positive Cabernet vintage, the Médocs being long-distance runners.	The 800th anniversary of *La Jurade de Saint-Emilion*, the longest track record of any of the many French wine fraternities.

Burgundy is wonderfully idiosyncratic: a region of individualist winemakers producing wines with a multitude of aromas and tastes from its varied landscape. A rich history has crucially influenced the region's extraordinary wines.

Burgundy

Anthony Hanson MW

The end of the 19th century and the start of the 20th were dominated by the phylloxera disaster. It arrived in Meursault in 1878, and in Chablis in 1890. The only dependable way to fight the scourge was complete replanting of the vineyards onto louse-resistant American rootstocks. This marked the end of centuries of renewal of the vineyards by layering: the

Until phylloxera, Burgundy's vineyards had been in a deep, humus-rich mulch of decomposing roots, vine-stocks and soil, pullulating with microbial life.

bending down to earth of a vine-shoot for it to take root, followed by the burying of the old vine-stock. Until phylloxera, Burgundy's vineyards had been planted in a deep, humus-rich mulch of decomposing roots, vine-stocks and soil, pullulating with microbial life. Cultivation was entirely manual.

In the replanted vineyards, the vines were laid out in rows. This allowed horses to plough between them, and for a methodical training of vine-shoots along steel wires rather than up

annually installed vine poles. Vineyard owners could also choose different varieties of Pinot Noir and Chardonnay. Some chose higher-yielding varieties than had been used in the past, or productive root-stocks, to make up for the dreadful losses they had suffered.

No sooner had the reconstitution of the vineyards gathered pace than war broke out in 1914. Large numbers of men were called to the Front, and most Burgundian villages suffered heavy losses of manpower and know-how.

The wine market must have been chaotic in the early years of the 20th century, with fraudulent 'wines' made from ingredients other than grapes flooding in to make up for shortfalls. The state reacted in 1905 with legislation aimed at protecting consumers. At the same time the concept of appellation was introduced so that wines might bear their names of origin.

The law did not go far enough, however. Unscrupulous owners started planting vine types unconnected with the wines of France's famous regions, and in unsuitable soils. A new law of 1919 allowed local courts to specify where the boundaries for a given name of

1900	1905	1910	1911
Foundation of the *Station Oenologique*, Beaune.	France's first legislation was enacted to eliminate fraud from winemaking and to protect wines' names of origin. Further laws followed in 1919 and 1927.	Wet weather brought disease and decimated the crop. The *Hospices de Beaune* auction did not take place.	A small harvest but excellent in both whites and reds, and from Chablis to Beaujolais.

origin should be drawn. In 1927, a further law enabled local courts to state which vine varieties could be planted in the greatest plots, and outlawed hybrid vines. Vicious battles took place in the courts. The wine-growers' leaders, Marquis d'Angerville (Volnay) and Henri Gouges (Nuits-Saint-Georges), were set against many famous local *négociants* who resented any restrictions on their freedom to buy, blend and label according to traditional practice. Reputations and fortunes were lost at this time. In Nuits-Saint-Georges, the owner of Maison Liger-Belair was so outraged by the arrival of fraud inspector Paul-Louis Murat to check his records that he locked him in the cellars for half a day. 'I will have your skin', said Murat when he was let out; and he did: the Liger-Belair company never recovered its strength, and the family had to part with its finest plot (La Tâche) in Vosne-Romanée.

It was in 1930 that Pinot Noir came to be defined as Burgundy's noble grape (with Gamay permitted for *crus* Beaujolais). A further law in

◁ Henri Gouges a specialist producer and long considered Nuits-Saint-Georges' top grower. His newly reinvigorated estate produces rich and complex wines.

◁ The Marquis d'Angerville (left) owns a clutch of fine Volnay vineyards from which he produces some of the best-structured, silky reds of the Côte de Beaune.

1921	1923	1927	1929
A superb year, both whites and reds.	A great year, but little of it. Foundation of La Chablisienne cooperative cellar. Comte Jules Lafon hosted a party for friends which was to become the *Paulée de Meursault* vintage banquet.	Creation of the *Revue du Vin de France* by Raymond Baudoin. Marquis d'Angerville of Volnay and Henri Gouges of Nuits-Saint-Georges campaigned for authenticity and typicity.	A famous vintage and the best of the decade, giving superbly rich wines.

▷ The 16th-century Château du Clos de Vougeot – a former Cistercian vat-house and cellar, now provides a sumptuous setting for high-profile dinners, banquets, enrolment ceremonies and tastings.

1935 established the *Appellation d'Origine Contrôlée* (AOC) system. Minimum ripeness was specified, along with maximum yields, and methods of cultivation, harvesting and winemaking.

Needless to say, the local *négociant* market had closed against Domaines D'Angerville and Gouges, so they had to sell their wines directly. Other leading estates such as Romanée-Conti expanded estate-bottling at this time, but the concept was not new. D'Angerville had been supplying his estate wines to the Thienpont family in Belgium since at least April 1912.

> *Many pale-coloured, weak productions sold to local négociants would then have been blended with Rhône wines.*

The man credited with inventing the modern concept of *vin de propriétaire* – wine direct from the grower, rather than signed by a *négociant* – is an American, Frank M Schoonmaker, who criss-crossed France persuading growers to bottle their wines for him. Alexis Lichine followed in his footsteps from the summer of 1939.

The wine market was moribund during the Depression of the early 1930s. Burgundians reacted by forming the *Confrérie des Chevaliers du Tastevin* in 1934. Leading figures in its early days were Georges Faiveley and Camille Rodier of Nuits-Saint-Georges and René Engel of Vosne-Romanée. Enthusiasts were ritualistically enthroned into the brotherhood, which from 1944 made the Château du Clos de Vougeot the scene of its sumptuous banquets to which politicians, astronauts, writers, opera singers, film-makers and many other consumers were invited. The *Confrérie* has served Burgundians well, and been widely copied.

Burgundy was invaded by the German Army on June 17th, 1940. Major houses in the villages were commandeered, *swastikas* flew over town

halls and cellars were pillaged. The 1940 harvest was lost. A black market developed and accommodations were made with the invading forces, until Beaune was finally liberated on September 8th, 1944.

Until the 1930s many vineyards were still cultivated by hand. Horse-drawn ploughs were phased out after the first vine-straddling tractors became available from 1954. The arrival of tractors stemmed the drift away from the land by the younger generation of *vignerons*.

By the 1950s and '60s, the ageing vineyards of the post-phylloxera reconstitution needed to be replanted. The key figure involved in improving the health, variety and quality of Burgundy's vines has been Raymond Bernard, who came from Poitiers to Burgundy in the mid-1950s. At that time there were many Gamay and Aligoté plantations, as well as pockets of directly rooted hybrid vines from the post-phylloxera replantings. Bernard found

1930	**1934**	**1935**	**1940**	**1943**
Pinot Noir is legally defined as the classic red burgundy grape.	An excellent vintage. Formation of the *Confrérie des Chevaliers du Tastevin* in Nuits-Saint-Georges, to promote Burgundy's wines.	First wines from leading domaines despatched to the United States by Frank Schoonmaker. Creation of the *Institut National des Appellations d'Origine*.	In June, Burgundy was invaded, cellars pillaged and buildings requisitioned. Central Chablis burned, after bombardment by German planes.	A great vintage, Romanée-Conti reported to be fabulous – two years before its pre-phylloxera vines were finally grubbed up.

much of the Chardonnay stock to be pitiably degenerate and riddled with virus. He was also stupefied by the varietal diversity of the Pinot Noir, which yielded assorted qualities. Although his recommendations were sometimes met with aggression by the locals, Bernard instituted a programme of clonal research, but it takes 15 years of growth, multiplications and trials before a healthy vine clone can be released onto the market. Today, in Burgundy, about 85 per cent of all Chardonnay replantings and 75 per cent of Pinot Noir replantings are with clonal stock.

Chemical weed-killing started to replace ploughing from the 1960s, the pace increasing rapidly in the 1970s. In the 1960s André Vedel, a technical advisor at the *Institut National des Appellations d'Origine* (INAO) and a respected taster, argued that potassium fertilizer would result in beautiful vineyards. It did, but at the cost of unbalancing the soils and fundamentally damaging the acidity of the wines. Chemical fertilizers, when used to excess, also encouraged grey rot, mildew and other diseases.

Harvesting machines, which appeared in the 1980s, are now widely used in Chablis and the Mâconnais (but not in Beaujolais, where grapes and stalks need to ferment intact). In 1999, about 40 were operating in the Côte d'Or.

In the 1990s the crucial development has been a growing awareness of environmental issues, which has led to a return to old methods of soil cultivation and the adoption of ecological approaches to vine protection.

The pioneers of organic viticulture in Burgundy have been Alain Guillot (Mâconnais), Jean-Claude Rateau (Beaune) and Didier Montchovet (Nantoux). Great domaines have now adopted such approaches (Domaine de la Romanée-Conti), sometimes also embracing biodynamic methods (Leroy, Leflaive, Lafon). Adopting a carefully thought-out programme of spraying with natural, rather than synthesized,

products, as well as re-balancing over-fertilized soils, has become *de rigueur* for leading growers. By the mid-1990s over 100 of the best growers had grouped together to cooperate in the production of composts to add humus to their soils.

WINEMAKING CHANGES

It is hard to know how red burgundy tasted at the beginning of the century. The means to combat vine diseases and rot were undeveloped, as were winemaking skills. Many pale-coloured, weak productions sold to local *négociants* would then have been blended with Rhône wines, Gamays from Beaujolais, or bone-setter reds from the Midi or Algeria. This gave consumers a false idea of the true tastes of pure burgundies. Burgundy's best sites were known and valued, but the concept of *terroir* was half a century away, and the serious teaching of winemaking skills dates only from the second half of the century.

△ Clos Saint-Jacques – once regarded as the best vineyard in Gevrey, after Chambertin – is walled like so many of the old monastic sites in Burgundy.

1945	1946	1947	1959	1961
A small harvest, but of excellent quality, richly concentrated wines.	Creation of the *Musée du Vin de Bourgogne* in the old Palace of the Dukes of Burgundy, in Beaune. Prototype vine-straddling tractor invented in Meursault.	A hot vintage, giving famously powerful wines. 1949 was also superb – as were most years ending in '9' during the century.	A superb vintage for reds, deep, flavoursome wines.	A great vintage, but little of it. Prices rise as interest in wine worldwide begins to grow.

The mastery of fermentation temperatures has been widespread in Burgundy only since the mid-1980s. Earlier systems were expensive or slow and ineffective. If a vat over-heated, you drew off the juice to finish fermentation away from the skins (resulting in a pale colour and limited-flavour extraction), or let it cool in the night air outside before returning it next morning to the skins. Or you threw in ice chunks, if you could obtain them. Until the arrival of running water in villages like Volnay, in 1955, winemakers had to travel to the stream in Pommard to draw water for rinsing vats or barrels.

Burgundy's barrel-makers were struggling to make a living. Then, from the 1970s, New World vineyard areas provided welcome new markets.

During the 1960s the *Station Oenologique* in Beaune engaged in heat-treatment experiments to extract additional colour from fermenting musts. We now know that colour extracted in this way was rarely stable, and the method made wines difficult to clarify. It was 20 years later that wine consultant Guy Accad was to be influential in persuading growers to equip themselves with cooling systems, but he also advocated more powerful doses of SO_2 than most were prepared to countenance, and his following melted away. He was an important catalyst of change, however, and many Burgundians awoke to the colour- and perfume-extracting potential of pre-fermentation cold macerations. And there was a blessed link with 'traditional' methods here. For vats often used to soak, quite naturally, for days without any fermentation starting, when the harvest was a chilly one and no means of heating was in place.

Today, fine burgundy is aged in small barrels known as *pièces*, which are renewed much more often than barrels were in the past. For most of the century, France's leading coopers were Bordeaux- or Cognac-based. In the 1960s and '70s some *grand cru* wines were still being aged in enamel vats. Few growers had the means to buy new barrels and Burgundy's barrel-makers were struggling to make a living. Then, from the 1970s, New World vineyard areas – particularly California – provided welcome new markets, and Burgundy coopers began to prosper.

NEGOCIANTS AND THEIR ROLE

Négociants have long played an important and sometimes controversial role in Burgundy. Until the mid-1930s, many red wines bought on the Côte de Beaune were sold as Pommard, and those from the Côte de Nuits as either Gevrey-Chambertin or Nuits-Saint-Georges. 'We used to buy on quality. The *appellation contrôlée* legislation caused the quality of burgundy to fall,' remarked the father of Yves Thomas (of *négociant* Moillard-Grivot). It is an interesting point, and perhaps true in the short term, for after the legislation certain wines had the absolute right to be called Pommard, Gevrey and so on, irrespective of their quality.

At the start of the century, 99 per cent of Burgundy's production was sold by *négociants*, and everything dispatched in barrel. By 1999 the figure was 64 per cent, the balance being sold by cooperatives and domaine-bottling private estates. In Beaujolais today, 85 per cent of the production is marketed by *négociants*.

Leading *négociants* have included the dynamic marketeer Louis Latour, whose lateral thinking led him to expand into the Ardèche before most of his competitors had perceived the need to look beyond Burgundy for growth. Robert Drouhin at Joseph Drouhin has delivered consistent quality since the 1960s, concentrating exclusively on Burgundy's authentic wines. J Faiveley of Nuits, with a large vineyard estate,

1964	1972	1977	1978	1985
A hot year, giving great, long-lasting wines. Foundation of Georges Duboeuf (by mid-1990s, the largest firm in Beaujolais).	A late harvest gave wines with high acidity, which aged well for decades.	A grape-sorting table invented and first used at Domaine de la Romanée-Conti.	A fine vintage, the best of a dreary decade for the region.	A fine vintage for whites and supple reds. Increasing recognition that soils saturated with herbicides and pesticides, and compacted by multiple tractor passages, were unable to nourish vine roots effectively.

◁ Georges Faiveley in his ceremonial robes as co-founder of the principal *Confrérie* in Burgundy. The J Faiveley firm of growers and merchants produces consistently high-quality Nuits-Saint-George.

names. In the final decades of the 20th century there were new arrivals, particularly for white wines. and a flowering of mini-*négociant* firms, often emanating from successful domaines.

Négociant Yves Thomas ended the century disquieted: 'Red burgundy is only good when it is aged, and mature. People have lost the taste for old wine. Today, burgundy is wasted. It is not drunk when it should be. *Vignerons* who sell directly have no stock. They are transforming the client's taste by selling their wines immediately.' Concerning the *négociant*'s role, he adds : 'We no longer have much choice when buying. I am worried for my profession.'

Négociants have certainly lost their once-dominant position in Burgundy, but they are not on the ropes. Consumers have surely benefited from the wider ranges of wine style and sources of supply.

CHABLIS

In the last 100 years, the chilly northerly region of Chablis has been transformed. Production in 1900 was tiny: crops were often ruined by spring frosts, against which there was little protection. The name Chablis was also being borrowed by traders worldwide to label their white wines. In 1908, it was estimated that over one million hectolitres of wine circulated each

In 1908... over one million hectolitres of wine circulated each year under the name Chablis.

year under the name Chablis, while the local, true production averaged just 15,000 hectolitres.

From the 1970s determined efforts were made to combat frost damage by installing spray systems which covered the vine-shoots with protective ice when temperatures dropped dangerously low. This coincided with frenzied debate between those in the district (led by Jean

has produced wines that are full of character and true to type. Louis Jadot, now solidly backed by American family investors, has moved to a dominant position in the United States and other leading markets. The late André Boisseaux of Patriarche finished the war wealthier than some of his competitors, allowing him to build brands, sponsor yachts, and venture into television and radio long before other traders had woken up to the possibilities offered by the new media.

Bouchard Père et Fils, a respected firm by the 1950s, has since been bought by Joseph Henriot in Champagne. Bollinger acquired Chanson Père et Fils in 1999. And Burgundy's oldest firm, Champy (founded 1720), is being revitalized by the Meurgey family. The largest firm in the region today is the publicly quoted Jean-Claude Boisset of Nuits-Saint-Georges, which has absorbed many old-established

1988	1989	1990
The red wines were sound, with ample tannins and acidity, maturing slowly. Creation of Domaine Leroy, Vosne-Romanée by Lalou Bize-Leroy, who later adopted biodynamic methods.	Formation of *Bureau Interprofessionnel du Vin de Bourgogne* (BIVB) in Beaune. Publication of *Le Sol, La Terre et Les Champs* by Claude Bourguignon, which awakened many Burgundians to the possibilities of ecological vineyard tending.	A magnificent year for both reds and whites. A decade later, most of the best were still immature.

△ The annual auction of the new vintage at the *Hospices de Beaune*, raises large sums of money for charity while boosting the image of Burgundy's wines.

THE HAUTES COTES

One area of Burgundy which has recently come back to life (if not yet real prosperity) comprises the 40 communes of the Hautes Côtes on the hillsides to the west and above Beaune and Nuits. The vineyard area had dropped to 40 hectares by the late 1950s, but by 1990 over 1,000 hectares were in production. Trellissing the wide-planted vines on high wires was permitted for the first time – a revolutionary departure from tradition – which may prove a valuable experiment for growers of regional appellations like Bourgogne Rouge.

BEAUJOLAIS

In 1900, in Beaujolais 28,000 hectares were in production. The wines went to Lyon and its region, and up to Paris bistros and restaurants. But two world wars dramatically reduced the labour force, and by 1947 the land planted with vineyards was down to 7,000 hectares. Most of the region was extremely poor, though the villages producing *crus* Beaujolais (Juliénas, Moulin-à-Vent, Morgon and so on) enjoyed brief prosperity from 1947–57 when their wines sold regularly to Côte d'Or *négociants*, who used them to bolster weak-kneed Pinots.

The person most closely associated with the region's climb to prosperity since the 1960s is Georges Duboeuf. His family have long been wine-growers in Chaintré, and his company is now the largest in the region. Duboeuf set up a mobile bottling plant in the late 1950s, enabling growers throughout the region to estate-bottle their wines in their own courtyards. Top local restaurateurs helped to promote the region's best wines, and Duboeuf's bright, floral labels transformed the way Beaujolais was presented.

By 1999 over 23,000 hectares were in production, more than tripling the 1947 area, and 170 million bottles are produced each year. These wines, when they are good, have wonderful

Durup) who believed in expanding the vineyard area, and those who opposed this (led by William Fèvre). The expansionists won, and the vineyard area has grown enormously, particularly the regional appellations Chablis and Petit-Chablis. Annual production rose from an average of 50,000 hectolitres in the mid-1970s to 240,000 hectolitres 20 years later, and now represents 30 per cent of all white burgundy production.

THE COTE CHALONNAISE

The major names of the Côte Chalonnaise are Mercurey and Givry for red wines and Rully, Montagny and Bouzeron for whites. Before the appellation legislation, Mercurey reds were often bought by *négociants* for use in blends of Beaune or Pommard. The wines can be richly structured, so were ideal *vins médecins* to bolster weaker Pinots. Only the best pockets of the region were replanted after phylloxera, the names of the villages being little-known. The region was heavily replanted during the 1970s and '80s, so has been suffering a dominance of young vines. In the 1990s there were still some vineyard hillsides being replanted for the first time in 100 years.

1992	1993	1995
Foundation of the *Institut Universitaire de la Vigne et du Vin Jules Guyot*, an integrated research and post-graduate teaching faculty of Dijon University, whose new buildings were inaugurated in January 1995.	A well-structured vintage, particularly good for long-keeping reds.	A vintage of fine whites and slowly maturing reds. Foundation of *Groupement d'Etudes et Suivi du Terroir* (GEST). Around 100 domaine members embrace organic cultivation.

soft fruitiness and richness, but many are dreary due to excessive yields, with sugar-bags compensating for their lack of natural richness.

The Beaujolais Nouveau phenomenon greatly contributed to the region's new prosperity. Wine for immediate consumption represented a mere ten per cent of production back in 1960, but over 50 per cent of the two appellations Beaujolais and Beaujolais-Villages by the mid-1980s. The proportion dipped back to 40 per cent in the early 1990s, when traditional markets (United Kingdom, Belgium and Holland) became bored or more demanding, but Beaujolais Nouveau – at its best, ripely fruity and easy to enjoy as soon as purchased – has a strong following within France, as well as in many far-flung countries.

Has Beaujolais always tasted supple and fruity? It is hard to know, and likely that lower yields and regular ageing in wooden tuns at the beginning of the century gave richer, spicier wines than are enjoyed today. The person responsible for establishing the modern style during the 1960s was a much-respected vineyard-owner, *négociant* and taster, Jules Chauvet of La Chapelle de Guinchay.

MACONNAIS

Mâconnais growers have been operating near the breadline for most of the century: there are few specialist merchants or major estates. Cooperatives have dominated the scene since the early 1930s, and today account for nearly 80 per cent of white Mâcon production and 65 per cent of red.

Only since the 1970s has Mâcon-Villages begun to raise its reputation above that of a country wine, coinciding with consumers' love affair with Chardonnay. The reds are made from Gamay, and can have surprisingly rich texture and spiciness if they come from mature vineyards and the right spots.

For the first two-thirds of the century grape-harvesting proceeded in rhythm with the manually operated wine presses. The *pressée* took place during the night – the *vigneron* often working a 20-hour stretch. Today, the wine

Duboeuf set up a mobile bottling plant in the late 1950s, enabling growers throughout the region to estate-bottle their wines in their courtyards.

harvest is child's play by contrast, and top domaines have specialized, investing in new presses, cooling equipment and sometimes small barrels. Ninety per cent of Mâcon-Villages is now machine harvested. Vines are rarely ploughed. Weed-killers do the work instead, though organic and biodynamic growers have at least established a foothold.

BURGUNDY IN THE 21ST CENTURY

Growers and merchants have woken up to the fact that the style and quality of their red wines had drifted away from the excellence that made Burgundy's reputation, and they are addressing the challenge to win it back.

What concerns me most today is the glorification of deep colour, mouth-puckering tannin, new-oak aromas and powerful structure, particularly by influential American commentators. When growers slavishly follow such market demands, they undermine the individuality, excitement and silky complexity of burgundy at its best. Today's best practitioners know that what happens in the humus-rich soil and in their carefully selected plants govern the quality of the wine. Top Burgundians need to multiply their commitments to making wines that express their origins with crystal clarity. If they can, then prosperity, respect and affection will surely reward them in the new century.

1996	1998	1999
Great year for white and red, both evolving slowly.	A good vintage, less charming than 1997 but with fine potential.	A record harvest of healthy grapes, mostly picked before September rains. In Vosne-Romanée 200 hectares of top vineyards were protected from grape-berry moths by natural predators instead of insecticides. Volnay, Pommard and Meursault are taking the same route.

From the *soirées* of the Belle Epoque to the late '80's New Golden Age, Champagne has symbolized celebration, but the real story is one of repeated struggle against the odds. Serial lurches from boom to bust have characterized the Champenois' history in the 20th century.

Champagne

Tom Stevenson

The reputation of Champagne as the ultimate celebratory drink is undisputed, with sales since 1996 breaking all previous records. Yet, as recently as the early 1990s Champagne sales had lost their fizz, while just a few years earlier they were at an all-time high. This trend of going from boom to bust and back again is caused by the very name of Champagne being regarded as the

For centuries the fashionability of Champagne had vied with that of burgundy.

epitome of celebration and luxury. Its image is a double-edged sword that hacks at sales whenever public spirits become dejected. Although Champagne is perhaps the only wine famous worldwide, its image creates the perception that few of us can actually afford to drink it on a regular basis. Champagne is thus consumed by a disproportionately large number of occasional drinkers, which makes its sales highly vulnerable.

Champagne's reputation can be traced back to the *nouveau riche* society of the 1890s and 1900s. The Industrial Revolution had created a new

class of conspicuous wealth, peopled by those who loved to travel and relished dining out in public. Wherever they went this new moneyed class demanded higher and more luxurious levels of service. This era saw the dawning of lavish new hotels and restaurants such as the Savoy (1890) and the Ritz (1898). For centuries the fashionability of Champagne had vied with that of burgundy, so it was only by chance that Champagne happened to be in vogue in the 1870s when the *nouveaux riches* were on the rise. They quickly made it the most chic drink in London, Paris and New York.

Champagne's patronage by the rich, powerful and famous gave it the aura of a luxury product and celebratory drink. In the decades prior to 1870, annual Champagne sales averaged less than ten million bottles, but during the rise of the *nouveau riche* sales doubled. The decades either side of 1900 found new Champagne-drinkers amongst the rapidly swelling ranks of the ambitious middle-classes. The average annual sales of Champagne rose to 32 million bottles, culminating in 1910 when almost 40 million bottles were sold.

1904	1907	1911
One of Champagne's greatest vintages. A large crop of elegant wines, including an extraordinary Pommery still in good condition in the mid-1980s.	In 1998, thousands of bottles of Heidsieck & Co 1907 Goût Américain were salvaged from the Baltic wreck of the Jönköping. The wine was in exceptional condition, tasting 50 years younger than its years, thanks to storage at a constant 2°C and the low salinity of the sea.	A small crop of classic quality wines, promising great longevity. But, few have survived with their mousse and fruit intact, although Pommery was in excellent condition in the early 1980s.

CHAMPAGNE THEN AND NOW

Sparkling Champagne was originally a dessert wine and very sweet indeed. The first dry Champagnes appeared in the mid-19th century, but the quantities produced were insignificant until the late 1880s, when the *brut* style accounted for five per cent of total sales. This grew to 15 per cent by the turn of the century, 25 in the 1920s and 40 in the early 1940s, but dropped back to 25 per cent in the late 1940s (due to the desire for all things sweet following the rationing of sugar). It was not until the early 1970s that *brut* Champagnes began to dominate the market. Now the styles have completely reversed, with no less than 92 per cent of all Champagne sold as *brut*. Even traditionally sweet-toothed markets such as Eastern Europe and South America buy very little *demi-sec* Champagne nowadays, although their domestic sparkling wines are produced in this style.

Although sales were at record levels in 1910, the harvest that year was abysmal, with just one million bottles produced instead of the normal 30 million. This was the final straw for the growers: the following year the Champagne region was torn apart by riots; cellars were ransacked and up to 40,000 soldiers were drafted into Epernay to avert a civil war. The glory years were well and truly over and Champagne was about to experience its first collapse, setting a familiar pattern for the future.

THE CHAMPAGNE RIOTS

To a large extent the riots were the fault of the French Government. It had been asked to legislate on the boundaries of Champagne to protect it from sparkling wines outside the region, which were trading on its name and reputation. Realizing that there was a dispute over whether the Aube should be included,

◁ Early in the 20th century vines in Champagne were planted in thick clusters rather than in neat rows.

◁ Teams of harvesters sort the grapes in the vineyard before they are dispatched to the press-house.

◁ Thousands of bottles being laid down for ageing in the immense, deep chalk tunnels and quarries beneath the city of Epernay.

◁ Even in the early years of the 20th century marketing, advertising and promotion were central components of the Champagne industry.

1914

A very good, rather than truly great vintage, which was harvested in part by more than 20 child pickers, who crawled through no-man's land to harvest the grapes. The most miraculous of all 1914s must be Pol Roger, which was disgorged in 1944 to celebrate liberation. It should have deteriorated rapidly, but is still fabulous 55 years later.

1921

Moët produced its greatest ever vintage and 15 years later some of this wine was transferred into special bottles for the first release of Dom Pérignon. Moët remains the greatest living 1921, but the transferred Dom Pérignon 1921 was over the hill decades ago. In 1921 the tiny house of Salon was established, and created the first *blanc de blancs* Champagne to be commercialised.

1927

The Dom Pérignon brand was presented as a gift to Moët et Chandon by Mercier in 1927, six years after the first vintage of Dom Pérignon. Previously Mercier had owned the brand, but never used it.

▷ In 1911, thousands of growers in the Aube region took to the streets to protest against restrictions placed on the use of their grapes in Champagne. One woman's placard reads 'we are ready to shed our blood to regain our rights'.

historically part of the Champagne province , the government tried to avoid trouble by not specifying precise boundaries in its 1905 law. However, after pressure from the Champagne houses, a new law named communes in the Marne and Aisne *départements* in 1908. The Aube growers did not object but continued to sell their grapes to Champagne houses. The Marne growers were mortgaged to the hilt following the dismal harvests of 1907 to 1910, whereas the Aube growers were well-off, benefiting from a slightly warmer climate.

When the growers in the Marne realized that some houses were still buying Aube grapes they protested, and in 1911 the government issued a tougher law restricting the use of Aube grapes. Now it was the turn of Aube growers to protest: over 8,000 of them marched through the streets to Bar-sur-Aube where they set fire to their tax forms. An effigy of Prime Minister Monis was burned in 36 towns throughout the Aube while their bands played, and 36 mayors resigned.

The ever-appeasing Monis government backtracked again, announcing its intention to annul the laws of 1908 and 1911. This placated growers in the Aube, but angered those in the Marne, who gathered to march in protest. The protesters quickly swelled into a mob and the march became a riot, as they sacked the cellars of producers in Damery and Aÿ. It took the presence of 40,000 troops to calm the situation.

The government drafted a new law recognizing the Aube, but as a separate district called *Champagne Deuxième Zone*. It is doubtful whether such a two-tier classification could have worked in the long term, but neither the growers in the Marne nor those in the Aube had the stomach for any more disruption and soon they would have other, much more important things on their mind.

THE FIRST WORLD WAR

On September 3rd, 1914, Reims fell to German forces and three days later so did Epernay, but the advance faltered, giving French forces time to regroup. Joffre, who commanded the French

1928	1929	1937	1947	1949
Quite possibly the greatest of all 20th century Champagne vintages. The best still have freshness, fruit and fizz, whereas most of the best 1929s do not. Salon is without doubt the greatest of all the 1928s I have tasted.	A great enough vintage that it took 50 years for its wines to be overshadowed by the magnificent Champagnes of 1928. Perrier-Jouët is the greatest living 1929 and owes its longevity to the Chardonnay of *grand cru* Cramant.	A large and great vintage. Veuve Clicquot is the best. Pol Roger stands out as the finest recently disgorged example, with its extremely fresh and complex aromas and huge capacity for further development.	This top vintage competes with 1964 for being second in ranking to 1928. Its wines are big, rich and almost over-generous. So many are still alive and kicking – Salon is the greatest, with Pol Roger, Krug and Veuve Clicquot close by.	Although overshadowed by the 1947s, these wines have more acidity and sometimes taste a decade fresher. Veuve Clicquot is probably showing best, but Krug gives it a close run.

Army on the Western Front, swiftly launched a counter-attack, liberating Epernay on the 11th and Reims on the 13th of September. From here on the warfare in Champagne would be confined to the high ground of the Montagne de Reims, where trench lines moved barely 100 yards over four long and bloody years.

In October 1917, while France was preoccupied by battles on its Western Front, Russia rose in revolution. For 50-odd years the Russian court and aristocracy had consumed one tenth of all the Champagne produced, but the revolutionary government halted shipments and refused to pay any bills. The entire Champagne trade suffered great difficulties as a result and looked elsewhere to fill the void in sales. However, Germany and the former Austro-Hungarian Empire were bankrupt and in 1920 Prohibition cut off yet another market. After the war, the subject of the Aube's *Deuxième Zone* arose, but this time a more astute French Government handed the matter to the courts. After six years of litigation, the case was decided in favour of the Aube and in 1927 a law establishing Champagne's AOC regulations dispensed with the *Deuxième* designation.

THE 1920S AND '30S

Champagne had been fashionable in Britain since the mid-19th century and its popularity was boosted when British soldiers returned from France with a taste for wine. The Roaring Twenties were perfect for Champagne: a time for celebration, a time to forget the war and look forward to happier times. Despite Prohibition, sales started to rise in America, as bootleggers managed to smuggle in significant quantities of Champagne. But in 1929, America's economy dived and prices on Wall Street collapsed, heralding the Depression, which eventually engulfed all the world's industrialized nations.

With little money about and no cause to celebrate, the demand for Champagne dried up. By 1933, the cellars in Reims and Epernay contained the equivalent of 33 years of stock and the last thing needed was a large harvest, yet that was exactly what 1934 provided. Many houses refused to purchase any grapes, while some paid a mere pittance, causing widespread hardship amongst the growers. In 1935, the government therefore ruled that the price of grapes should in future be fixed by a committee composed of houses and growers.

The Montagne de Reims, where trench lines moved barely 100 yards over four long and bloody years.

With export markets unresponsive, most houses turned their attention to the home market. Nowadays France consumes twice as much Champagne as the rest of the world put together, but at the beginning of the 20th century it was the other way round. Within a few years, the houses managed to triple French sales, but while this provided a quick financial fix, it created a long-term imbalance in the economy of the Champagne trade.

In 1935, an interprofessional body called the *Commission Spéciale de la Champagne* was created and, because its meetings were held in Châlons-sur-Marne, it soon became known as the *Commission de Châlons*. Its aims were to ensure the respect of local custom and tradition in order to preserve the quality of Champagne, but it was toothless, and thus ineffective.

THE SECOND WORLD WAR

From May 1940 until August 1944 the region of Champagne was occupied by German troops. The Champenois were not unprepared, having sealed up their most precious stocks in parts of

1952	1953	1955	1959
One of Champagne's greatest vintages, producing exquisitely balanced wines. Pol Roger disgorged in 1977 evokes happy memories, but Gosset and Pommery are at least on par, yet all three are pipped at the post by Clos des Goisses.	Fuller in body and higher in alcohol than either the 1955 or 1952, with a deft balance of fruit that enabled early disgorgement. Bollinger, which had just three years on yeast, and Krug, with no less than 30 per cent Meunier, are the best wines.	Although not quite in the class of the other three classic years of the 1950s, Veuve Clicquot made its greatest vintage in 1955 and on an individual basis this Champagne is a match for the best from 1952, 1953 and 1959.	The last of the really big, bruising vintages of the century because the wines were still fermented in wood. The perfectly balanced, amazingly fresh Billecart-Salmon disgorged in 1964 is the best living example of this extraordinarily hot year. However, Salon, Clos des Goisses, Pommery and Pol Roger are all stunning. Veuve Clicquot produced its greatest ever rosé.

▷ *Remuage* or riddling was once all undertaken by hand. The bottles held by the neck in *pupitres* are gradually inverted to allow the sediment to collect in the cap. This process can take up to two or three months to complete.

△ German soldiers in the trenches of northern France during the First World War show an appreciative interest in the local produce.

their cellars, but the more famous the brand, the more careful they had to be. A famous firm claiming blatantly low stocks or declaring cellars too small for its recorded production would attraction attention, inviting the Nazis to make an even more thorough search.

In November 1940, the Vichy government abolished the *Commission de Châlons*, intending to replace it with another organization called *Le Bureau de Repartition du Vinicole de Champagne*, but two clever Champenois had other ideas. Robert-Jean de Vogüé, a legendary head of Moët et Chandon, and Maurice Doyard, the growers' leader, persuaded the Germans to establish the *Comité Interprofessionnel du Vin de Champagne* (CIVC) by suggesting that the Third Reich had more important things to do than to get bogged down in the day-to-day machinations of the Champagne industry. This not only enabled the Champenois to run their own industry under the noses of their invaders, but also resulted in the most powerful interprofessional organization in the French wine industry (although this power declined in 1990s).

Champagne was liberated on August 28th, 1944, when General Patton swept into Epernay before the Germans could blow up the cellars.

THE POST-WAR PERIOD

Although the second half of the 1940s was a time of relative joy and celebration, sales of Champagne were slow to take off. This was

1961	**1964**	**1966**	**1966**
The best have surprised everybody over the last ten years or so, and as they acquire further finesse, so the assessment of this vintage continues to rise. Dom Pérignon comes out top, with Pommery in magnum giving chase.	This vintage competes with 1947 for being second to the greatest vintage of the century, 1928. The best? Salon, Krug, Pol Roger, Dom Pérignon, Dom Ruinart, Taittinger Comtes de Champagne – take your pick!	Elegant, stylish wines that sometimes appear more seductive than the 1964s, although they are not intrinsically as great. Salon, Clos des Goisses, Pol Roger, Dom Pérignon, Taittinger Comtes de Champagne Rosé and Dom Ruinart are currently fighting it out for top honours.	Bollinger releases its Vieilles Vignes Françaises, a very special wine made from overripe grapes grown on ungrafted vines.

primarily due to the domination of the French market, which was hindered by the troubles of the Fourth Republic. Global sales reached a modest peak of 35 million bottles in 1951 (which was less than the 1910 figure), but dipped in 1953, and so Champagne's cyclical fortunes continued. In 1957, Champagne sales topped 48 million bottles and the cost of a kilo of grapes was indexed to the previous year's price of a bottle of Champagne. This effectively doubled the growers' income, but the houses were achieving record sales and felt they could afford it. Until the very next year, that is, when Champagne sales crashed once more and, with more than a hint of *déjà vu*, the houses refused to purchase grapes. To prevent this happening again, an interprofessional contract was agreed in 1959 in which the houses guaranteed to buy a minimum percentage of the growers' harvest, while the growers undertook to sell a minimum percentage of their crop. Obviously this pleased the growers, but there would come times when the houses would benefit from the arrangement and no doubt they realized this.

Under General De Gaulle's popular leadership, Champagne sales in France rose as never before, pushing up the global total to 93 million bottles by 1967, but the bottom dropped out of the market when Paris experienced the student riots of May 1968. The next boom came in 1973 when sales surged to 124 million bottles, another all-time high, only to be followed by Champagne's worst-ever slump in the midst of the oil crisis of 1974. In a bid to lessen the effects of France's volatile market, the largest Champagne houses decided to target export countries and, within just four years, sales were pushing well over 185 million bottles. Another peak – but with the pressure off, French sales dived. Exports also began to falter and within another four years global sales had plummeted by no less than 40 million bottles.

◁ Comte Robert-Jean de Vogüé, head of Moët et Chandon, helped found the self-regulatory bodies that continue to guard the interests of the Champagne industry today.

The second biggest boom in history occurred in 1989, when a staggering 249 million bottles were sold. This was aided by the short-lived economic boom of the late 1980s and abetted by a number of greedy firms who sold far more Champagne than they should have. The only way for such houses to sell excessive amounts was by depleting their own stocks to dangerous levels; buying stocks from other less successful houses, growers or cooperatives and slapping

The largest Champagne houses decided to target export countries and, within just four years, sales were pushing well over 185 million bottles.

on their own famous labels (regrettably legal and known as *sur lattes*, after the point in production at which they are purchased); or both depleting stocks and buying *sur lattes*. The interprofessional contract did not allow houses any other strategy. Each house was forced by

1971

A freak year in terms of weather, which even included tornado damage, yet the small harvest produced some stunning Champagnes. Salon leads the way, with Krug, Dom Pérignon and Dom Pérignon Rosé in the chase.

1976

One of Champagne's greatest vintages, but hammered by many critics because of its high alcohol and low acidity. The fruit found in the best wines is often quite exotic. The top wines include Taittinger Comtes de Champagne, Krug, Diamant Bleu, Clos des Goisses and Salon.

this contract to buy up to a certain volume based on its previous year's sales, relative to the size of the actual crop. If, for example, one house sold two million bottles and the crop was ten per cent larger than average it would be

This anti-Champagne campaign was followed by a global economic slump... few had money for luxury products and fewer had any desire to celebrate.

allowed to buy enough grapes to produce 2.2 million bottles of Champagne and no more. If the crop was ten per cent smaller, then it would be able to buy only enough grapes to produce 1.8 million bottles of Champagne.

From a superficial stance, this seems fair. Champagne is a delimited wine region with a finite yield and the contract appeared to ensure that everybody received enough grapes to continue business. But all it did was maintain the status quo, ensuring the largest houses remained the largest, the smallest houses remained the smallest and, of course, that no new firms could muscle in on their lucrative industry (because they would have to demonstrate sales of Champagne in the year before they were allowed to purchase the grapes necessary to make that Champagne!). The infamous interprofessional agreement had to go and in 1990 it did, as did the fixed price.

The grapes purchased in the first year achieved ridiculously high prices as the high-volume houses desperately tried to build up stocks. It would be another three years before the finished Champagnes from these grapes could start filtering onto the shelves. In the meantime, however, Champagne came under attack from the media, primarily in the United Kingdom, for its poor quality. And what could the Champagne houses say? After all, the wines were either too young or of dubious origin. It

was at this point that Jean-Claude Rouzaud, the head of Roederer and new chairman of the *Syndicat de Grandes Marques* stated that he wanted quality criteria for membership, and that if he could not get agreement on this he would resign (later, in 1997, when Rouzaud finally admitted failure, he not only resigned, but also disbanded the *Grandes Marques*).

This criticism from the press had hit some brands more than others, although a few escaped any blame whatsoever. Some merely because they managed to buy better Champagnes *sur lattes* than they could make themselves! This anti-Champagne campaign was soon followed by a global economic slump and the Gulf War, so few people had money to spare for luxury products and fewer had any desire to celebrate. It was these circumstances that set Champagne up for its most damaging crisis and, ironically, the fall-out from this debacle would save the industry from an even worse one as the new millennium approached. As sales slumped, so the price of Champagne dropped and by 1993 it was at its lowest ebb, just as the first Champagnes made from the most expensive Champagne grapes ever started to hit the shelves. That year more than 30 Champagne houses made an operating loss and the amount owed by the trade to the banks reached FF15 billion, which was one billion more than the entire industry's annual turnover.

PREPARED FOR 2000 – BY ACCIDENT
As sales dwindled further, so stocks built up and it soon became accepted wisdom that the industry was so grossly overstocked that it needed to divest itself of 250 million bottles. Since this roughly equated to one year's harvest, someone came up with the idea of not picking the next harvest. Not only would this redress the balance of stocks, but it would save the cost

1981	1982		1985
Probably the most underrated vintage of the century. The crop was tiny and came when stocks were low, thus relatively few houses declared a vintage. Krug is the finest example, but there are a dozen or so great 1981s around.	A large harvest that every house declared. The wines shone early, requiring minimal yeast contact, yet possessing the balance to age gracefully for many decades. Consistent quality across houses and styles, but Krug Vintage, Krug Clos du Mesnil, Laurent-Perrier Cuvée Alexandre Rosé, Dom Pérignon and Dom Pérignon Rosé manage to stand out.		This vintage continues to surprise even the Champenois. There is so much undeveloped extract in the best wines that they will just get better and better. It will be impossible to pick out any clear leaders for a decade or more.

of picking, pressing and making the wine. Other incidental savings would include the cost of 250 million bottles, labels, corks, *muselets* (metal caps that protect the corks) and wire cages, not to mention the 37 million kilos of sugar required for dosage. Apparently this creative accounting would instantly have turned 30 operating losses into 30 massive profits, but it fell down on one fundamental premise – that Champagne was overstocked. In reality, it was not. If any boom is predictable, it must surely have been the millennium boom.

After all, the Champenois even had the last new century to go by, when Champagne houses made their greatest profits ever, and that was just a 100 year celebration. This would be the big three zeros! Yet an examination of the trade press at the time shows that the word 'millennium' did not enter Champenois vocabulary until late 1995. Earlier that year the Champenois were still desperately trying to rid themselves of 250 million bottles. History shows that they never managed to do that and thus by accident had one billion bottles in stock for the turn of the millennium.

What will the future bring? If the houses and growers could not bond for once in a thousand years, there is nothing to suggest they will come any closer over the next 999, but there are at least two crucial things that are easy to predict. Both concern misrepresentation: one involves *vins sur lattes*, the other concerns the misuse of the Champagne appellation.

It is grossly misleading for a Champagne house to develop brand loyalty, then when stocks are low to buy Champagne from another house, usually a less well-known one, slap on its own famous label and pretend to its customers that it is their own handcrafted wine. After much media criticism, Jean-Claude Rouzaud persuaded the *Syndicat de Grandes Marques* to ban *vins sur lattes* in 1994. As the *Grandes Marques*

were themselves disbanded in 1997, this ban had no effect, but its ephemeral enactment has at least set a moral precedent, so the Champenois must act to make it illegal to use *vins sur lattes* for anything other than second wines or Buyers' Own Brands. In the meantime, however, the only Champagnes that can legitimately claim to be *sur-lattes*-free are those made by the *Récoltant-Manipulant* (authentic grower-producers with RM preceding the matriculation number on the label).

The second important change concerns those Champagne houses that produce sparkling wine as Champaña in Argentina and Chile, and Champanha in Brazil. It is both hypocritical and self-defeating to do this when the CIVC takes firms in other countries to court in defence of their appellation. The companies involved fund a large proportion of the CIVC's budget and dominate its committees, which may be why the CIVC has persistently failed to take any action against them. It has no jurisdiction over companies in other countries, hence its recourse to diplomacy or foreign judicial systems, but it has jurisdiction within Champagne itself. If the CIVC does not use its powers to penalize such companies, then the organization will become a laughing stock.

If the houses and growers could not bond for once in a thousand years, there is nothing to suggest they will come any closer over the next 999.

Other expected developments include the replacement of Champagne's single-wine appellation with a multiple *Appellation d'Origine Contrôlée* that specifies more stringent quality criteria for superior sub-appellations; an expansion of the land classified as AOC Champagne; and legislation preventing disgorgement to order of vintage Champagnes.

1990

Not only one of Champagne's greatest vintages, but one of its most extraordinarily consistent across the different houses and styles. Although hard to believe, the 1990s are more alcoholic than the 1976s – their success is due to high levels of ripe acidity. Too early to whittle the leaders down to a handful of names.

1996

On paper this year's superior to 1990 and could even vie with 1923 as the greatest vintage of the century but only time will tell how successful the winemakers have been in capturing this potential in the bottle.

Inspiring example and an increasingly acceptable cooperative mood have triumphed in France, despite the blinkered attitudes and short-term outlook of many. Now winemaking outside the classic regions is squaring up to modern consumer demands.

Rest of France

Joanna Simon

If this chapter had been written at the half-century, it would have told a story of disease, depression and difficult harvests, of struggle, despair, government intervention, regulation and not a lot else. True, the century had seemed to open on a hopeful note for some: in Paris the exuberance of Belle Epoque society was inescapable and, with it, the demand for fine

Vineyards in most of France were in a parlous, post-phylloxera state. From Alsace to the Pyrenees, they lay abandoned or neglected.

wine; Bordeaux had enjoyed two splendid vintages in 1899 and 1900. But away from the metropolis and Bordeaux, the picture was largely bleak – and even in Paris and Bordeaux the optimism faded fast.

Vineyards in most of France were in a parlous, post-phylloxera state. From Alsace (then under German rule) to the Pyrénées, they lay abandoned or neglected. In Cahors, for example, where vines had been everywhere, growers had mostly been unable to afford

phylloxera-resistant grafted vines and so had replanted with ungrafted stock – with swift and tragic results. Not until the 1950s did Cahors begin to show signs of recovery – and then it suffered another setback, the great killer freeze of 1956. In the Loire and the Rhône, many growers simply switched to other crops. It was not until the 1980s that some of the finest (and steepest) vineyards of the northern Rhône began to be replanted, in response to sudden demand for these great, long-lived, serious reds. Where vineyards were replanted after phylloxera, it was often with resistant, but low-quality, heavy-cropping hybrids and crossings. They were the last thing anyone needed. Nowhere was this more evident than in Alsace and Languedoc.

When phylloxera arrived in Alsace in 1904, it was only the last, and not the worst, of a series of ruinous diseases. Growers were ordered to plant the new, resistant hybrids by the German authorities. Some refused but, as Alsace had by then become little more than a source of blending wine for Germany, most succumbed to the lure of large yields and flat land. By

1907	1918	1921	1923
Surpluses of low-quality wine, much of it beefed up with Algerian red, cause wine prices to collapse, sparking riots in Narbonne.	Alsace is returned to France from Germany.	As perfect a vintage for Vouvray *moelleux* as it is possible to imagine. Still worth drinking – if you can find any. Legendary in Jurançon, too.	Baron Le Roy draws up rules for the wine laws of his region, Châteauneuf-du-Pape. These were to act as the foundations for the subsequent AOC system.

◁ Alsace, fought over for centuries, was twice reoccupied by Germany. By the close of the Second World War many of the small-holders and *négociants* who had dominated the wine business faced ruin.

the time the region was returned to France in 1918, the traditional grape varieties were heavily outnumbered.

It was immediately clear that there was no French market for this poor-quality wine, since Languedoc did the same thing more cheaply. Some growers started to pull up their hybrids and, a few years later, a newly formed growers' association voted not only to ban hybrids but to restrict planting to the slopes. But this was not the end of Alsace's difficulties. The Second World War brought further occupation and hardship, and hybrids were still making their presence felt in 1962 when Alsace finally achieved full *appellation contrôlée* status. There remains work to do – on limiting yields and achieving a more even standard among the 50 *grands crus*, for example – but, compared with the vast Languedoc region, Alsace seems to have dealt with the vagaries of the 20th century relatively tidily.

It wasn't until the late 1980s, after spending most of the century on its knees, that Languedoc began to emerge as one of the most dynamic

regions in Europe. Investment in 'the California of the old world' came both from within the Languedoc region (from the likes of Robert Skalli and his enormous, hi-tech Fortant de France enterprise), and from without (the Sichel family of Bordeaux and BRL Hardy and Penfolds of Australia, among others).

Australian-trained winemakers – with their kitbags of enzymes and yeasts, their enthusiasm for hygiene and the flavours of new-oak and soft tannins – flooded in to hose down and shake up dozy, down-at-heel cooperative wineries and, where they were still clinging on, old-fashioned *négociant* merchants.

Growers were encouraged to plant the fashionable varieties – Chardonnay, Sauvignon and Viognier, Cabernet, Merlot and Syrah – and these were made into varietal (single variety) wines. Not only did these wines have a flavour of the New World, they looked New World. The *vin de pays* category – created in 1973 to encourage the move away from the basic *vin de table* that was increasingly filling the European wine lake – allowed wines to be

1929

Remarkable Hermitage – some whites as well as reds have seemed almost indestructible, particularly from Chave. Châteauneuf-du-Pape was also outstanding. In Alsace, 1928 was marginally better.

1935

The creation of the *Comité National des Appellations d'Origine* and the ACC system.

named and labelled by grape variety, instead of predominantly by place of origin. With the exception of Alsace, this was a practice proscribed for AOC wines: the spirit of place had always been the cornerstone of French wine.

INSPIRATION AND REPUTATION

All this outside influence helped to raise the average standard of Languedoc wine and gained respect for it, but there was another strand of development which was at least as important. Deserted and run-down estates in the *garrigue*-covered hills began to be reclaimed and revived, along with their traditional grape varieties, and new estates started to appear on equally inhospitable-looking soils: the inimitably French concept of *terroir* was being established for the first time outside the classic regions. Low-yielding, old Grenache and Carignan vines were rehabilitated. The wines produced began to gain recognition. Their prices rose to viable levels – and higher – and reputations were made.

The first such reputation, and a source of inspiration to all who followed, was that of Mas de Daumas Gassac in the Vin de Pays de l'Hérault area. Neither Aimé nor Véronique Guibert, who bought the estate in 1970, had

The wines produced began to gain recognition. Their prices rose to viable levels – and higher – and reputations were made.

any experience of vines or winemaking, but they were encouraged by the opinion of a wine geology expert, Professor Henri Enjalbert. He thought the soil had the potential to produce a *grand cru*. Mind you, he also said it might take 200 years and that the Guiberts would have to be crazy to attempt it. Perhaps they were, for they went ahead – clearing, planting

and choosing Cabernet Sauvignon, despite Enjalbert having compared their soil to that of Burgundy, where Pinot Noir reigns. If Cabernet was in vogue internationally, thanks largely to California, planting uncloned, original vinestocks was not. Dependence on one or a small handful of clones was far more normal, but Aimé Guibert believed the uncloned material he had tracked down in the Rhône region was more likely to produce a wine of distinction and individuality.

From the first vintage in 1978, Mas de Daumas Gassac proved to be precisely that: a distinguished, original wine. Rich in fruit, dark and densely tannic, it needed years to mature – and that was a problem. Even with the endorsement of Professor Emile Peynaud – consultant to the Bordeaux glitterati and, after much pestering, consultant also to Daumas Gassac – it proved almost impossible to sell this unknown newcomer, from France's least-regarded region, at a decidedly un-Languedoc price. The breakthrough came in autumn 1982. Guibert had persuaded a few restaurateur friends in Paris to list the wine and one of them recommended it to a director of *Gault-Millau* magazine. Shortly afterwards, the magazine described it as the 'Lafite du Languedoc'. The rest is history.

No one would pretend that the Midi is not still a huge producer of relatively modest-quality wine (and some that is fit only for distillation), but in this huge terrain – by far the largest in France and with an output many times that of Australia – there is room for great diversity. There are pockets of true excellence and potential yet to be realized.

SHIFTING IMAGE

While all this may have come as news to us in the last decade or two, it would not have been

1947

An extraordinary harvest of sweet Loire wines, especially Vouvray and Bonnezeaux: perhaps even superior to 1921. Exceptional Alsace – the best since 1934. Great red Rhônes, but now tiring.

a surprise in the middle of the 19th century. Languedoc had a reputation not only for the quality of its wine but for its pioneering developments. Indeed, it was researchers at the University of Montpellier who came up with the vine-grafting solution for phylloxera. Two things changed Languedoc's image and position: the coming of the railways, opening up expansive new markets; and, despite Montpellier's ground-breaking discovery, phylloxera in the 1860s.

With not an inkling of how vulnerable they were making themselves, growers took the opportunity to replant on the easy-to-cultivate plains and to switch to poor-quality, highly productive varieties. Other regions planted hybrids, but Languedoc went for monoculture and on an industrial scale. The resulting wines were so thin and weak that they were widely beefed up with imports from Algeria (a custom that continued until after Algeria gained independence in 1962, and was then partly replaced by the Italian equivalent). By 1900, with huge surpluses, prices were collapsing.

Out of this desperate situation, which culminated in fatal riots in Narbonne in 1907, came the first of many steps to regulate the French wine industry – regulating and restricting it being one of the growth industries of the 20th century, one might add.

These early measures had two aims: to protect growers from fraudulent copies (the growers, who saw this as their salvation, seemed not to appreciate that there was no incentive to fake abysmal wines that couldn't even be sold at cost); and, secondly, to impose controls that would balance supply and demand – an equilibrium the French government has been trying to achieve ever since. To this end, wine was for the first time legally defined as the fermented product of fresh grapes, and every grower was henceforth required to submit a crop declaration.

A few years later, the first laws delineating regions were also passed. The identity of these regions says much about the reputation of wines at the time. Among the first were Banyuls – its sweet, fortified *vins doux naturels* already famed for their longevity; Clairette de Die in

Out of this desperate situation, which culminated in fatal riots in Narbonne in 1907, came the first of many steps to regulate the French wine industry.

the Drôme Valley, east of the Rhône – now mainly a sparkling wine but then a still dry white; and Madiran in the southwest, despite the fact that it was one of the areas hardest hit by phylloxera and very little authentic Madiran was being produced. Another was Bordeaux, which fought off the demands of growers in the Dordogne and Lot et Garonne, who argued that they should be included, as their wines were regularly used to 'improve' those of Bordeaux. It was to be another 60 years before wines such as Bergerac, Buzet and Côtes du Duras began to emerge properly from Bordeaux's shadow.

The real importance of these moves to delineate regions lay in what they presaged or, in effect, evolved into – *Appellation d'Origine Contrôlée* (AOC), a system which has been both the saving grace of the French wine industry and, equally, one of its most frustrating and inflexible icons. Only in France would one of the most original, high-quality wine creations of the century be demoted from AOC status to humble *vin de pays* because it fell outside the appellation rules when the rules – not the wine – were changed. Eloi Dürrbach, former Paris architect and godson of Picasso, started creating his wine estate, Domaine de Trévallon in

1956

A killer freeze devastates the region of Cahors.

1959

A hot summer produced excellent sweet Alsace and Loire whites and fine, long-lived northern Rhône reds. Châteauneuf-du-Pape was a little less favoured, although Château Rayas was highly acclaimed.

Provence, at much the same time as Aimé Guibert was embarking on his in Languedoc. Like Guibert, he planted Cabernet Sauvignon, although he also planted the local Syrah grape. From the first vintage, 1978, Trévallon was widely acclaimed and, though expensive, over-subscribed. Perhaps it was the success and, even more, the perceived audacity of the prices, set by an outsider, that rankled with the local Coteaux d'Aix appellation authorities.

Dürrbach's relationship with them was never warm and when they halved the permitted Cabernet component to 20 per cent in 1994, Trévallon was unceremoniously demoted to a Vin de Pays des Bouches du Rhône. It has not made a jot of difference to the success of Trévallon, but it has highlighted the shortcomings – notably the sometimes farcical intractability – of the AOC system.

△ Mas de Daumas Gassac, a pioneering Languedoc estate whose successful *vins de pays* have inspired other producers to develop new wines and establish individual reputations in previously unappreciated areas.

▷ Baron Le Roy de Boiseaumarié, investigator of the system of *Appellation d'Origine Contrôlées*, first defined the region of Châteauneuf-du-Pape in the Rhône Valley.

SHAPING REGIONS

When *Appellation d'Origine Contrôlée* emerged on the statute book in the mid-1930s, however, the situation was very different. As the regulations introduced in the early years of the century had also been, AOC was a response to the desperate plight of growers.

The short-lived period of prosperity at the end of the 1920s had been replaced by global depression, exacerbated for the wine industry by yet more disease, particularly mildew, and dwindling French consumption from the peak of 136 litres per capita in 1926. 1932 was the blackest of black years. Although the concept took legal form in 1935, with the creation of the *Comité National des Appellations d'Origine* (later INAO), AOC had been shaped some years earlier in Châteauneuf-du-Pape.

This was a wine with a celebrated and historic reputation, but that didn't prevent much of the output from all but the most

1961	1962	1964
A superb vintage for white and red Hermitage, and the best of both are still holding up. Jaboulet's La Chapelle and Chapoutier s white are fabled. Very good vintage in Alsace, too.	Alsace is awarded *appellation contrôlée* status.	A great Rhône vintage, though small in Châteauneuf-du-Pape: the best red Hermitages should make it to their 40th birthday. Exceptional Vouvray.

◁ The Sauvignon Blanc harvest in Sancerre, one of the uppermost of the mainstream Loire vineyards. The wine's easily recognizable style – pungent and cutting – has profoundly influenced modern tastes in white wine.

revered estates – and sometimes even from those – ending up with other southern Rhônes in the blending vats of Burgundy *négociants*.

It was against this background that, in 1923, an enlightened and prominent producer of Châteauneuf-du-Pape, Baron Le Roy de Boiseaumarié of Château Fortia, drew up rules for the wine of his region. He was a lawyer and realized that the protection of the wine's integrity and reputation from fakes and blending – and the protection of producers' livelihoods – required more than geographical boundaries: wine from a given place needed to be produced in a given way, in accordance with local custom. His detailed specifications ran to grape varieties (no fewer than 13), soil types, pruning, ripeness levels, yields and cellar practices – and they were all enshrined in the AOC of Châteauneuf-du-Pape 12 years later.

The other maiden AOCs were Cassis in Provence and Arbois in the Jura, both of which

have subsequently shown that *appellation contrôlée* does not guarantee protection and survival. Cassis has spent much of its subsequent history trying to hold the creeping Marseilles suburbs at bay – and at last managed to do so during the 1990s, slightly increasing its tiny vineyard total to 175 hectares.

The vineyards in Jura might have disappeared altogether had it not been for the determination of the producer Henri Maire in the 1950s and '60s. Before he began his campaign to revive them, the area under vine had dropped from a pre-phylloxera total of 18,500 hectares to a mere 500 hectares. It is now three times that and the Jura's distinctive indigenous grape varieties and styles have survived.

With the rules in place, all that remained was for hundreds more appellations to be drawn up and ratified and for growers to form local *syndicats* – a new phenomenon – to help press their case. Cooperatives played a part in this,

1970	**1971**	**1976**	**1978**
Aimé Guibert buys the estate that will become Mas de Daumas Gassac in the region of Vin de Pays de l'Hérault.	Not quite in the 1921/1947 league, but some fabulous Vouvrays nevertheless, especially from Huët. It was also a memorable year for Jurançon and northern Rhône, but the latter need drinking.	The greatest Alsace vintage since 1959, many producers making *vendange tardive* and *selection de grains nobles* wines for the first time. Exceptionally rich Coteaux du Layon, Bonnezeaux and Vouvray.	Big, concentrated reds from Cahors and throughout the Rhône and impressive debuts from Mas de Daumas Gassac in Languedoc and Domaine de Trévallon in Provence. Top-class Jurançon also.

too, and their numbers burgeoned in the 1930s, especially in the southern Rhône and the Midi. By 1939 the total had swelled to 838 from just 92 in 1902.

The incentives for growers were obvious. Apart from pushing for AOC status, the heavily government-subsidized cooperatives had modern equipment, such as concrete vats and new hydraulic presses, which growers alone could rarely afford. The average holding had doubled to between five and six hectares in the inter-war years, but this was still not enough to enable most growers to invest in anything more than a horse-drawn plough and rudimentary equipment. Where it existed, no less an incentive in these frequently straitened inter-war years, was the market provided by those cooperatives which also sold the wine on behalf of their members.

The rise of the cooperative movement in the 1930s and '40s also reflected the stirrings of something deeper: a desire among growers to escape the clutches of the merchant-blenders – previously the only significant outlet for many growers. But this was not the disaster it might appear for the merchants. It was certainly not the beginning of the end (when their

The rise of the cooperative movement in the 1930s and '40s also reflected the stirrings of something deeper: a desire among growers to escape the clutches of the merchant-blenders.

power waned much later, it was more to do with supermarkets coming on to the scene and dispensing with middlemen). Cooperatives had wines to sell and merchants were happy to buy them: they were often more reliable than the wines merchants had been buying direct from growers.

ADVANCES IN FIELD AND CELLAR

The Second World War reintroduced many problems the wine industry had faced in the First: lack of resources, human and otherwise, and consequently deteriorating vineyards. In Jurançon, despite having been favoured by such individuals as Henry IV and Colette, the area under vine had fallen from a pre-phylloxera 3,000 hectares to only 300 by the 1950s, and the winemaking was appalling, with excessive sugar being used to disguise other evils.

But the war was also a turning point. Where the first four decades had been characterized by crises and the government's regulatory reaction, the second half of the century was characterized by viticultural and vinicultural revolutions and by the changing demands of changing markets. Indeed, the developments in field and cellar came, increasingly, to be dictated by the evolution in consumption and taste, rather than the reverse.

First came the domestic decline in consumption of *gros rouge*, which started with the war. Then, with economic prosperity in France in the 1960s, came increasing demand for AOC wine, especially wine that did not need cellaring for years in cellars that fewer and fewer people possessed. In the southern Rhône and Midi, carbonic maceration became an important method for achieving less aggressive-tasting wines. Stainless steel, bringing with it the possibility of temperature control, began to replace cement and enamel – although the costs involved mean that, even now, old-style vats are still in use. Some cooperatives simply cannot persuade members that it would be money well spent.

By the 1980s the market was shifting again – this time the impetus coming more from abroad. In Britain, wine was increasingly being sold by supermarkets to people for whom it was a new habit rather than an occasional

1990	1991
The third of a trio of celebrated vintages in many regions, with Hermitage comparable to 1929 and 1961; powerful Madiran and Cahors, and tremendous, sweet Loires. For Châteauneuf and Alsace, 1989 was slightly finer.	The first in a run of punishing vintages, which coincided with widespread economic recession.

celebratory treat, and one that involved buying a bottle for the same evening or, at a stretch, the next weekend. Typically, over two thirds of sales were white wine, which was not a great help to the Midi, but turned out to be perfect for the grape-growers of Gascony when Armagnac hit the doldrums.

Between them, André Dubosc of the Plaimont cooperative and Yves Grassa of Château de Tariquet turned a surplus of Armagnac grapes into an eminently saleable crisp, light white wine and, in so doing, put Vin de Pays des Côtes de Gascogne on the international map. Dubosc's achievement is all the more remarkable in that he conceived the idea after a trip to Germany in 1973, when all was well with Armagnac, and later managed to coax the traditional, insular Gascon growers into believing that their future lay in a completely different product.

TAKING STEPS FORWARD

By the late 1980s, Britain's wine-drinkers were also being introduced to the delights of Australian wines – bold, fruity, instantly appealing, alluringly flavoured with new oak and, no less important, of unequalled reliability.

French producers and exporters were slow to respond, largely because most could not see that something they were apt to dismiss as alcoholic fruit juice could possibly pose a threat to French hegemony. They reckoned without a punishing run of vintages which, starting with 1991, affected most regions and coincided with widespread economic recession. Plus they reckoned without the flexibility of the Australian industry. Australian producers gave buyers the style and quality of wine they requested at the price specified. The French attitude was still inclined to be: geography dictates style and quality; weather dictates price

take it or leave it. By the time the generally superior 1995 vintage arrived, France's grip on the British wine market had been bruisingly weakened in favour of New World wines – especially Australian. The industry reacted,

In Britain, wine was increasingly being sold by supermarkets to people for whom it was a new habit rather than an occasional treat... Typically, over two thirds of sales were white wine.

finally, in the right way. The last five years of the century saw new investment in equipment and in people: sometimes the reins were handed to the more skilled and ambitious younger generation; sometimes itinerant Australasian winemakers were hired.

Quality and consistency – aided by a run of better vintages – took another step forward, and perhaps nowhere more so than in the Loire Valley, where a strong *négociant* presence seemed to have held back progress (in contrast to the Rhône Valley where *négociants* such as Jaboulet, Guigal and Chapoutier have been beacons of quality).

In the excellent trio of vintages 1995, 1996 and 1997 some extraordinary, ground-breaking sweet wines were made in Anjou by the likes of Jo Pithon, Patrick Baudoin and Philippe Delesvaux. But as much of a breakthrough was the improvement in the dry and medium white wines – the bread and butter of the region – and the red wines. The last may be small in volume but, in a world turning to red wine, they are vital.

As for the other regions, only Alsace must be hoping that the pendulum will swing back in favour of white wines before we are far into the third millennium. And all must be hoping that the first years of this century will not repeat those of the last.

1995

The first of four pleasing vintages in many regions. Glorious sweet Loires (and dry wines, but not for keeping); intense, ageworthy red Rhônes; and good Alsace, Cahors and Madiran.

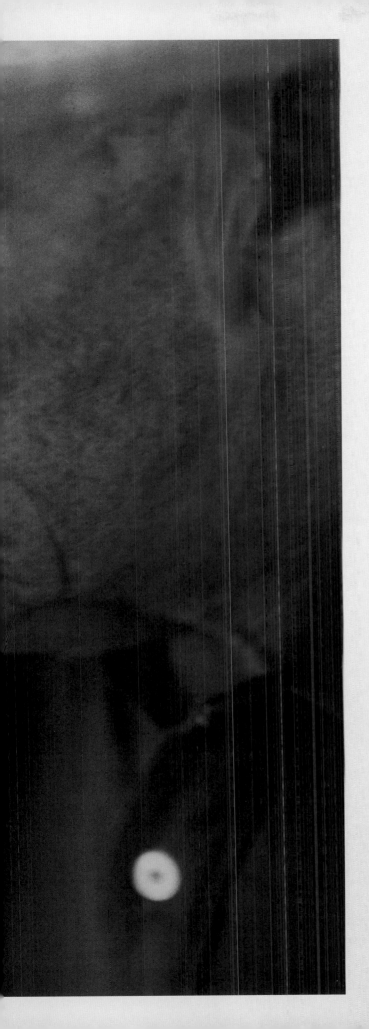

OLD WORLD

When phylloxera drove a thirsty market to Italy's cellar door, exports soared, but short-term solutions and disaffected sharecroppers hindered progress towards quality output. Then the Super Tuscans emerged to take the lead and the Italian wine revolution really took off.

Italy

David Gleave

Italian wine entered the 20th century in 1904, when the first vintage of a Chianti Riserva was produced by the newly established firm of L&P Antinori. Founded in San Casciano, just outside Florence, in 1895, the driving forces behind the new company were two brothers, Lodovico and Piero Antinori, and their brother-in-law, Guglielmo Guerrini.

People produced wine themselves, and had no need to buy it from a couple of noblemen in San Casciano.

There are two versions of the way in which this Chianti Riserva (later Villa Antinori Riserva) was born. The first, told by Lodovico's grandson Francesco Giuntini, has it that the wine was produced in 1904, while the second, told in Emanuele Pelluci's book, *Antinori Vintners in Florence* (Vallecchi, 1981) claims that the wine was first produced and named in 1928. The two versions are similar in substance, but Giuntini's dovetails more neatly with our own story. It was, explained Lodovico to his attentive grandson, a

blend from four properties in Tuscany: the Antinori's Santa Cristina estate at San Casciano, Nippozano and Remole (belonging to the Frescobaldis) in what is now Chianti Rufina, and Altomano, situated in the Val d'Arno, south of Pontassieve. To this blend was added a small amount of Bordeaux wine. 'If you wanted to be successful in international markets,' said Lodovico, 'you needed to make a wine that appealed to international tastes. And the international standard at that time was Bordeaux.'

In the first decades of its existence, the Antinori business was built primarily upon exports, since the market for quality wines in Italy, outside of a few grand hotels and restaurants in major towns, was virtually non-existent. At the turn of the century, the bulk of the population lived on the land. Most people produced wine themselves, and had no need to buy it from a couple of noblemen in San Casciano.

The export markets opened suddenly and dramatically, when phylloxera struck the vineyards of France in the late 19th century. As the French searched for a solution to the pest, their production declined. And once a solution

1901	1902	1904	1906
The Pieropan family buys the Calvarino v neyard in what is today Soave Classico; 70 years later, at the beginning of the country's quality revolution, they produce Italy's first single-vineyarc white wine.	The Mayor of Greve calls on growers in Chianti to form an association to protect the name of Chianti. This is in reaction to widespread fraud.	Antinori produce its first vintage of Villa Antinori Riserva.	Pieropan wins an award at an expostion in Milan for its *Recioto* – the sweet white wine made from dried grapes in Soave.

◁ An Italian fisherman braces himself for a long, cold day on the water with a fortifying draught of wine.

had been found, production declined even further as the vineyards were replanted. As a result, the markets that had traditionally bought their wine from France searched elsewhere.

The Italians stepped into the breach, and the 1880s saw a huge increase in exports, particularly of wines as well-known as Chianti. The demand for exports was further stoked by the Italian diaspora created by mass emigration. It is hardly surprising that the major markets for the young Antinori firm were New York, Buenos Aires and São Paolo, all cities that had been magnets for Italian emigrants.

The Antinoris were unusual in their approach at the time. Their use of wine from four outstanding properties, enhanced by a dollop of decent claret, set them on the road of quality from which they have not deviated since. Many other Italian firms opted for quantity rather than quality. Quality meant growing good grapes, a difficult undertaking for much of this century, especially when it was so much easier to buy good, inexpensive blending wine from the south of Italy.

The boom in exports coincided with the efforts of the new government (Italy became a country only in 1861) to link the diverse regions of the peninsula by railway. The railway also enabled producers in search of good, cheap, deep-coloured and high-strength blending wine to move tanks up from the south. These blending wines were indispensable in giving

1919

The South Tyrol (Alto Adige) and parts of Friuli became part of Italy as a result of the punitive break-up of the Austro-Hungarian empire at the end of the First World War. Italian white wine is much the richer today as a result.

1921

A law outlining the characteristics of *vini tipici* (typical wines) is crafted. Unfortunately, it wasn't passed by the Senate until 1924. In any case, it did not define producing zones, so did little to lift Italian wines from the mire.

colour and backbone to some of the cheap and feeble wines produced from Tuscany's poor vineyards. The boom presented the Tuscans in particular with the possibility of establishing their wines with a quality image on export markets. There was a move at the time to introduce production controls to ensure that wines exported as Chianti were authentic and of good quality. Unfortunately, the opportunity was

Italian wine woke up with a hangover on January 1st, 1900: a bulk producer occasionally capable of producing decent wines.

missed. A few merchants, such as Antinori, followed the quality route, but the image Italian wine would project for the rest of the century was already set when Italian wine woke up with a hangover on January 1st, 1900: a bulk producer occasionally capable of producing decent wines.

MEZZADRIA

The beauty of the villas in the hills of Tuscany and the Veneto bears testimony to Italy's wealth in past centuries. These grand houses were built not only as retreats from urban congestion, but also as dwellings from which to survey the agricultural land in which the owners had invested.

Agriculture, of great importance to the economy, was in the hands of the wealthy mercantile and noble classes. Their large estates were often split into smaller units, *poderi* (farms) in Tuscany. Each of these farmhouses – today tastefully transformed and rented for a week for the sort of money that would once have fed a family for a decade – were inhabited by one or two families of *mezzadri*, or sharecroppers, who would work the land surrounding their *podere*.

In order to make the most efficient use of the space at their disposal, the sharecroppers planted vines amongst olive and fruit trees in a system of 'promiscuous culture'. Wheat and maize would be planted in a particularly fertile field; chickens and the occasional cow would also be kept. Half of what was produced by the *mezzadri* went to the estate, while the other half was retained for subsistence or barter.

Mezzadria had existed in virtually every region of Italy since the 14th century, but was on its last legs at the beginning of the 20th. A lack of investment had left agriculture in a sorry state. The landowners had no incentive to put money into the farms, as they would receive only a half return on their investment, while the *mezzadri* lived in penury, and lacked capital to buy land of their own.

The large estates of Tuscany, the magnificent houses among the hills of Valpolicella and the great *masserie* of Puglia, were all underpinned by *mezzadria*. Only in Piemonte, where earlier land reform and the influence of the Kingdom of Savoy had resulted in smaller estates, and farmers' being able to buy land for themselves, were Italian agriculture, and hence wine, free from the influence of *mezzadria*.

Mezzadria ensured that the quality of the grapes wasn't always what it should have been. In most cases, the estate owners had neither the knowledge nor the inclination to produce the sort of grapes which would have provided their *fattore* (estate manager) with the raw materials needed to produce good wines. And as the *mezzadri* received half what they produced, not half the price their wine was sold for, they preferred to concentrate on quantity rather than quality.

The estates would usually bottle a small amount of wine for themselves, but most left the commercialization to the merchants. A few estates – Brolio and Selvapiana – were well-known enough to sell in large cities, but the market was dominated by merchants such as

1931	1939	1945
The Dalmasso Commission reports, having been set up to resolve the chaos of Italian wine. As a result of the report, producers are allowed to use the name of specific zones on bottles of their wines. Pieropan bottles its first vintage of a dry white wine known as Soave. 1931 is a great vintage in Barolo. The old timers say it is the best vintage of the century. The best wines are now rare.	At the end of this decade, for the first time ever, less than half the population is involved in agriculture.	The end of the Second World War sees the beginning of the exodus from the country to the city that will eventually transform Italian agriculture. A great vintage in Barolo to celebrate the end the war.

Ruffino, Melini and Antinori. Some estates, however, had better reputations for the quality of their wine, either because of their felicitous position or because their owner or *fattore* was particularly driven to produce the best possible quality. It was estates such as these that the Antinoris would have sought when making up the blend for their Chianti Riserva in the early years of this century.

PHYLLOXERA

The louse gave Italian wine a great opportunity to establish itself on export markets. This opportunity, characteristically, was not grasped, and by the time phylloxera struck Italy's vineyards in the early 20th century, Italian wine was already taking the broad road of quantity rather than the straitened path of quality.

Phylloxera struck Piemonte in the second decade of this century. Replanting was carried out relatively quickly and, according to Aldo Conterno, a producer whose family has been growing grapes in Monforte d'Alba since the 18th century, was finished by about 1920. In Tuscany, the louse's destructive progress was slowed by the 'promiscuous' system of culture, and many vineyards were not replanted until the 1920s and '30s. Piemonte apart, replanting proved more devastating for Italian wine than the louse itself. Prices for wine were low, so there was little confidence on the part of estate owners when it came to replanting.

Mezzadria remained a problem, as did social upheaval and political uncertainty. These factors combined to result in the replanting of high-yielding grape varieties, an error compounded by the fact that these lesser varieties not only replaced many of better quality, some of which are now virtually extinct, but they were also planted on sites with more fertile soil that were easier to work.

△ Harvest time in the 1920s, when almost every agricultural smallholding encompassed a few vines, promiscuously interspersed with other household staples.

THE DALMASSO COMMISSION

This 'quantity revolution' was further entrenched by the report of the Dalmasso Commission in 1931. Mussolini may have made the trains run on time, but his contribution to Italian wine was to reinforce the seemingly inexorable march (or was it a goosestep?) to homogeneity and low quality. The commission was asked to resolve the question of, among other things, Chianti. This best-known of all Italian wines takes its name from the hilly area north of Siena. The name had been used for its wines since the 14th century

The louse's destructive progress was slowed by the 'promiscuous' system of culture, and many vineyards were not replanted until the 1920s and '30s.

and, like all well-known names, has often been subject to fraud and passing off. It was so prevalent at the beginning of the 18th century that the Grand Duke of Tuscany introduced the world's first delimited wine regions in

1952	1953	1958
An outstanding vintage in Barolo. Not quite up to the standard of 1958, but the best wines still have some life left in them.	Bolla and Bertani produce the first wines in Valpolicella that were labelled as Amarone. These wines, made from dried grapes, are, at the end of the century, enjoying unparalleled success.	A great vintage in Barolo and Chianti. Few wines remain from Tuscany, as most ended up in the merchants' blends, but there a few bottles of magnificent – albeit aged and old-fashioned – Barolo and Barbaresco still in existence.

1716 in an attempt to protect Chianti and other Tuscan regions.

The success of the law was short-lived, however, and fraud became increasingly widespread in the early 20th century, and intensified through to the late 1920s. In 1902, the mayor of Greve, in what was then northern Chianti, urged producers to form an association to protect the name Chianti. And as if to prove that the problem of fraud was not confined to Tuscany, the National Congress of Alba (the town bordered by the Barolo and Barbaresco zones) called for legislation to protect the names of typical Italian wines.

In 1921, a law setting out the characteristics of *vini tipici* (typical wines) was passed, but it was not approved by the Senate until 1924. And since the law did nothing to delimit the producing areas for the better-known Italian wines, it did little to stem the flow of fraudulent wine that was flooding the market. Dalmasso's brief was to delimit the zones for Chianti. It was

a name that sold well, said the other Tuscan producers, so we would like to sell our wine as Chianti too. Dalmasso considered this proposal, and rejecting the example set by the recently-established system of *appellation contrôlée* in France, perversely imposed a political structure on a vinous problem.

Chianti the area became Chianti Classico to distinguish it as the original zone. To please its neighbours, the zone was extended to take in communes in the province of Florence, many of which had never previously belonged to Chianti – and with good reason, said those in the know. The soil and altitude were completely different from that which prevailed in Gaiole, Castellina and Radda, the heart of the historic Chianti-producing zone, and the wines were markedly different – inferior, some would say.

Every other province in Tuscany – apart from Grosseto in the south – was given a Chianti of its own. Outside Classico, the hills of Siena (Colli Senesi) and Florence (Colli Fiorentini) were

▷ Local women give the traditional *fiaschi* bottles the straw jackets that signal fresh, fruity young Chianti to the world. Wines that are intended for ageing are now bottled in Bordeaux bottles, which can be stacked.

1961

Another great vintage. Aldo Conterno remembers plunging blocks of ice into the fermenting vats in his fathers cellar in Barolo to the cool the temperature. They succeeded, and made wonderful wine.

1963

The law for the *Denominazione di Origine Controllata* (DOC) was passed in parliament. The aim was to introduce some order to the chaotic world of Italian wine.

1964

The Barolo producer Prunotto made and sold a wine from the Bussia vineyard in Monforte. For the first time this century, the concept of *cru* entered Italian wine.

joined by those of Pisa (Colline Pisane) and Arezzo (Colli Aretini); Rufina, northeast of Florence and, to the west, Montalbano.

This may have appeased the politicians, but it did little to further the cause of quality. Indeed, it institutionalized the philosophy of defining wine zones by political boundaries, rather than by *terroir*. And it was a philosophy that was to do far greater damage in the decades to come.

A NEW INDUSTRIAL REVOLUTION

The end of the Second World War saw Italy pick up where it had left off in the 1930s. Rural depopulation intensified. In the 1930s, for the first time in Italy's history, less than half the active population was involved in agriculture. Between 1951 and 1975, the numbers working in agriculture fell from 8.6 million to 3 million.

Italy's economy expanded rapidly in the post-war years: industrial production grew by 8.1 per cent a year, and by 1966 was treble its 1951 level. These changes sounded the death-knell for *mezzadria*, which had relied upon a constant pool of cheap labour. Emigration from country to city robbed estates of their traditional source of labour, and many, unable to change, foundered. Those that did survive needed to modernize, and looked for inspiration to the very same industries that had forced change upon them by luring away their workers.

The breakneck speed of Italy's industrial growth was matched by a huge increase in agricultural output. Food production doubled between 1950 and 1970 as new techniques, and a move within a generation from peasant to industrial cultivation, resulted in greatly increased yields. The same was true of wine. Estates were gradually replanted as the last of the *mezzadri* left for the city, a trend that was slower in Tuscany than in the Veneto. As in the period after phylloxera, quantity was preferred above quality. The Trebbiano Toscano grape became Italy's most widely planted variety, thanks largely to its prodigious yields. And it wasn't, of course, planted on the poor soils of hillside sites; it was more likely to be found on flatter, fertile plains.

Francesco Giuntini recalls the typical day of the last of his *mezzadri* at this time. 'In the summer, they would begin work at five, when the sun was up but before it was too hot. They would work until nine and then stop for breakfast, a meal that would usually include at least half a litre of wine, which was often their major source of energy. They would go back to work until noon, when they would break for lunch, which would include more wine, and then a sleep. They would start work again at about four, when the worst of the hot midday sun was over, and work until seven, when they would have more wine with dinner.'

Such a lifestyle meant that Italy had a per capita consumption of 120 litres in 1970. To keep pace with this consumption, it was producing about 25 per cent of all the world's wine by the late 1960s. It was also a huge exporter, not only in bulk to Germany and France but also in bottle to America and Britain.

Italy had a per capita consumption of 120 litres in 1970... it was producing about 25 per cent of all the world's wine by the late 1960s.

This vast increase in production was also due to the advice proffered by the universities of the 1940s and '50s, at the time when Italy was regenerating its vineyards. The professors' view was that the new urban consumers would require a lower calorific intake from wine, especially if they were working in a factory. The wines, therefore, needed to be lighter. This was achieved by encouraging higher yields, and

1966

Vernaccia di San Gimignano, a white Tuscan wine, became the first Italian wine to be sold with the DOC status.

1968

The first commercially produced vintage of Sassicaia is made in this vintage. Now rare, but still one of the best.

▷ Meat and poultry, black cabbage and herbs are some of the abundant local produce in Tuscany, that complement the region's rustic wines.

by planting varieties such as Trebbiano and the more prolific clones of Sangiovese, Molinara in Valpolicella and Barbera in Piemonte.

Expanding production also led to another export boom, fuelled largely by Veronese viniculture. There were at the time positive signs of quality. The old merchant house of Bolla, for instance, was responsible for the first commercial release of Amarone from the 1950

Amarone, a wine style that traces its origins in the Valpolicella hills back to Roman times.

vintage, while the venerable family estate of Bertani followed a few months later with their own release. Amarone, a style of wine that traces its origins in the Valpolicella hills back to Roman times, is made from dried grapes. Requiring several years' ageing before release,

it is an expensive wine to make. The bold step taken by both Bolla and Bertani no doubt reflected the optimism prevailing at the time.

A similar measure of optimism was the fact that the fertile plains on the northern lip of the Po Valley were quickly transformed from the cereal crops with which they had been planted before the war to the more remunerative vine. Yields that might, before the war, have been as high as four to five tonnes per hectare were soon reaching 15 to 20 tonnes.

The professors were delighted. Such yields ensured that the wines were lighter, as natural alcohol levels of anything higher than nine or ten degrees were virtually impossible to obtain with such crop levels. And, added the professors, with our new technology, we will be able to remedy in the winery any defects derived from the vineyard.

1970	1971	1974
A Chianti Classico from the Tignanello vineyard is produced by Antinori. Despite its quality, it fails to have the expected impact on the market, probably because people aren't willing to pay such high prices for a Chianti.	Antinori releases Tignanello as a *vino da tavola*. This spawns a whole generation of *vini da tavola*, wines that redefine the world's image of Italian wine. A great vintage in Barolo and Tuscany.	An excellent vintage in Piemonte and Tuscany. Few of the wines have lived long, however.

THE ADVENT OF DOC

This was the prevailing philosophy when Italian wine producers and politicians turned their thoughts towards a system of control similar to *Appellation d'Origine Contrôlée* (ACC). The system of *Denominazione di Origine Controllata* (DOC) became law in 1963, and the first DOCs came into being in 1966.

While better than no system at all, however, DOC did institutionalize the trends that had developed during the previous six decades. This meant that the tradition of quantity – high yields, poor sites and even poorer grape varieties – was enshrined in law, and that of quality, by now eclipsed in the minds of most producers, was excluded. A huge wave of optimism followed the introduction of DOC, and between 1967 and 1973 tens of thousands of hectares of new vineyards were planted in preparation for the brave new world of wine that was to be ushered in. Scant regard was given to such chimerical concepts as quality, so considerations such as site, grape variety and clone were not allowed to influence these massive plantings.

In Chianti, for instance, 7,000 hectares of vineyard were planted between 1967 and 1972, leaving only about 10 per cent of vineyards planted before 1964. Production quadrupled, and the new vineyards started to produce fruit at the same time as the global economy shifted into a reverse gear when faced with the 1973 oil crisis. Fatefully, production increased dramatically just as the price of wine plummeted.

As a result, the merchants stopped buying. A number of estates in Chianti decided to bottle their own wines, without realizing the perils lurking on the road from producer of bulk plonk to bottler of fine wines. The Burgundians, possessors of outstanding vineyards, had found the journey fairly easy once they learned the difference between making wine to sell to a *négociant* for blending, and making it to bottle in

your own cellars unaided by what the Italians called a *correttivo* (a helpful blending component). The Chiantigiani, however, had poor vineyards, so not only did they need to modernize their winemaking, but they also needed to overcome the deficiencies presented by their mediocre grapes. The viticultural advice provided by the

In Chianti, for instance, 7,000 hectares of vineyard were planted between 1967 and 1972, leaving only about 10 per cent of vineyards planted before 1964.

universities in the 1950s and '60s turned out to be the greatest handicap suffered by Tuscan wine specifically, and Italian wine generally, for the rest of the century. And the fact that this advice was largely enshrined in the DOC laws only increased producers' difficulties. The route that Italy's quality-oriented producers had to follow if they were to extract themselves from the mire of quantity had been signposted a decade earlier by a group of producers from the Langhe. Led by Renato Ratti, these men had travelled to the classic regions of France. 'We were all rather shocked,' recalls Aldo

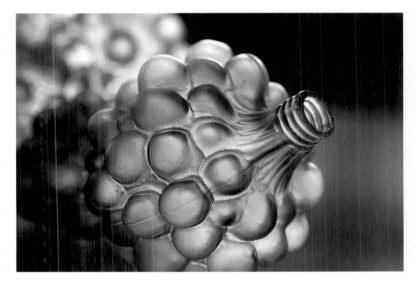

▽ The artist's homage to the winemaker's art: there is little mistaking the intended contents of this strange bottle – but storage and pouring must have proved problematic.

1977

The Chianti estate Montevertine release a *vino da tavola* called Le Pergole Torte, made solely from Sangiovese.

1979

Denominazione di *Origine Controllata e Garantita* (DOCG) the superior version of DOC, is introduced. The first wines sold as this are Vino Nobile di Montepulciano, Barbaresco, Barolo and Brunello di Montalcino.

Conterno. 'We thought we were producing the best wines in the world in Barolo, but when we saw what they were doing in Burgundy and Bordeaux, we realized that, in fact, we had been left behind.'

It was all the more striking that such sentiments should be expressed on the back of outstanding vintages such as the 1958 and the 1961. At the time, the concept of learning from other wine-producing regions was virtually unheard of in Italy. As a result, these hill farmers from the Langhe, convinced that they were at the vanguard of quality-wine production, were surprised to encounter the early signs of the Peynaud revolution that made their own approach in the cellar seem dated and parochial.

They returned, determined to modernize their winemaking. This meant reducing the levels of both oxidation and volatile acidity. This was to be achieved by better housekeeping and by ageing the wine in oak for a shorter period. This was the start of a trend – and a heated debate – that has continued into the 1990s.

We thought we were producing the best wines in the world in Barolo, but when we saw what they were doing in Burgundy and Bordeaux, we realized that, in fact, we had been left behind.

At the same time, there was also a move to rescue individual vineyard sites from the anonymity of the merchants' blending vats and bottle them as separate *crus*. This was once again following the French lead, where the *terroir* of certain sites is held to produce a distinctive style that deserves to be bottled separately. In Piemonte, as in the rest of Italy, the merchants had little incentive to bottle these *crus* individually, as the market was unwilling to acknowledge any such differentiation.

The first *cru* wine was produced by Prunotto in 1964. Its Barolo Bussia was still stunning when tasted in 1989. It was also a wine of historic importance, representing the first step out of the blending vat of quantity that was to set Italian wines back on the road to quality.

THE SUPER TUSCANS

Wines such as Prunotto's 1964 Barolo Bussia were produced in small quantities, so had little impact on the market. They did, however, influence other winemakers. By the late 1960s, numerous producers in Barolo and Barbaresco were producing single-vineyard wines and commanding premium prices for them.

At the same time, a young Piemontese winemaker who had emigrated to Tuscany was carrying out experiments at his employer's cellars in San Casciano and at a smaller property on the Tuscan coast. Giacomo Tachis was employed as technical director of Antinori, working alongside the dynamic young scion of this venerable firm.

Piero Antinori realized that Italy had to free itself from the lower sector of the market in which it was shackled. The only way to do this, he concluded, was to pursue quality. This, said Tachis, could only be done if the basic precepts of the Peynaud revolution – better extraction of colour and flavour, cleaner and fresher wines, the intelligent use of oak, the completion of the malolactic fermentation – were applied in the cellar.

Tachis mastered many of these techniques while working at a property belonging to an Antinori cousin, Mario Incisa della Rocchetta, on the Tuscan coast at Bolgheri. The resulting wine, made solely from Cabernet Sauvignon planted on the estate in the 1940s, was named after a vineyard on the Tenuta San Guido property, Sassicaia. Tachis replicated these experiments on a larger scale at San Casciano,

1982

A very good vintage in Barolo and Barbaresco, though the wines have not lived very long, and are, for the most part, past their best.

1984

The first vintage for Chianti DOCG. Viewed as fitting in some quarters that the introduction of watered-down regulations coincided with a wet, dreadful vintage.

working with grapes grown in a single vineyard on the Antinori's Santa Cristina estate. Trebbiano, then a key component of the Chianti blend, was replaced with a higher percentage of Sangiovese. And instead of ageing the wine in large old chestnut and Slovenian oak casks, Tachis introduced the small French *barriques* that Peynaud was, at the time, compelling the Bordelais to use for ageing – as distinct from storing – the wine.

The 1970 vintage saw Antinori release a single-vineyard Chianti Classico. Though its intrinsic quality was clearly evident, most people's view of it was obscured by the use of the name Chianti Classico on the bottle. As a result, in 1971, Antinori put only the vineyard name on the label: it was sold as a *vino da tavola* from the Tignanello vineyard.

Tignanello was probably the most important wine produced in Italy in the 20th century. By dispensing with DOC status, it also proved that the production practices enshrined in the law were an impediment to making quality wine. Antinori and Tachis had to step outside the DOC law to make Tignanello, a fact emphasized by the inclusion of Cabernet Sauvignon in the 1975 vintage. The wine was met with critical rapture in some quarters, mostly on the export markets, but with adverse reactions closer to home. 'People in Florence thought the wine was corked,' recalls Piero Antinori, when in fact it was the new oak that was lending the wine such a distinct character.

'They said it wasn't typical,' says Tachis, 'but if by typical they meant a wine that was lightly coloured, oxidized, tannic and volatile, like those I found when I first came to Tuscany, then they were right. Tignanello was modern, and showed what Tuscany was capable of.'

Tignanello and Sassicaia proved to doubting consumers that Tuscany could make something other than Chianti in a straw-jacketed *fiasco*, and to doubting producers that quality wines could indeed come from their vineyards.

Producers were equally certain, as Antinori and Tachis had been, that quality wines could not be made within the confines of the DOC

In 1971, Antinori put only the vineyard name on the label: it was sold as a vino da tavola from the Tignanello vineyard.

laws. Sassicaia was made solely from a French grape variety that, at the time in Tuscany, was not included in the blend for any of the DOC wines. Though it had been planted in Tuscany since the middle of the 19th century, it was atypical by the time the DOC laws were framed. As a result, it was excluded from Chianti Classico, yet the blend for Tignanello – stabilized at about 80 per cent Sangiovese and 20 per cent Cabernet Sauvignon in the late 1970s – proved its worth. Others in Tuscany, perhaps alarmed at the sudden influx of French grape varieties, decided to concentrate on their native cultivars.

In 1977, Sergio Manetti of Montevertine, a small property in Radda in the heart of Chianti Classico, produced a pure Sangiovese, Le Pergole Torte. Once again, this wine had to be sold as a *vino da tavola*, as the DOC laws did not permit the use of Sangiovese on its own.

These wines, free of the lumpen ballast of DOC, soared to price levels producers dared only dream of a decade earlier.

These wines, free of the lumpen ballast of DOC, soared to price levels producers dared only dream of a decade earlier. Perhaps because of their elevated prices, or because of their innovative style and quality, the

1985

An outstanding vintage in Piemonte, Veneto and Tuscany. The best wines are still going strong, though many were tough and tannic.

1989

A poor, wet vintage in all of Italy, apart from Piemonte, which enjoyed its best vintage of the decade. The best of the Baroli and Barbareschi are still young, and are showing outstanding ageing potential.

▷ The fashionable Bordeaux varieties Cabernet Sauvignon and Merlot are the current favourites at Orne Iaia, near Bolgheri on the Tuscan coast. This dynamic estate was developed by Ludovico Antinori.

wines became known as Super Tuscans. The Super Tuscans inspired a generation of wine producers, first in Tuscany and then throughout Italy, to innovate in the pursuit of quality. In this respect, they have had an indelible mark on Italian wines.

DOCG

The official reaction to these wines was one of bemusement. Just when the law had caught up with what was actually happening and introduced the DOC laws, the winemakers suddenly took off in another direction. The lawmakers responded by introducing the concept of DOCG – where the name and origin of a wine was not only controlled (DOC) but also *garantita*, or guaranteed.

In 1979, DOCG was introduced in Barolo and Barbaresco, and for Vino Nobile di Montepulciano and Brunello di Montalcino.

The laws had been tightened and maximum permitted yields had been reduced. In 1984, Chianti became the biggest test for DOCG. The law was altered in an intelligent manner, but the concept of the Super Tuscans was not directly addressed.

It was only in 1992, when the Goria Law (named after the reigning minister of agriculture) was passed, that some provision was made for bringing these innovative renegades under some form of control. A new category, *Indicazione Geografica Tipica* (IGT), was introduced which would give the Super Tuscans laws to which they had to conform.

The term *vino da tavola* was no longer an option in respect of these wines. As usual, the wines were far ahead of the laws, but at least some attempt was being made to move away from the Dalmasso mentality to a philosophy that recognized the intrinsic superiority of certain pieces of earth over others. It was only fitting

1990

Another stellar vintage. The best of the Tuscans are still young and backwards, while many of the Baroli and Barbareschi have developed much more quickly than the 1989s.

1992

The Goria Law is passed. This is the first major overhaul of the Italian wine laws since 1963. It introduces *Indicazione Geografica Tipica* (IGT), the Italian equivalent of the French *vin de pays*. Appears positive, but its later implementation is bungled by bureaucrats.

that Sassicaia became the first wine, under the new philosophy that imbued the Goria Law, to be granted its own DOC, Bolgheri – Sassicaia. First produced in 1994, this DOC officially marked the victory of the Super Tuscans.

The Super Tuscans' influence spread to other regions. Piemonte, perhaps because of its great wealth of native varieties like Nebbiolo, Barbera and Dolcetto, was slower than Tuscany to pick up on the French varieties, despite having first planted Cabernet Sauvignon in 1827. However, the spirit of innovation and experimentation that characterized the Super Tuscans was taken up by the Piemontese, and wines such as Darmagi from Gaja, Il Favot from Aldo Conterno, Vigna Larigi and Vigna Arborina from Elio Altare, Vignaserra from Roberto Voerzio and Arte from Domenico Clerico were early examples. The experimentation undertaken on these wines slowly fed through to the DOCG wines, thus altering the style of Barolo and Barbaresco, making them more modern and 'user friendly' than the tannic beasts of old.

The Veneto has been slower to catch on to the Zeitgeist, but Allegrini's La Poja, made solely from the native Corvina grape, has shown others the way. Today, virtually all of Italy's wine-producing regions have at least a handful of producers who are propagating – and in some cases even proselytizing – the philosophy of quality and innovation that evolved in the cellars of Bolgheri and San Casciano 30 years ago.

THE WINEMAKERS

The evangelists have most often been itinerant winemakers who act as consultants to several producers. Tachis is the most famous, though Giulio Gambelli, consultant to the estate of Montevertine, deserves a special mention. They set the stage for the likes of Franco Bernabei, Maurizio Castelli and Vittorio Fiore to emerge in the 1980s, all of whom improved the quality of the wines from estates they oversaw. They have now been joined by Riccardo Cottarella in Umbria, Lazio and Campania, and Donato Lanati, whose expert services have been confined largely to his native northern Italy.

It was only fitting that Sassicaia became the first wine to be granted its own DOC... officially marking the victory of the Super Tuscans.

Throughout the 1980s, these consultants gradually improved the technology and production practices in the cellars of Italy. The new generation of consultants is tackling the next great problem: the vineyard. Alberto Antonini, Stefano Chioccioli and Fabrizio Molthard are agronomists by training, and view the regeneration of Italy's vineyards as the only way to improve upon the quality they inherited from the previous generation.

It seems that the fight for quality grapes, the enduring battle of the 20th century, is finally being won. For proof, we need look no further than Antinori. The company that has defined the 20th century for Italian wine now has almost 1,000 hectares of vineyard, making it self-sufficient for its top wines.

It seems that the fight for quality grapes, the enduring battle of the 20th century, is finally being won.

How it develops those vineyards – and where, for it now owns Prunotto in Piemonte and another producer, Vigneti del Sud, in Puglia – will no doubt play a large part in the story of Italian wine in the 21st century.

1996	1997	1998	1999
An outstanding vintage in Barolo and Barbaresco, the best since 1989. The wines will be very long lived.	A much heralded vintage throughout Italy. A hot summer resulted in wines with explosive fruit, but only those in the cooler positions will have produced classic, long-lived wines.	In many ways, a better vintage than its predecessor, producing wines in Piemonte the Veneto and Tuscany that are better balanced and for longer ageing.	In Piemonte and Tuscany, early indications are that this will be the vintage of the decade. What a note on which to end the century!

German wines, once the most prestigious of all, have been boxed into a cheap and sweet corner, chiefly by dismally low minimum standards. But with leading growers now regularly selling out for healthy prices, the country's wine industry is poised at a critical turning-point.

Germany & Austria

Stuart Pigott

The wine in the glass was a deep amber colour, shading towards mahogany in the centre, which meant that it could only be old white wine. The aromas of chocolate, caramel and spices were enticing and surprisingly free from dustiness or decay. This hardly prepared me for the taste, which was so lively that had this been a real blind tasting – with blindfolds – I would have guessed that the wine was about 30 years old. In fact it was the 1893 Deidesheimer Langenmorgen

Prices were higher than for any other wines, including those of the great Bordeaux châteaux.

Riesling Auslese from Dr Bassermann-Jordan of Deidesheim in the Pfalz. I tasted it in 1999 in the estate's cellars. In the first years of the 20th century, high society throughout the western world esteemed late-harvest German wines like these more highly than any others.

German wines as we know them started to be produced during the latter decades of the 18th century. This was the first Golden Age, when the Rheingau region and the Mittel-Haardt area of the Pfalz region were synonymous with great white wine around the world. The Belle Epoque, or Wilhelmine Period as the Germans call it in reference to Kaisers Wilhelm I and Wilhelm II, was a period of prosperity, not just for the aristocracy and industrialists, but also for the growing middle-classes.

The international wine market was vital and growing, and the production of top-quality German Rieslings could not meet the demand. Prices were higher than for any other wines, including those of the great Bordeaux châteaux. The price pinnacle was dizzying indeed. In the spring of 1907, for example, a 300-litre cask of 1893 Steinberger Trockenbeer-Auslese was auctioned at Kloster Eberbach in the Rheingau for 17,410 Gold Marks, the approximate contemporary equivalent of DM5220 per bottle! While the regular quality dry wines which then made up most of Germany's wine production were much cheaper than this, their prices were still very healthy. No wonder wine consumption in Germany in the year 1900 averaged only 3.7 litres per person per year.

Such prices made the 'stretching' or counterfeiting of wine an attractive proposition.

1909	1911	1918	1919
The first German wine law was passed creating the *Naturwein* designation for unchaptalised, unblended wines.	Finest German vintage of the pre-First World War years, giving wines of marvellous structure which sold for stratospheric prices. Even the cream of the crop is now sadly past its best.	The First World War ends, Kaiser Wilhelm II flees Berlin, the German and Austrian republics declared.	The Treaty of Versailles imposes massive reparations on fledgling German democracy that will dog it until its end in 1933. The Austro-Hungarian empire is divided up.

◁ In the early 19th century much of Austria's output was still consumed in local taverns, making 'shipment' an uncomplicated affair.

The wine law of 1909 tried to prevent such practices by establishing that a vineyard name on the label had to mean that the wine actually originated from that site, but it left the door wide open for the exploitation of certain famous vineyard names. It sanctioned the use of the names of vineyards lying in more than one parish – for example, the famous Marcobrunn in the Rheingau and the Brauneberg on the Mosel – on the wines of nearby vineyards and villages, 'so long as they are of similar character and quality'. The result was chaos.

The present German wine law has created similar difficulties today, but this is not the only parallel between the industry's situation a century ago and that of today. Then, too, controversy raged about the legalization of new winemaking techniques – then it was about chaptalization, today it is about artificial concentration – and then, as now, high labour

1920	1921	1923	1929
A small vintage in quantity, but German late-harvest wines had a rare combination of intensity and brilliance. Top wines can still be magnificent.	A vintage of the century, with opulence and extravagance far exceeding the norm in Germany. It was received with international enthusiasm leading to premature bottling of many wines. First *Trockenbeerenauslese* in the Mosel-Saar-Ruwer. Many *Beerenauslese* and *Trockenbeerenauslese* are still superb.	Hyper-inflation brings chaos to the wine market and almost ruins the German economy.	Wall Street Crash precipitates economic crisis which bankrupts many wine-growers and leads to mass unemployment.

List of the Wines, &c.

BERRY BROS. & CO.,

3 ST. JAMES'S STREET.

— LONDON, S.W. —

'CLARET.

	Per doz.
Much recommended for ordinary use	18/-
Older 21/- ... ... Finer	24/-
Château Leboscq, 1888	30/-
,, Citran, 1888	36/-
,, Cantenac	36/-
,, Meyney, 1888	36/-
,, Citran, 1890	42/-
,, Palmer	40/-
,, Rausan	45/-
,, Léoville, 1888	50/-
,, Margaux	60/-
,, Pichon Longueville, 1878 ...	60/-
,, Léoville, 1878	80/-
,, Langoa, 1874	80/-
,, Lafite, 1878	140/-
,, Lafite 1870 Magnums ...	144/-
Also a selection of vintages from 1890 and 1893.	

CHAMPAGNE.

	Per doz.
Le St. Cyr. Vin Brut, a pure Reims wine,	50
Clos St. Jacques, 1880, 1884, 1892 vintages	72/-
Verzenay 1889	66/-
Dagonet, Special Cuvée	70/-
,, Brut, Full body and colour, 1889	90/-
,, Dry (medium dry and color)	90/-
,, Cuvée Excep^lle Brut (fine flavour, pale and delicate) 1889	90/-
Duc de Montebello	84/-
Laurent-Perrier Brut Sans Sucre, 1892	84/-
,, ,, ,, 1889	90/-
Pommery ,, 96/- Clicquot ...	100/-
Binet Sec, 1880 100/- 1884	90/-

HOCK.

	Per doz.		
St Jacobsberg	20/-	Nierstein	30/-
Rudesheim	40/-	Oestrich	50/-
Liebfraumilch	62/-	Rudesheim	66/-
Stein Wein	50/-	Marcobrunn	74/-
Rauenthal			96/-
Rudesheimer Rottland Cabinet, 1886			120/-
Steinberg Cabinet, 1886			150/-
Marcobrunn Cabinet, 1886, 180/-		1862	200/-
Rudesheimer Hinterhaus, 1862			200/-
Red Hock, 50 - 60/- Sparkling Hock, 48 - 64/-			

BURGUNDY.

	Per doz.		
Beaujolais	24/-	Beaune	36 - 42/-
Volnay	60/-	Pommard 60 - 66 - 72/-	
Corton	66/-	Romanée	90 - 130/-
Chambertin 72/- 96/-			130/-
Clos de Vougeout		84/-	150/-

△ This London price list of 1896 confirms that German wines were once as esteemed as the best bottles from France.

costs were eroding the industry's profitability. Between 1830 and 1915, vineyard workers' wages increased fourfold as employers were forced to match the wages offered by other industries. This was the background of the struggle by the leading estates of the period to establish legal designations which would identify quality wines clearly.

Dr Albert Bürklin of the Dr Bürklin-Wolf estate in Wachenheim in the Pfalz region was the first to raise this matter in the

Vineyard workers' wages increased fourfold as employers were forced to match the wages offered by other industries.

German Reichstag – then more talking shop than the legislative chamber it is today – in 1877. The 1901 wine law was a victory for this lobby since it introduced the designation *Naturwein* for unchaptalized, unsweetened and unblended wines; the basis for *Qualitätswein mit Prädikat*, the highest category of German wines today.

AUSTRIA'S FALTERING PROGRESS

The situation of Austria's wine industry was very different. During the 19th century most of it lagged far behind that of Germany, and of its 'partner' in the Austro-Hungarian Empire. Most of Austria's wine was sold in bulk, much of it to be drunk in taverns belonging to vineyard owners. Only at the end of the 19th and beginning of the 20th centuries were many of the noble grape varieties that account for much of the nation's fine dry white wine today imported from Germany and France. This process was accelerated by the phylloxera plague, which forced thousands of growers to replant.

The shortage of new vine material from domestic sources prompted producers to import. Often the Weissburgunder (Pinot Blanc) vines that Styrian growers thought they had planted were actually Chardonnay. When it became apparent that they had a different variety in their new vineyards they christened it Morillon, a name still used today.

Some wine-growers in the Wachau region in the Danube Valley and the neighbouring Kremstal and Kamptal regions claim that Riesling has been in their vineyards for centuries, but everything points to its having been imported to Austria by pioneers of quality-wine production just over a century ago.

The First World War and the economic shocks of the 1920s affected Germany and Austria's wine industries in very different ways. In Austria, the quality-wine industry was halted in its tracks, while in Germany, the wine culture that had been built up during the previous century or so was decimated.

Nowhere was this more serious than in the Mosel Valley. Political changes during the 19th century – the Napoleonic invasion, absorption into Prussia in 1815, the expanding German customs union, then German unification – put the industry through a rollercoaster ride of

1933

Hitler becomes chancellor and seized complete power. Persecution of Jewish community begins, crippling many regions' wine marketing.

1937

Finest German vintage of the inter-war years, similar in style to 1920 but more concentrated; the top wines are still impeccable today.

violent up- and downturns. It was only with the string of excellent vintages from 1893 that the Riesling wines from the Mosel and its tributaries the Saar and Ruwer finally gained international recognition as being of equal standing to those from the Rheingau and Pfalz.

1921 was a truly momentous year for the Mosel, not just because it was a great vintage, but because it was the first time that *Trockenbeerenauslese* wines, the highest level in the hierarchical German wine classification (*Prädikat*) system, had been produced here. The most famous was the 1921 Bernkasteler Doctor Riesling Trockenbeerenauslese from the Dr H Thanisch estate of Bernkastel – to this day an incredibly intense, honey-like essence of the Riesling. But the rug was about to be pulled from beneath the Mosel wine-growers' feet.

Many of the Germans who bought the 1921s were *nouveau riche*, a class which was to be significantly expanded during the hyper-inflation of 1923 to 1924, since only ruthless opportunists benefited from the economic chaos. Hyper-inflation left many members of the upper- and middle-classes stripped of their inherited wealth and savings, and the consequent loss of their custom was to hit wine-growers hard.

There were many bankruptcies, and countless families survived only by bartering wine for food and goods. The Wall Street Crash of 1929 and the mass unemployment that followed made matters worse. Indirectly, these events were to have far more damning consequences though, for the humiliation and indignation felt by those whose circumstances were reduced as a result of these economic upheavals were to provide Hitler's National Socialist party with much of the support which swept them to power in 1933.

Even in its early years the Nazi dictatorship had serious consequences for the German wine industry. For example, most of the wine production in the Pfalz was marketed by Jewish brokers and merchants. From 1933–39 these people were either interned in concentration camps, expelled from the country, or fled. This left most of the region's growers without a market. To fill the vacuum each important German town was forced to adopt a Pfalz wine-growing parish. To publicize the region's wines the *Deutsche Weinstrasse* was created, a road connecting all the region's significant wine-growing towns and villages. During this period not only the wine industry, but every other aspect of German business, culture and public life lost dynamic

Even in its early years the Nazi dictatorship had serious consequences for the German wine industry.

and talented figures because they were Jewish, socialist, homosexual or openly opposed to the regime in some manner.

A string of good to outstanding vintages during the 1930s provided short-lived optimism in the industry at least. 1937 was a great vintage for *Auslese*, *Beerenauslese* and *Trockenbeerenauslese* dessert wines, though little was exported before the outbreak of the Second World War.

Only small stocks of pre-war wines were to survive the destruction of the latter war years as British and American bombing reduced virtually every major German town and city to ruins. The pillaging of the French occupation troops in Mosel-Saar-Ruwer and the wine-growing regions on the left bank of the Rhine mopped up most of what was left. Given the scale of the destruction it is astonishing how quickly many of the nation's leading wine estates bounced back after the Nazis surrendered on May 8th, 1945. While there was no crop that year in many parts of the country due to an acute shortage of labour, Schloss Johannisberg

1945	1949
Defeat of Nazi Germany, beginning of Allied occupation of Germany and Austria, and a minuscule harvest of great wines. Due to the immediate post-war chaos in Germany these regal wines are extremely rare.	Foundation of German Federal Republic within three sectors under occupation of Western powers; and the greatest vintage of the post-war years in both Germany and Austria, the wines matching richness with elegance. The best wines are at their peak. The Seitz company of Bad Kreuznach introduces affordable modern filters for winemaking.

in the Rheingau was not the only famous estate to pick a tiny crop of exquisite wines. It was the introduction of the Deutschmark in the American, French and British sectors of occupied Germany on March 20th, 1949 that provided the most important stimulus for the re-emerging wine industry and for the West German economy as a whole.

This was the prelude to the creation of the Federal German Republic out of these three zones on May 23rd of the same year.

Given the scale of the destruction it is astonishing how quickly many of the nation's leading wine estates bounced back.

From this moment, economic growth was rapid. Wine was a way for those who had money to spend to divert thoughts from the hardships of the immediate post-war years.

A TECHNICAL REVOLUTION

There was another string of good vintages from 1945, the greatest of which was 1949. With his sensational 1949s, Sebastian Alois Prüm (1902–1969) established the reputation of the Joh Jos Prüm estate of Wehlen on the Mosel as one of the leading white wine producers in the world. Prüm, one of the most positive examples of a German winemaker, always searched for new technical possibilities to help him make better wines. However, during the post-war period not only did the German wine industry undergo a technical revolution, but a large part of it adopted a narrowly technocratic approach. Had the Nazis not denuded the industry of so much talent, this modernization might have taken another, more positive, course.

The first phase of this revolution was the arrival of tractors narrow enough to be used for vineyard cultivation, which led to the rapid mechanization of wine-growing. It also created pressure for a *Flurbereinigung*, or vineyard reorganization. The Napoleonic regime in the German provinces on the left bank of the Rhine had introduced the Napoleonic Code inheritance law, which required a dead man's property to be divided equally between his children. This led to the fragmentation of vineyard holdings. But mechanical vineyard cultivation eases vineyard work and brings the wine-grower a financial advantage only when vineyard parcels are relatively large.

The modestly scaled, privately administered reorganizations that began during the late 1950s and early 1960s were to be followed by ambitious state-sponsored drives. During the 1970s these brutally transformed many vineyard landscapes, removing fruit and nut trees that had once interrupted the monoculture, and turning hillsides' narrow ancient terraces into a few massive shelves resembling giant's steps.

Growers often used the *Flurbereinigungen* as an opportunity to plant large areas of new vineyards on flat land which had been orchards, meadows or fields. Here mechanization could reduce the labour needed for cultivation to as little as 400 hours per hectare per year, from up to 3,500 hours needed in Germany's steepest vineyards. Thankfully, later *Flurbereinigungen* such as those of Forst in the Pfalz or Piesport in the Mosel were undertaken with great sensitivity for both landscape and ecosystem.

A similar process of modernization took place in cellars. While sheet filters capable of the sterile filtration of wine were developed in Germany during the 1920s, they were so expensive that only the largest estates could afford them. In 1949, the Seitz company of Bad Kreuznach introduced the first moderately priced modern filter. This was to be a mixed blessing, enabling winemakers to bottle sweet

1955	**1956**	**1959**
Russian occupation troops leave Austria and the modern nation is founded as a neutral state. The wine industry slowly picks itself up.	Catastrophic spring frost brings a decade of good and great vintages to an end.	A great vintage of atypically opulent, soft wines. Initial fears they would not age well turn out to be misplaced. Some Austrian and German wines are slightly over-blown, but the best will be virtually immortal.

late-harvest wines which were completely stable, but it also facilitated mass-production of cheap sweet wines. Such filters can be used to produce *Süssreserve*, a sterile-filtered grape must that can then be used to sweeten any wine.

From the beginning of the 1960s the German market for sweet wines grew steadily, encouraged by the economic boom. Consumers wanted something that tasted like a great German late-harvest wine but cost a fraction of the price. Many growers whose vineyards were not good enough to produce these great wines began looking for ways to produce cheap imitations of the classics to capitalize on this demand.

The first solutions they found were the so-called *Neuzuchtungen*, or new grape varieties. The first of these was Müller-Thurgau, bred in 1882 by the Swiss wine scientist Dr Hermann Müller (1850–1927) from Tägerwilen of Thurgau in Switzerland. It was long thought to have been a crossing of Riesling with Silvaner, but recent gene analysis research has revealed that it is in fact a crossing of Gutedel (Chasselas) and Silvaner, which were the dominant white grapes in Switzerland at this time. Müller-Thurgau did

not become a runaway success until the wave of vineyard replanting that followed the end of the Second World War, the area of cropping vineyards in Germany having fallen from 73,300 hectares in 1938 to 51,161 a decade later.

At first Müller-Thurgau was planted on traditional vineyard land where the microclimate was too cool to ripen noble grapes like Riesling or Ruländer (Pinot Gris), and it was successful there. From the 1960s it was planted on alluvial

△ The Mosel slate of the fine Erdener Prälat vineyard in Mosel-Saar-Ruwer is so inhospitable to the phylloxera aphid that ungrafted vines still flourish on its steep slopes.

◁ One of the first modern wine filters was introduced by the Seitz company of Bad Kreuznach in 1949.

1961

First important Eiswein (ice wine) vintage of the modern era in Germany.

1969

The European Economic Community requires Germany to reform its wine law to bring into conformity with European Law.

or clay soils, producing huge crops of mediocre wine; the source of most base wines for Liebfraumilch and other modern German generics. Worse than this was the spread of *Neuzuchtungen* bred for sugar production rather than wine character, such as Optima, Ortega and Siegerrebe. They all ripen very early and easily achieve the extremely high sugar content necessary for making late-harvest wines. During the 1960s the possibilities they offered were exploited to only a limited degree due to the restrictions which the wine law of the time imposed. Right up to the end of the decade the international image of German wines remained excellent, their being widely regarded as more reliable than the white wines of Burgundy, for example. However, during the 1970s *Spätlese*, *Auslese*, *Beerenauslese* and *Trockenbeerenauslese* wines from these grapes poured onto the market with no less disastrous consequences than the Liebfraumilch boom they accompanied.

> *By 1989 it had been reduced to 'sugar water'... The reputation of Liebfraumilch was devalued in direct proportion to its expansion in sales.*

It was the German wine law of 1971 and the commercial structures that developed in its wake that unleashed the boom and subsequent collapse. The aim of the law-makers was laudable: the clear division of German wine production into three categories – in ascending order *Tafelwein*, *Qualitätswein*, *Qualitätswein mit Prädikat* (the last subdivided into *Kabinett*, *Spätlese*, *Auslese*, *Beerenauslese*, *Eiswein* and *Trockenbeerenauslese*) – each accounting in volume terms for roughly one third of the country's production. However, effectively the only factor defining these categories is grape-sugar content at harvest. Fatally, the planned analytical minimum requirements for the upper categories

were lowered at the request of the German Wine-growers Association. Most producers of bulk wine consequently focused their work in the vineyard on reaching the minimum level necessary for the wine to qualify for *Qualitätswein*. As a result, from the beginning *Tafelwein* accounted for less than five per cent of production and all kinds of simple wines could be legally sold as *Qualitätswein* (the equivalent of AOC in France).

THE 'SUGAR WATER' FLOOD

With their 'flowery' bouquet, soft, sweetish taste and modest prices, the new generic German *Qualitätswein* had a great appeal for the flood of new wine-drinkers, particularly in the English-speaking world. From 1971 to 1980 German wine exports to the UK increased by over 450 per cent and between 1980 and 1989 trebled again. Much of the 150 million litres of German wine imported into the United Kingdom in this – the peak sales year – was Liebfraumilch. Prior to 1971 this had usually been a branded wine of mild taste but respectable quality. By 1989 it had been reduced to 'sugar water', usually sold under the name of a supermarket where it was the cheapest wine. The reputation of Liebfraumilch was devalued in direct proportion to its expansion in sales.

The 1971 wine law ordained the same fate for many of the geographical designations once synonymous with great German wine. Most damaging were the *Grosslage* within whose boundaries lay the vineyards of anything from one to a dozen villages, but which read like single vineyard names. For example, Piesporter Michelsberg and Niersteiner Gutes Domtal are *Grosslage* under which names large volumes of mediocre blended wines are marketed, most of it originating from vineyards not belonging to Piesport or Nierstein. On the other hand,

1970	1971	1976	1977
Enormous expansion of vineyard area begins, often through flagrantly illegal plantations.	New wine law passed, leading to disastrous mid-term consequences. Extremely fine elegant wines both in Austria and Germany, now at their peak. However, few of them will make really old bones.	In Germany a vintage of big lush dessert wines, many of which were overblown. No better than average for Austria.	A mediocre vintage in Germany, but a great one for the dry wines from the Wachau and neighbouring regions in Austria. Rich but beautifully balanced wines.

Piesporter Goldtröpfchen and Nierste ner Pettental are single vineyards whose names some of the greatest Riesling wines carry. The success of cheap *Grosslage* wines such as Piesporter Michelsberg and Niersteiner Michelsberg was at the cost of the genuine wines from these parishes.

The 1971 wine law gave the big wine blenders and bottlers an instrument for the cannibalization of Germany's wine-growing traditions, a process they pushed forward energetically. The result was that producing wines of world-class quality no longer made economic sense. If it had not been for individualists like Egon Müller of the eponymous estate in Wiltingen, Dr Carl von Schubert of Maximin Grünhaus, Wilhelm Haag of the Fritz Haag estate of Brauneberg and Dr Manfred Prüm of Joh Jos Prüm – all in the Mosel-Saar-Ruwer – Germany would have made no great wines during the late 1970s and the 1980s. However, their very limited productions were not enough to persuade the new, international generation of wine-consumers that Germany produced great wines.

As these consumers began trading up from Liebfraumilch, they almost invariably switched to wines from other countries. The prime beneficiaries were the New World wine countries. During the 1980s the German wine industry boxed itself into the cheap and sweet corner, precipitating the fall in total exports which began in 1993 and continues to this day.

While Germany's top wine-growers had adopted new technology which enabled them to influence how much unfermented grape sugar wines retained (and thus their balance) Austria's leading white wine producers had chosen a strictly dry wine path. Here Josef Jamek of Joching and Franz Prager of Weissenkirchen in the Wachau were standard-bearers. However, not only did the nation get

a wine law that followed the German model, but the large Austrian wine companies took the sweet and cheap path like their German colleagues, some of them doing big business with cheap wines bearing the highest *Prädikat* designations. Since the end of the 1960s large

The 1971 wine law gave the big wine blenders and bottlers an instrument for the cannibalization of Germany's wine-growing traditions.

amounts of dessert wines in these styles were being produced in the province of Burgenland on the eastern bank of the Neusiedlersee. The best proved that Austria could produce German-style dessert wines of no less remarkable quality than the Tokaji-like Ausbruch wines from Rust on the western bank of the Neusiedlersee, but many of the dessert wines sold in bulk were nothing special. Several of the big Austrian bottlers who marketed them succumbed to the temptation to 'improve' them, thus unleashing the Austrian wine scandal of 1985.

Diethylene glycol, a substance used in some kinds of antifreeze, was found to have been added to a number of Austrian dessert wines. There was no evidence of harm to health, but the damage done to Austria's wine exports was catastrophic. The consequences, however, were ultimately positive, leading to a dramatic

During the next decade there was a revolution in the quality of Austrian dry white wines.

improvement in the legal control of Austrian wine production. During the next decade there was a revolution in the quality of Austrian dry whites. Suddenly, after the scandal, Austrian wine-drinkers wanted handcrafted dry wines of integrity and were willing to pay healthy prices.

1984	1985	1989
A group of growers in the Wachau, Austria, form the revolutionary *Vina Wachau* association, taking the region's destiny in their own hands.	The Austrian diethylene glycol, or so-called 'anti-freeze' scandal spreads to Germany where Austrian dessert wines were blended with German ones.	The Berlin Wall falls, leading to the collapse of the German Democratic Republic and the reunification of Germany in the following year.

This presented leading wine-growers, such as Toni Bodenstein (of Franz Prager), Emmerich Knoll, Franz Hirtzberger, Franz Xavier Pichler

The 1970's flood of soft, kitschy sweet wines... turned sophisticated domestic consumers off German wine.

in the Wachau, Willi Bründlmayer in the Kremstal, and Erich Polz and Manfred Tement in Styria, with a great opportunity. They seized it, and since the 1988 vintage they have produced a string of great dry white wines in a variety of distinctively Austrian styles.

Because the scandal had involved sweet wine, it took longer for the nation's dessert-wine producers to win over the Austrian press and public, but with his *Beerenauslesen* and *Trockenbeerenauslesen* of the 1991 vintage, Alois Kracher of Illmitz in Burgenland succeeded.

▷ Hans-Günther Schwarz of Müller-Catoir in Neustadt, Pfalz, whose pioneering did much to prompt the quality revolution of the 1980s.

The reputations of several German companies were also tainted in the scandal, but although the press reaction in Germany was no less extreme than it had been in Austria, no political action was taken there. This was not the only factor making life arduous for the young ambitious winemakers emerging in Germany at this time. The flood of soft, kitschy, sweet wines produced during the 1970s turned sophisticated domestic consumers off German wine, a process which the glycol and other scandals accelerated.

Many growers found the only way to win them back was to produce wines of the opposite in style: acidic, neutral and bone-dry. However, harvesting the grapes when they are half-ripe so that the resulting wine has a biting acidity, then vinifying it in a technocratic manner that strips it of the modest aroma and character it has, is not the recipe for great wines in a cool climate like Germany's, nor is it the way in which the great German wines of the past were produced. Top German winemakers had to free themselves from this thoroughly mistaken approach and rediscover that wine quality grows in the vineyard and requires super-ripe grapes. This took several years.

Both instinctively, and through trial and error, those growers who began pushing for higher quality found their way back to the wine-growing and -making ideas of a century earlier, combining these with modern technology where it could help. In the vineyard, the 1990 harvest, where nature drastically reduced yields to give the best vintage in decades, pointed the way.

In the field of dry wines, where the well-meaning experimentation of the 1980s had been most misguided, the transformation of the 1990s was most dramatic. Here the pioneer work of the Pfalz's leading wine-growers, and most particularly Hans-Günther Schwarz of Müller-Catoir in Neustadt, Pfalz, was crucial. They proved that a healthy alcoholic content was necessary to make exciting dry wines from Riesling, the Pinot family of grapes and other varieties, and that with a combination of modest yields and cautiousness in the cellar, even 14° of natural alcohol need not stand in the way of a balanced wine. These wines represent a new style of German wine, since in the past grapes of this ripeness would never have been deliberately vinified to give dry wines.

The exciting new wines of the 1990s also proved conclusively that the prophets of vineyard

1990

A great vintage for Austria and Germany – wines with concentration and brilliance that should age magnificently – ushers in a new era for the leading producers of both nations; the rest of the German industry, however, continues its decline.

1994

The last Allied occupation forces withdraw from Germany and the nation acquires full sovereignty.

classification in Germany were right; in the hands of a talented wine-grower the difference in character between wines from different vineyard sites is as pronounced in Germany as it is anywhere in France. Unfortunately, this message was rejected by most growers because it did not assist them in selling mediocre wines from inferior vineyard sites.

During the boom years the cropping area of vineyards in Germany had climbed from 73,700 hectares in 1970 to 103,266 in 1995. The great majority of these vineyards are not capable of regularly producing wines worthy of the title *Qualitätswein*, and are thus irrelevant for a vineyard classification. However, the wine-growers who cultivate them represent a powerful lobby in the German Wine-growers Association, and only two bodies exert a significant influence on German wine law: the Association and Brussels. Neither is a force for positive change.

Germany stands at a turning point in the development of its wine industry. On the one hand the leading growers – including large estates such as Robert Weil of Kiedrich in the Rheingau, with plenty of wine to market – are regularly selling out for healthy prices. On the other hand prices on the bulk wine market are at rock-bottom levels, making sections of the industry completely uneconomic. Already many of the leading estates have expanded their vineyard holdings significantly as land in the top vineyard sites has come onto the market.

Inferior vineyards have also begun falling out of cultivation, particularly where they are steep and expensive to maintain. This process, in itself a kind of vineyard classification, will accelerate during the first years of the 21st century. By 2020 there will be perhaps no more than 85,000 hectares of vineyards, but if the leading estates at least maintain the current quality standards, then the international profile of wines from Germany's top sites will surely be raised. And thanks to the

◁ After the devastating wine scandal of 1985, Alois Kracher led the successful campaign to restore Austria's reputation for world-class sweet wines.

dedication of winegrowers like Georg Prinz zur Lippe and Klaus Zimmerling in Sachsen and Udo Lützkendorf in Saale-Unstrut both these ex-East German wine regions will be recognised for their distinctive dry white wines, rather than regarded as footnotes to the German wine story.

Given a talented grower, the difference in character between wines from different sites is as pronounced in Germany as it is anywhere in France.

In Austria a more modest reduction in the vineyard area also seems likely as some inferior vineyards fall out of cultivation – which will help those white wine producers committed to quality. As the achievements of the 1997 red wine vintage are built on, both Austrian and German red wines will earn serious evaluation.

Interestingly in Switzerland, the abolition of the once strict import controls for white wines during the late 1990s seem to have been a real stimulus for the nation's wine-growers to produce fine wines. The nation's reputation as a producer of quality dry white wines may lag behind that of Austria, but it, too, should begin to share the limelight.

1995

A milestone vintage for Austrian late-harvest wines, the vineyards of Burgenland producing world-class dessert wines for the first time this century.

1997

A turn-round vintage for German and Austrian red wines from top producers, showing they are capable of making wines of international class.

The chance to re-equip with stainless steel and re-enter the quality wine market woke Spanish wine producers with a start. The country's response to 20th-century technological advances may be late, but it is impressively confident and all embracing.

Spain

John Radford

Table-talk in *bodega* tasting-rooms in the early 1900s would have been dominated by one topic – phylloxera. The louse had appeared in Málaga in 1875 and reached Rioja in 1899. Some areas escaped its attentions for a few years more, but the damage was already done. The major vineyards had been devastated. Politically, too, Spain was demoralized by losses in the war with the United States which had ended in 1898 with the surrender of her remaining American colonies.

With few or no grapes to sell, most were ruined. Poverty and hopelessness dominated hundreds of thousands of lives.

At home there had been political equilibrium for a decade or more: María-Cristina, the widow of the late king Alfonso XII, was ruling as regent on behalf of her son, who turned 14 in 1900. Her policy of alternating conservative and liberal governments had brought peace and stability at home. Spain was still a largely agricultural nation and much of the country had survived through self-sufficiency, allowing government policy to consider 'weightier' matters. Phylloxera changed all that. At that time, as for most of the century, grapes were supplied to the *bodegas* by small independent farmers whose livelihood depended on the price per kilo at the winery gate. With few or no grapes to sell, most were ruined. Poverty and hopelessness dominated hundreds of thousands of lives and contributed towards a rise in revolutionary, republican and separatist movements; the echoes of the last are still being heard today.

María-Cristina's son became Alfonso XIII in 1902. He continued his mother's policy of alternating governments, but couldn't resist interfering: 33 governments held office in the 21 years after his accession. Alfonso won respect in other ways: his humanitarian and strictly neutral position during the First World War won him friends in Spain and abroad. But his disastrous intervention in government policy over the Moroccan War in 1921 led to a successful coup by General Miguel Primo de Rivera in 1923.

Meanwhile the wine industry had been struggling to its feet. In spite of the political turmoil in Madrid, work had progressed in

1915

Marqués de Riscal produced a lovely wine, which still has quite a bit of fight left in it. Delicate, perfumed, a hint of richness. At this time they were putting anything up to 50 per cent Cabernet Sauvignon in the mix.

◁ Row upon row of casks at the Freixenet winery in northern Spain. The business was started in 1889, when it simply sold wine, but has grown into an international concern respected for its efficient mechanized methods and strict quality standards.

vineyards all over Spain. Growers who had been experimenting with American *Vitis labrusca* vines to try to beat phylloxera noticed that these continued to flourish, although their grapes were too poor to make decent wine. Several regions discovered grafting around the turn of the century.

By 1923 the vineyards had largely been restored and the business began to advance after a 20-year retreat. There were still problems, however. Spain was becoming industrialized and, as well-paid jobs became available, the drift of population to the cities became a flood. The cost of harvesting grapes started to rise and in many rural areas it was almost impossible to find people to work on the land and in the wineries. The result was the establishment of *Consejos Reguladores* – the regional regulating councils which oversaw wine production and guaranteed its basic quality. The first was in Rioja in 1926, followed by Alella and Cariñena in 1932. Spain's oldest wine – sherry – didn't get its *Consejo* until 1933, along with Montilla-Moriles and Tarragona. But, some confidence and stability had returned.

It couldn't last. Primo de Rivera fell by another coup, this time headed by General Dámaso Berenguer in January 1930. He was determined to restore democracy, and municipal elections were held in April 1931. The vote favoured the republican tendency, and there were calls for the King's abdication. The military, which had supported Alfonso, was unwilling to get involved in a civil war and withdrew its support. The King refused to abdicate, but left the country for ever, passing his succession rights to his third son Juan-Carlos de Borbón y Battenburg (1913–93) who eventually returned to Spain as the Conde (Count) of Barcelona.

Spain declared itself a republic under president Niceto Alcalá Zamora y Torres and, after a general election, the socialist/republicans were elected under Prime Minister Manuel

1923	1926	1928
Vineyards were restored after 20 years of political and economic turmoil.	Introduction of the first regional regulating council – *Consejo Regulador* – in Rioja.	Long-lived Marqués de Riscal still has a soft, elegant, perfumed nose. Drying out on the palate but still with a hint of greatness.

▷ In the 1930s, Bodega Torres in Penedès suffered bomb damage during the Civil War, as did its famous giant vat, a 132,000 gallon vessel which once held a banquet for 50 guests, including King Alfonso XII. Today both the *bodega* and the vat have been restored.

Somehow amid this turmoil Málaga got its *Consejo Regulador* in 1937, but by then the country was riven by war and, even when it was over, the wine industry was hardly a priority. The confidence of the 1920s and early 1930s had disappeared and, although wines that were strong in the export business (for example Málaga, sherry, Rioja and cava) continued to trade abroad with some success, war was on its way to the rest of Europe and even that small compensation was about to disappear.

During the Second World War Spain was nominally neutral, as Franco knew that another war would be disastrous for an already exhausted and demoralized country. As it became clear that the Axis powers were going to lose the conflict he distanced Spain from Germany and Italy and tried to win the favour of the Allies.

TORRES BUCKS THE TREND

During this period the wine business staggered along, but there were no new *Consejos* created and many wine producers were grateful to scrape a living serving their local customers and doing what little export business they could.

One man who bucked the trend was the late Miguel Torres Carbó. He had taken over the family firm in Vilafranca del Penedès in 1932 at the age of 23. The Torres *bodega* was badly damaged by shelling during the civil war. However, Torres realized that if his business were ever to get back on its feet the export market was the key. Along with his wife Margarita Riera, he set forth to sell the Torres name all over the world. Most of his export markets had been shattered by war – some of them were still involved in it, but the couple travelled widely visiting South America, the Far East, the Pacific Rim, the United States and Europe. The Torres name became almost

Azaña, who embarked on a programme of reform. Early euphoria faded and the government called another general election in late 1933, which was won by a centre-right coalition. The white heat of reform was quenched by the cold water of pragmatism, which in turn galvanized those on the left, who felt betrayed. The next general election, in February 1936, threw up a marginal socialist government which pressed ahead with reform, but it was doomed from the start. Hitler and Mussolini expressed their support for the 'nationalist' cause – headed by General Emilio Mora – in the burgeoning civil war. Stalin supported the republicans and an international brigade of supporters joined up to fight alongside them, but their resistance was eventually destroyed under General Francisco Franco, who had taken over from Emilio Mora in 1936.

1932	1937	1939	1954	1955
Miguel Torres Carbó takes over the family firm in Vilafranca del Penedès. *Consejos Reguladores* established in Alella and Cariñena.	Málaga is alotted its *Consejo Regulador* after a tumultuous political year.	Tasted in 1996, the Marqués de Riscal was a surprisingly lively old wine with a dreaming, honeysuckle nose and enough fruit to speak up for itself.	*Denominaciónes de Origens* (DOs), a development of the *Consejos Reguladores* are established, with Priorato designated first.	Spain is admitted to the United Nations, allowing some stability of the nation.

▽ Spanish workers take a break in a traditional tapas bar in the 1940s. The word *tapa* (cover, lid) comes from the slice of bread, cheese or ham that was laid on a glass of wine to protect it from flies and dust.

better known than that of Spain itself in emerging markets, an early advantage which the company has maintained to this day.

The immediate post-war years were scarcely better for Spanish wine. Export markets in Latin America and the Far East were growing, but Europe and North America were giving Spain the cold shoulder over Franco's links with the defeated Axis powers. Franco, however, had correctly perceived that the next threat to peace would be the Soviet Union under Stalin, and Spain's strategic position would eventually bring the country back into the European fold. The first step was made in 1953 with the establishment of American military bases in Spain.

By now some elements of normality were creeping back into the trade. *Denominaciónes de Origen* (DOs – a development of the simple appointment of a *Consejo Regulador*) came into

1959

A very good vintage. Bottles still occasionally crop up and have been uniformly excellent, if a little faded.

1964

An excellent year, widely regarded as the 'vintage of the century'. Magical wines, still available from a few of the great Rioja houses. Outstanding in their longevity, style, and character.

1966

The Miguel Torres *bodega* installs a full-scale winery with stainless steel.

being in 1954 (Priorato), 1957 (Valencia, Ribeiro, Valdeorras, Alicante, Utiel-Requena), 1958 (Navarra) and 1959 (cava), and some confidence was returning to the market. In 1955 Spain was admitted to the United Nations.

The 1960s also saw the introduction of stainless steel for fermenting vessels and holding tanks.

At home, the wine business was almost entirely production-driven: prices were governed by the annual yield. Export markets stagnated. With the traditional exceptions of sherry and Rioja and, increasingly, cava (then known as 'Spanish Champagne'), most of northern Europe and America saw Spanish wine as, at best, cheap and cheerful. The United States had its own emergent wine sector in California, and the formation of the Common Market in 1957 meant that Spain, an outsider, paid customs duties on wines entering the market. The United Kingdom and Ireland were still major customers, but the main trade was in bulk wines for blending: many a fond-remembered claret vintage from this era had a helping hand from vineyards further south.

Then came the 1960s, and the first Spanish 'revolution' – tourism. Obscure fishing villages on the east coast suddenly sprouted tower-block hotels and holiday villas, marinas replaced harbours, new roads were driven through coastal

Export markets stagnated…. Most of northern Europe and America saw Spanish wine as, at best, cheap and cheerful.

plains. This was more than merely an economic revolution: in wine terms, it introduced increasing numbers of tourists from the affluent north of Europe – and particularly Britain and Germany – to wine. Many had not tasted wine at all; most had never tasted Spanish wine. Quite a few

vowed never to taste it again, given the lamentable quality of much that was available, but the export-minded *bodegas* of the established DO zones realized that here was an opportunity. The UK wine trade responded immediately – by shipping vast quantities of anonymous bulk wine and blending it into 'Spanish Claret', 'Spanish Burgundy', 'Spanish Sauternes' *et al*. Much of it was thoroughly vile but some good stuff slipped through and a few wine merchants were bold enough to start listing other Spanish wines alongside sherry and Rioja. This decade saw the creation of DOs in Penedès and Méntrida (1960), the Condado de Huelva and Valdepeñas (1964), and Jumilla, La Mancha and Almansa (1966).

The 1960s also saw the introduction of stainless steel for fermenting vessels and holding tanks. Bodegas Torres is credited with the first such installation: his round-the-world travels had brought him into contact with all kinds of new thinking about wine and winemaking, and in Australia and southern France in the 1950s, experiments with stainless steel had shown promising results – albeit originally simply for chilling grape-must to make non-alcoholic grape juice. Stainless steel was expensive, and it was a bold move to invest a large amount of money in new kit, but Torres decided to make the leap of faith. He started experimenting in 1962 and installed a full-scale winery in 1966.

By 1969 Franco was in failing health and, at the age of 76, finally named his successor as Juan-Carlos de Borbón y Borbón (known as Don Juan-Carlos), then aged 37, son of the Conde de Barcelona (who had waived his claim to the throne) and grandson of Alfonso XIII. The 1970s was a momentous decade, beginning with executions of members of *Euzkadi Ta Azkatsuna* (ETA – 'Basque Homeland and Liberty'), the Basque terrorist organization. This did little

1971	1972	1973	1978
Nationalist groups stake their claim for autonomy – the first Assembly of Cataluña.	Francisco Hurtado de Amezaga establishes the first 'new-wave' winery in Rueda.	Marqués de Griñón plants Cabernet Sauvignon and Merlot, which later sets the tone for maverick winemakers to produce non-DO wines.	Very good wines, as were 1970 and 1975, but improving vineyard and *bodega* practices meant that 1978 reached a wider public. The wines were performing well in the early 1990s, although starting to fade now.

for Spain's image abroad (especially since the method of execution was the garrotte) and galvanized other nationalistic groups within the country to stake their own claims for autonomy, most notably the Assembly of Cataluña in 1971. Franco appointed Carlos Arias Navarro as Prime Minister, who promised reform as late as 1974 but was unable to deliver. However, the situation resolved itself on November 25th, 1975, when Franco died, nine days before his 82nd birthday.

The new king quickly established his democratic credentials: he had seen enough to know that constitutional monarchy was the only way Spain could pull together both the monarchists and the republicans. He immediately encouraged the revival of political parties and ordered the release of political prisoners. Juan-Carlos appointed Adolfo Suárez González as prime minister in 1976 and the first truly democratic elections in Spain since the 1930s were held in 1977 with Suárez's UDC (Centrist Democratic Union) party gaining 34 per cent of the vote. The Socialist Party came second. A new constitution in 1978 created 17 autonomous regions reflecting the old kingdoms, regions and cultures that make up the modern nation.

The 1970s brought something of a revolution in the wine world as well. Enrique Forner established a new winery in the village of Cenicero (Rioja) in 1970, based on the latest stainless-steel winemaking technology. He called his wine Marqués de Cáceres and promised a break away from the traditional heavily oaked styles that had until then been prevalent in Rioja.

Many (but by no means all) other winemakers in Rioja and beyond followed suit and the economy of scale provided by this tide of new technology swiftly made it cheaper to buy stainless-steel equipment than to rebuild the epoxy-lined concrete vats of yester-century when they came up for renewal. Winemaking

was clean and crisp and pin-sharp for the first time in an ever-expanding area of Spain, and all too often this exposed the inadequate quality of much of the fruit being delivered to the *bodegas*.

In 1972, Francisco Hurtado de Amezaga established the first new-wave winery in Rueda to exploit the local Verdejo grape and make a wine worthy of the name of his ancestor, the Marqués de Riscal. In 1973, in the province of Toledo (not formerly known for its grape-growing) Carlos Falcó, the Marqués de Griñón, planted a vineyard of Cabernet Sauvignon and Merlot and installed a new winery on his family estate. The success of his wines a decade later was to set the tone for winemaking mavericks for the rest of the century – 'damn the DO system, let's just make good wine'. Legally, however, only two new DO regions won their 'ticket' in the 1970s: Yecla and Ampurdán-Costa Brava ('Empordà-Costa Brava' in Catalan) – both in 1975. The Spanish government had its mind on other things.

If the 1970s saw the revolution in the winery, then the 1980s saw the revolution in the vineyard. *Bodegas* began to reject faulty, mouldy, damaged, oxidized and over-ripe grapes and (more importantly) started to offer more money per kilo for grapes in perfect condition.

The success of his wines… set the tone for winemaking mavericks for the rest of the century – 'damn the DO system, let's just make good wine'.

Forward-looking regions such as Navarra and (particularly) Penedès started to experiment with 'international' grape varieties and no fewer than ten new DO regions came into being, including Rueda (1980), Ribera del Duero (1982 – bringing Vega Sicilia into the DO fold), Somontano (1985), Toro (1987), Rías Baixas and Costers del Segre (1988 – bringing

1982

Excellent wines – the big vintage of the 1980s and the last of this quality for 12 years. *Gran Reservas* from 1982 should still be at their peak, and although *Reservas* may be starting to fade they may well be very drinkable.

1986

Spain joins the European Union.

1987

A very good year, giving wines that aged gracefully in oak. Starting to show its age a bit in 2000 although the best *Gran Reservas* are still magnificent.

stepping in and rallying the troops personally, and the moment was passed. Another coup plot in 1982 was neutralized with similar aplomb and this probably explains why, even among many people of a republican tendency, Juan-Carlos is regarded as a national hero.

Spain became a member of NATO in 1982, confirmed (just) by a referendum in 1986, the year in which the country joined the European Union, as it had become, and the year in which Felipe González was elected for a second term. He went on to win again in 1989 – albeit against a background of rising inflation and unemployment, but confidence was still running high. At the end of the decade a small group of young entrepreneurs started planting vines along the course of the River Siurana in the DO Priorato (Cataluña). Like Carlos Falcó in the 1970s they paid no heed to the bureaucracy of the DO system and set out simply to make good wine. René Barbier (son of the eponymous Catalan *bodeguero*) was one of the ringleaders and he, along with such entrepreneurs as Carles Pastrana, Alvaro Palacios and the Perez i Ovejero family succeeded so comprehensively that their wines were quickly assimilated into the DO and have now become some of the most respected (and expensive) in Spain.

Raïmat in). This was also the decade when the sherry bubble burst. After around 500 years of almost continual growth, exports peaked in 1979 and then halved within ten years. The consequences for the industry were horrendous: closures, redundancies, mergers and strikes dogged the formerly wealthy and stable business. Vineyards were grubbed up under government subsidy and the slimmed-down industry started to try to rebuild itself.

Politically, the world had welcomed King Juan-Carlos and his democratic approach, but there were still reactionary forces within Spain. Adolfo Suárez's reforming zeal got him into trouble and he resigned in January 1981, to be

The wine business was busier than ever, with new DO regions coming into being (some 22 in all).

replaced by Calvo Sotelo who was widely regarded as 'leftist'. In February of that year, one Colonel Tejero, with a few blimpish colleagues, tried to 'arrest' the *Cortés* (parliament) and, for a moment, democracy teetered. The King proved himself worthy of the title by

The start of the 1990s was a time of immense national pride and achievement for Spain. The Barcelona Olympics were a stunning success in 1992 and, if the economy was stumbling towards recession – along with most of the rest of Europe – no one seemed to notice. The wine business was busier than ever, with new DO regions coming into being (some 22 in all), including the first offshore DOs in Mallorca and the Canary Islands, ancient regions such as Ribera Sacra and Getaria, and 'promotions' for *vinos de la tierra* such as Ribera del Guadiana. Rioja was promoted from DO to DOCa (*Denominación de Origen Calificada*) amid

1991	**1992**	**1994**
Very good vintage, although it disappointed many producers. Rioja had just been promoted to DOCa and they wanted a really great vintage to show it off (it finally arrived in 1994). Some houses over-oaked their wines in a vain hope that it would improve them. Big-name wines are, however, superb.	The Barcelona Olympics generate excitement and optimism: 22 new DOs are designated during the 1990s.	Excellent, although a very small harvest after the worst drought in living memory. Severe shortages after the small and unexciting vintages in the drought years of 1992 and 1993 mean that these wines may already have disappeared, which is a tragedy.

argument over what the new epithet should mean; but, after an enduring flirtation with the New World, Europe had rediscovered Spanish wines and the range was wider than ever.

Modern equipment at bargain prices encouraged regions to experiment boldly and new, original wines were produced. As Europe began to emerge from recession in the mid-'90s, the third wine revolution of Spain became apparent. At last, producers had started to consult the market instead of simply making a large quantity of wine and trying to sell it to all-comers. Successful experimentation was widespread, in Navarra, Somontano, Murcia and (particularly) throughout Cataluña. The range of wines available, at home and abroad, had never been better. Even the sherry market clawed its way back – although the huge quantities of indifferent wines being made in the 1970s are unlikely to be seen again. A smaller quantity of better-quality wine was what the market was demanding, and, thanks to diversification and experiment, that is what Spain was finally providing.

Politically, the emphasis shifted in March 1996 with the election of José-María Aznar at the head of the *Partido Popular* as a minority government. As the century closed, economic growth continued at an encouraging pace and the wine market with it. The first 'regional' wines were created in 1999 – DO Cataluña and Vino de la Tierra de Castilla (La Mancha).

So which are the runners and riders in the Quality Wine Stakes that will lead the field in the next edition of this book, in 2100? From the classic stables, cava, at 128 years old, is second only to Champagne in world sparkling wine markets and continues to increase its penetration well above the general trend. Rioja has got over its original DOCa difficulties with a series of good vintages in the mid- to late 1990s and, if the *bodegas* can be persuaded not to sell the wines the moment they're weaned, promises

a golden era of magnificent (if expensive) performances. Even dear old sherry, once a carthorse, is now back on thoroughbred form in lighter and fresher – and older and finer – silks.

Even dear old sherry, once a carthorse, is back on thoroughbred form in lighter and fresher silks.

At the new-wave stables, Ribera del Duero and Priorato have established themselves as world-class wines (albeit at a fairly steep starting price) while Penedès, Navarra, Rías Baixas and Rueda have done well and show new promise in innovation and re-invention. Waiting in the paddock: comebacks by Ribeiro, Jumilla, La Mancha; new-entrants including Bierzo, Valdeorras, Cigales and Plá de Bages; and new contenders from 'obscure' areas such as Sierra de Alcaraz, Bajo-Aragón and the Alpujarra.

From phylloxera to fulfilment in 100 years? Perhaps not quite; perhaps not yet... but here comes tomorrow.

▽ The solemn cellars of Marqués de Riscal in Rioja, where vintages up to a century old are reverently stored.

EU investment has restored life and livelihood to rural Portugal. Native grapes are re-emerging and single *quintas* are replacing giant cooperatives in a country where growers have been trapped in a cycle of subsistence for decades as a result of political turmoil and inflexible bureaucracy.

Portugal

Richard Mayson

Portugal in the early 1900s must have looked much as it had a century earlier. True, the *burghers* of Oporto had recently benefited from long overdue civic improvements, but life in the rural vineyards was still largely medieval. Twenty years earlier Phylloxera had all but destroyed the rural economy; one British

The port trade enjoyed an unexpected war-time fillip… 'port and lemon' became the everyday drink in pubs across the land.

commentator compared the devastation to that caused by the potato famine in Ireland. Following wholesale vineyard replanting, the excellent and well-received 1896 port vintage marked a welcome return to near normality. George Warre wrote in his diary that the year's wines were 'better than any since 1878 and will, I hope and believe, start a new era in the port wine trade'.

It was a vain hope, for 1896 proved to be a brief calm before a series of storms. Cholera broke out in the north and a sanitary cordon imposed on Oporto effectively prohibited the port shippers

from visiting their vineyards. In Lisbon, politics were in ferment. Mounting republican pressure in the late 19th century finally ruptured the nation in the first decade of the 20th. King Carlos I was assassinated in 1908 and the monarchy petered out two years later when Manuel II abdicated. However, in what amounted to a legislative swan-song, the monarchist dictator, João Franco, followed the example set by the similarly dictatorial Marqués de Pombal 150 years earlier and demarcated seven Portuguese wine regions: Colares, Carcavelos, Dão, Madeira, Setúbal and Vinho Verde.

Far from enjoying a 'new era' the port wine region faced renewed crisis in the 1900s caused by falling exports and strong competition from the so-called 'ports' of Tarragona, Australia and California, as well as southern Portuguese wine masquerading as port. In response, it was decreed that wine with the legal right to the name 'port' must be shipped either across the bar of the River Douro or from the new port of Leixões north of Oporto. This, together with the creation of an *entreposto* or entrepôt at Vila Nova de Gaia in 1927 handed to the port

1900	1908	1910	1912	1916
A fine, generally declared port vintage to start the century. *O Portugal Vinicola* by Prof Cincinato da Costa provides a detailed post-phylloxera appraisal of Portugal's native grape varieties.	King Carlos I assassinated in Lisbon; outstanding port vintage, declared by the majority of shippers.	King Manuel II abdicates. Portugal becomes a republic.	One of the finest port vintages of the early 20th century.	Portugal enters the First World War on the side of the Allies.

shippers an export monopoly to the detriment of single *quintas* (estates) up in the Douro. The legislation remained in force until overturned by the European Union in 1987.

Early republican governments continued to pursue much the same regulatory course as their predecessors, but the regime quickly descended into anarchy. Between 1910 and 1926 (the so-called 'First Republic') there were 49 different administrations with over 60 ministers of agriculture. Corruption, strikes and riots were rife as weak governments failed to enforce the laws they passed.

Out in the Atlantic, Madeira had its own little local difficulty. The island's economy had been taken over by the Germans in the late 19th century, provoking a series of spats with long-standing British residents. When Portugal joined the First World War on the side of the Allies, German interests on the island were expropriated, severely damaging the island's economy. Madeira wine exports were badly hit by the collapse of the Russian market in 1917 and by the threat from German submarines. A British resident wrote 'the poverty is terrible, soup kitchens cannot keep up with the needs of the hungry'.

On the mainland, the port trade enjoyed an unexpected war-time fillip. Increased tax on spirits in Britain persuaded many to give up whisky and gin for a glass of port. 'Port and lemon' (a shot of cheap ruby port let out with fizzy lemonade) became the everyday drink in pubs across the land. This new-found business helped to revive trade for both growers and shippers and, despite the loss of the Russian market, port began to enjoy a minor boom.

In the early 1920s, the north of Portugal threatened to erupt into civil war and in May 1926, the liberal 'First Republic' collapsed. Fierce fighting took place in Oporto and the local correspondent for the *Wine Trade Review* reported that the bombardment 'was as good as

△ A girl carries vine cuttings to the steep terraces of the Douro Valley. Portugal's winemakers continue to resist take-over by French varieties, having excellent grapes of their own – and the will to use them.

any I've heard on the Western Front'. In the midst of this continuing chaos, the military prime minister appointed a shy young Catholic academic, António de Oliveira Salazar, as finance minister in 1928. By pruning expenditure and raising taxes, Salazar accomplished the near-impossible by balancing the nation's books. This put him in a strong position and in 1932 he became prime minister, a post which he held as virtual dictator for 36 years.

1919	1925	1927	1931	1932
Record Madeira shipments.	Madeira Wine Association (subsequently Madeira Wine Company) is established.	Outstanding port vintage declared by most shippers. Vila Nova de Gaia *entreposto* created.	Due to world economic crisis, a potentially great port vintage is generally overlooked.	António de Oliveira Salazar becomes prime minister of Portugal.

△ The celebrated port producer Ronalc Symington assesses the colour, aroma and flavour of a young wine.

THE STRONG ARM OF THE STATE

Back in Lisbon, Salazar was busy imposing his new one-party 'corporate state' founded on tiers of rigid bureaucracy. In 1932, he set up the *Casa do Douro* to instill 'discipline' into the wayward port industry, and followed this with the *Instituto do Vinho do Porto* (Port Wine Institute) and *Grêmio dos Exportadores* (Exporters' Guild) a year later. The government also established regional federations of growers and winemakers, charged with improving quality and regulating the market. These were reinforced in 1937 by the creation of the ominously centralized *Junta Nacional do Vinho* (National Wine Junta) which issued seals of authenticity to wines from demarcated regions.

Up until the late 1930s much of Portugal's wine trade (other than port and madeira) had been stuck in a cycle of subsistence. Apart from a handful of merchant firms based around Lisbon and Oporto, most of the country's wine found a ready outlet among the thirsty agricultural smallholders who had made it originally. A lucrative but dishonest trade had been established with France early in the century whereby Ribatejo and Estremadura wines were sold for blending with those of Bordeaux. Otherwise, the African colonies and Brazil were the only export markets of any consequence.

In the mid-1930s a serious financial crisis in Brazil upset this fragile state of affairs. Salazar responded by instituting a programme of cooperativization. The first cooperative winery was established in 1935, but only after the Second World War did cooperatives spring up all over the country: over 120 in total, mostly north of the River Tejo where land holdings are small and fragmented.

Portugal's cooperative wineries were built to a similar state-formulated plan and furnished with the most modern winemaking equipment. To protect them from private competition, they

Due to Salazar's protectionism and financial acumen, Portugal survived the worldwide slump of 1929–31 almost unscathed. The same could not be said, however, for the wine trade, which had steadily been losing out to the 1920s fashion for cocktails. With the notable exception of Quinta do Noval, nearly all the Port shippers passed over the outstanding 1931 vintage.

Prohibition in the United States helped add to Madeira's economic malaise. A number of shippers pooled their stocks to form the Madeira

Mateus Rosé subsequently became a huge international success with sales of millions of cases worldwide.

Wine Association which was cruelly labelled as the 'shippers' graveyard'. Nevertheless it remained a force to be reckoned with and eventually transmuted into the Madeira Wine Company, by far the largest producer on the island today.

1933	1935	1937	1940	1945
Port Wine Institute (IVP) established.	First cooperative winery set up at Muge in the Ribatejo.	The *Junta Nacional do Vinho* (JNV) established.	Portugal remains neutral in the Second World War.	'Victory vintage' – widely declared by Port shippers.

were handed a virtual monopoly in Dão and Colares – then two of Portugal's leading wine regions. Hailed as a significant advance, Portugal's bureaucratic cooperative system subsequently proved too inflexible. It remained cash-starved until the late 1980s and the standard of many Portuguese wines steadily deteriorated.

THE DAYS OF WAR AND ROSE

When the world went to war again in 1939, Portugal remained neutral and awash with inexpensive wine. At the height of the conflict in 1942, a group of friends sitting round the dining table decided to set up a new company to export Portuguese wine. Inspired by the spritzy Vinho Verde which was already popular in Portugal and Brazil, Fernando Van Zeller Guedes dreamt up a new wine with the same slight sparkle, but pink and medium-sweet in style. Production began on the northern margins of the

Douro at a winery close to the baroque palace of Mateus. Guedes offered the owners a payment for the use of the palace's name and the picture of its facade on the label. Faced with a choice of a lump sum or a royalty, the owners played safe and opted for a one-off payment. Mateus Rosé subsequently became a huge international success with sales of millions of cases world wide. Sogrape, the export company which is still controlled by the Guedes family, is now Portugal's largest wine producer.

Immediately after the Second World War, the port shippers expected a rapid recovery, but they were sorely disappointed. Even a duo of exceptional vintages, 1945 and 1947, failed to stimulate interest. As Cockburn's Wyndham Fletcher recorded, 'There was no new business... we spent our time examining stock; in other words tasting through our old vintage ports!'

With fashion turning against fortified wines, Madeira was similarly blighted and exports continued to decline. As France (generally an

◁ Autovinificators for the production of port give a rapid extraction of colour and tannin in the young wine...

▽ ...but treading by foot gives the best results, and is currently making a comeback at top estates.

1955	1960	1961	1963	1968
Fine, generally declared port vintage.	Imposition of the *Lei do Terço* (Law of a Third) causes difficulties for port shippers.	Guerrilla war breaks out in Portugal's African colonies.	Outstanding port vintage.	Salazar suffers crippling accident. Marcelo Caetano becomes prime minister.

outlet for bargain-basement cooking wine) picked up an increasing share of the market, bananas increasingly replaced vines as viable commercial crops.

The slump in port sales throughout the late 1940s, '50s and into the '60s meant that many shippers fell on hard times. The problem was exacerbated by the sudden imposition of the so-called *Lei do Terço* ('Law of a Third') in 1960 which required all port shippers to maintain a three-to-one stock ratio. Shippers fell over each other trying to acquire stock before the law came into force, some selling off treasured *quintas* or merging with other shippers just to survive. During the 1960s, the current structure of the port trade began to take shape with multinational-owned firms (Cockburn, Croft, Delaforce and Sandeman) competing alongside private, family-owned groups (Taylor/Fonseca and the Symington family's houses of Dow, Graham and Warre).

In the 1960s, ruled by the elderly and intransigent Salazar, the country embarked on a costly war to keep hold of its African colonies. The rural economy suffered a complete breakdown as the young and able-bodied left to fight in the colonies or emigrated to escape military service. Facing a serious shortage of

Strange as it may seem in our largely varietal world, few Portuguese growers had much idea about the grape varieties in their vineyards even in the late 1970s.

manpower, many wine producers were forced to abandon the time-honoured method of foot-treading grapes in stone *lagares*. The port shippers built large, centralized wineries equipped with an ingenious, self-perpetuating system known as autovinification. Although *lagares* have thankfully made something of a

comeback for high-quality port, autovinification still continues to be used. The outstanding and universally declared 1963 vintage was probably the last to be entirely foot-trodden.

REVOLUTION AND EUROPE

By 1974 the pressure of the colonial wars had become too great and the Salazar regime was summarily overthrown by the military. The '25th April' revolution began as a good-natured affair with a promise of 'democracy, decolonization and development', but within a year it had run out of control. In the summer of 1975 the communists made a bid for power. For a time the port shippers were threatened with nationalization and vast swathes of the Alentejo were seized by agricultural workers. The backlash that began in the north in the autumn of 1975 briefly threatened civil war, but by early 1976 Portugal had shed her African colonies and settled down as a mild-mannered (though economically devastated) European democracy.

A quarter of a century later, it is clear that the 1974 revolution had less of an impact on Portugal than the subsequent decision to join the European Union. Since 1986 Iberia's rural landscape has been literally and metaphorically transformed. The wine trade is one of the principal beneficiaries of this European largesse. It has been liberalized, old monopolies overturned, new wine regions created and, above all, finance has been made available to replant vineyards and re-equip wineries. Even Portugal's moribund cooperatives have been given a much-needed make-over.

Isolated geographically and politically for so much of the century, Portugal has kept a firm grip on old habits and traditions – such as using 'typicity' as an excuse for outdated winemaking. But the nation's innate conservatism has helped to safeguard its unique viticultural heritage.

1970–71	1974–75	1976–77	1979	1983
Salazar dies. First of a series of dams completed on the River Douro.	Military coup overthrows the Caetano government. Revolution and counter-revolution as communists attempt to seize power.	First democratic elections in Portugal for half a century. Dr Mario Soares elected prime minister. Fine port vintage declared by the majority of shippers.	Madeira Wine Institute established.	The start of the PDRITM (World Bank scheme) to replant the Douro's vineyards.

Strange as it may seem in our largely varietal world, few Portuguese growers had much idea about the grape varieties in their vineyards even in the late 1970s. The inter-planting of different grapes on the same plot had been practised from time immemorial. After phylloxera some high-yielding American hybrids were introduced, and for much of the century Portuguese wines were the result of an uncertain and often unsatisfactory pick-and-mix.

The problem in Madeira was particularly acute, the noble varieties (Sercial, Verdelho, Bual and Malvasia/Malmsey) after which the wines were labelled having declined to a derisory four per cent of total production. Since the start of the Douro's PDRITM (World Bank scheme) re-planting project of the early 1980s (the Portuguese adore acronyms), Portugal has once more been taking notice of her native grapes. Varieties such as Touriga Nacional, Tinta Roriz/Aragonez, Tinto Cão, Castelão Francês and Trincadeira have been singled out for block-planting and are starting to appear on labels. Since 1993 any bottle of Madeira that mentions a varietal name must be made with at least 85 per cent of the stated variety. Madeira is more honest as a result.

At the end of a turbulent century, the Portuguese have every reason to expect a calmer and more prosperous future. At home, per capita wine consumption has halved in 20 years with the growing urban middle-class drinking less but demanding ever better quality. Wine regions such as the Alentejo and Ribatejo, almost unheard of a decade ago, have found their way onto export markets as consumers satiated with Cabernet and Chardonnay begin to appreciate the distinctive flavours proffered by Portuguese grapes. New oak is making an impact, but fortunately not to the extent that its use is universal.

The structure of Portugal's wine industry has also taken a turn for the better, the giant cooperative *adegas* having divested much of their power to a bevy of enterprising single *quintas*. The port trade, in the doldrums for so much of the century, has made a full recovery, the North Americans having outstripped the British as the main customers for vintage port. Even Madeira, once seemingly in terminal decline, is showing a flicker of revival helped by the Symington family's takeover of the Madeira Wine Company. Life and livelihood have been restored to the countryside and, at the end of the 20th century, rural Portugal certainly looks different from the way it looked at the outset.

△ Dow's single-Quinta do Bomfin: one of many Douro properties owned by the large and dynamic Symington family.

1985–86	1991	1993	1996	1997
Port vintage universally declared. Portugal joins the European Union. *Junta Nacional do Vinho* abolished and replaced by the *Instituto da Vinha e do Vinho* (IVV).	Port vintage declared. The United States takes over from the United Kingdom as the principal market for vintage port.	One of the worst harvests of the century in northern Portugal	Bulk shipments of port are suspended.	Last declared port vintage of the century. Port shipments reach record high.

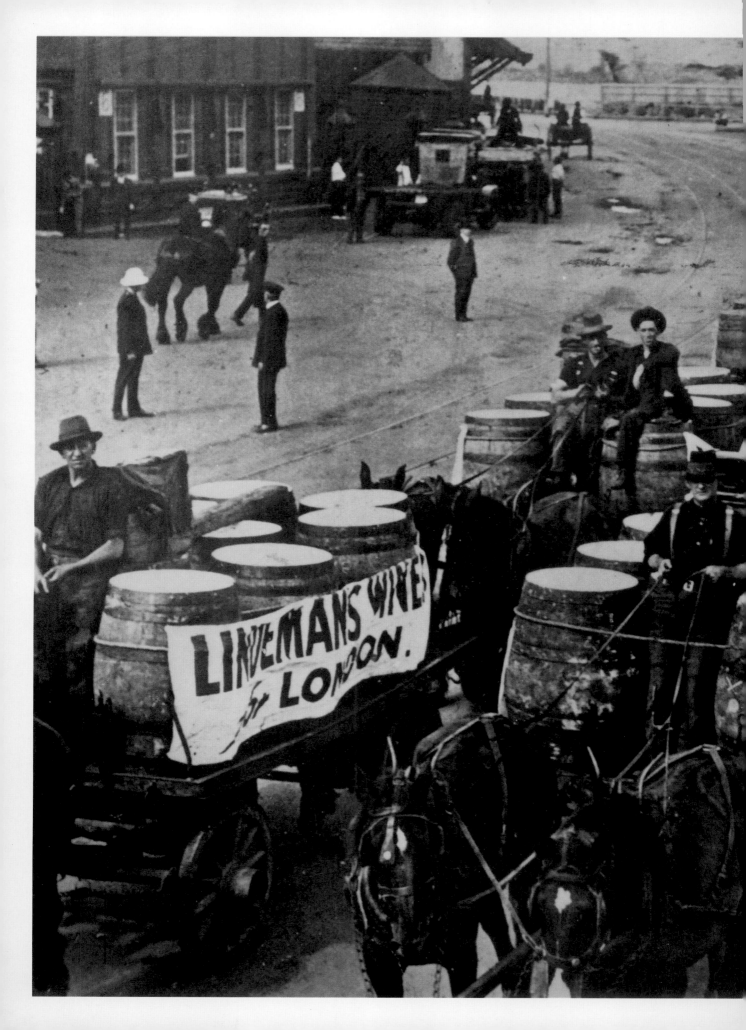

NEW WORLD

Having mastered easy-drinking styles, Australia is now making fine wines to challenge the world's best – and aiming to double production and treble exports. And New Zealand's development since the mid-'80s has propelled it straight into the fast lane.

Australia &
New Zealand

James Halliday

In both Australia and New Zealand, the 20th century falls in two pieces, marked in each instance by a watershed decade. For Australia, it was the 1950s; for New Zealand, the 1960s.

At the turn of the last century each country had a visionary whose message was 50 years ahead of its time. In Australia, it was Hubert de Castella who, in 1886, visited the Rutherglen Wine Show in North East Victoria and wrote:

Alcohol is the virtue, or rather the vice, which the growers are advised to secure.

'This state of things – a preponderant production of wines too strong for ordinary consumption – is due in a great measure to the influence of a certain commerce, which asks for a high degree of alcoholic strength in wine at a minimum of price, in order to effect manipulations afterwards. Alcohol is the virtue, or rather the vice, which the

growers are advised to secure. Thus influenced, even in their local exhibitions, the vignerons who organize them, forgetful of past lessons and indulging in self-glorification, instead of favouring clean, dry wines, as light as their climate can produce, adjudicate the greatest number of prizes to what their list of awards calls sweet full-bodied red, and sweet full-bodied white – abomination of desolation.'

'What will it serve them to fill their cellars with undrinkable wines, even if for a short time? Wine-sellers and grocers are ready to give a larger price for sweet and strong, which the prosperous Australian middle-classes prefer only until they are educated to lighter wines… consumption is limited, and the market soon glutted.'

De Castella's mantle passed to his son François, who became the Victorian state viticulturist, and watched in dismay as the Australian wine industry ignored his father's

1900

In the Barossa Valley the greatest of the Para Vintage Tawnies were made between 1878 and 1900, each drawn from cask when 100 years old. An avalanche of viscous toffee and plum pudding flavours.

1918

New Zealand narrowly escapes Prohibition, but suffers severely restrictive legislation on the sale of all types of alcohol.

warnings and became almost entirely occupied with the production of cheap fortified wine and high-strength red wine exported in cask to the United Kingdom (UK).

These wines came from the irrigation areas along the Murray River from Swan Hill through to Waikerie in South Australia and from Griffith on the Murrumbidgee River in New South Wales. Production of Australian wine leapt from a pre-First World War average of 25 million litres to a record 93 million litres in 1927. The grapes came mostly from a mix of Returned Soldier Settlement blocks (or properties) and from the first influx of Italian *vignerons* lured to Australia with tales of huge yields and easily won fortunes.

Aided by a combination of export bounties paid by Australia and a preferential empire tariff on wines imported into the UK, exports to the UK soared during the 1920s and '30s. In 1919, they amounted to a little over 2 million litres, and rose to a peak of 19 million in 1927, spurred by notice from the Commonwealth Government that the export bounty (introduced in 1924) was to be reduced by one shilling from two shillings and nine pence per gallon. However, the 50 per cent preferential duty introduced by the UK in 1925 continued, and exports remained strong. Indeed, from 1928 to 1940 the UK imported more wine from Australia than it did from France.

Indeed, from 1928 to 1940 the UK imported more wine from Australia than it did from France.

New Zealand's visionary was Italian-born and trained viticulturist Romeo Bragato, who was seconded to New Zealand by the Victorian Government. In 1895, he toured the country with the purpose of advising the government on suitable regions for viticulture and the types of varieties that should be grown. The extent of his vision can be gauged by his advice that (for example) Central Otago was 'pre-eminently

1921

Maurice O'Shea returns from Montpellier to Australia to the Mount Pleasant estate in the Hunter Valley.

1925

The UK introduces 50 per cent preferential duty on all imported wines

suitable' for winemaking. He was equally impressed with the Wairarapa region's potential, and advocated the planting of the classic *Vitis vinifera* varieties.

Just as Australia moved into fortified wine production, so did New Zealand. But the latter country added the burden of hybrids (Baco 22A and Seibel 5455) and *Vitis labrusca* (Albany Surprise). The only classic variety of note was

> *I have a dozen or so of those wines in my cellar which would almost certainly outlive me – if I gave them the chance.*

Palomino, an appropriate choice for fortified winemaking, of course. New Zealand also came perilously close to entering into Prohibition, stopping just short with 1918 legislation that placed severe restrictions on the sale of all forms of alcohol.

Although fortified wine sales accounted for 90 per cent of the market in both countries, there were a few immensely gifted table-winemakers making small quantities of world-class wines.

AUSTRALIA'S GREATS

Maurice O'Shea's father was Irish, his mother French; it was probably her influence that led to Maurice being sent to Montpellier to study viticulture and oenology. He returned to Australia in 1921 and became winemaker at a vineyard and winery that had been established in 1880 (by Charles King) on some of the best red volcanic soil in the Hunter Valley. He renamed the vineyard Mount Pleasant and the winery L'Hermitage; in 1932 he sold a half-interest to McWilliam's, subsequently selling the remainder also, but remaining absolutely in charge of winemaking until his death in 1956.

Over that time he made a series of wines of stupendous quality and longevity.

Over the past 30 years I have been privileged to taste many of them. As recently as 1996 a dinner was held in Melbourne at which the 1943 Mountain D, 1944 Mount Henry, 1945 Bin H4, 1945 Henry II and 1954 Robert Hermitage all opened superbly. In 1984, I shared in a bottle of 1937 Mountain A, a wine I shall never forget, although whether it was better than those wines from the 1940s is hard to say. I have a dozen or so of those and similar wines in my cellar which I recorked ten years ago, and which would almost certainly outlive me – if I gave them the chance. They are either 100 per cent Shiraz, or Shiraz with a little Pinot Noir.

Colin Preece graduated from Roseworthy Agricultural College and joined Seppelt at Seppeltsfield in the Barossa Valley in 1923, before succeeding Reginald Mowatt as winemaker at Seppelt Great Western in 1932. Over the next 30 years he made a series of wines – principally but not entirely red – as remarkable as those of O'Shea, and which I have also been privileged to taste.

Preece had a much broader varietal mix to draw on than O'Shea; he used Shiraz, Cabernet Sauvignon, Malbec, Mourvedre (known as Esparte at Great Western) and Pinot Meunier (known as Miller's Burgundy). Seppelt had vineyards at Rutherglen in North East Victoria as well as the Barossa Valley, and Preece was a master blender who did not hesitate to draw on these sources if he thought they would improve the blend.

The cellar blend books reveal that Preece sought grape flavours that can be attained only at sugar levels which would give wines of 15 degrees or more alcohol, so he often diluted the must with ten per cent water to reduce the strength. Moreover, he frequently blended wines from three or four vintages, so the

1945	1951	1953	1955	1956
Dry and warm in the Hunter Valley, producing the incomparable Maurice O'Shea Mount Pleasant Bin H4 (Shiraz). Most recently tasted in November 1999 and at the peak of its power.	Max Schubert experiments with a red wine that will eventually become Penfolds Grange.	In the Barossa Valley, an above average spring and early summer rainfall was followed by a very dry vintage, and produced the first commercial vintage of Penfolds Grange, still sublime in November 1999.	To quote Wynns: 'A good year; warm summer in Coonawarra. It produced an utterly freakish wine, Michael Hermitage, still satin smooth, elegant and fresh, the epitome of Coonawarra.'	Orlando releases its 'Barossa Pearl' – one of Australia's most successful wines.

vintage appearing on the label was either that of the youngest component or of a weighted average. Many think his 1953 Bin J32 Claret was his greatest wine. I tasted it at a dinner in 1993 in Melbourne; my note reads: 'Still vibrantly coloured, with a fine, elegant, scented bouquet and an entrancing mix of raspberry and blackberry aromas. The palate is classically constructed and balanced, still long and fresh, rich yet elegant.'

THE McDONALD LEGACY

New Zealand's answer to these Australian pioneers was Tom McDonald, who started work as a 14-year-old at Bartholemew Steinmetz's vineyard at Taradale, Hawke's Bay, in 1921. In 1926, Steinmetz returned to his native Luxembourg, and leased the business to McDonald and George Hildred, eventually selling it to McDonald.

Fortified wines were the main product, but McDonald did make small quantities of table wines from Chasselas, Pinot Meunier and Cabernet Sauvignon. In 1944, in a move echoing that of Maurice O'Shea, he sold the business to Christchurch brewers, Ballins, but remained in sole charge of winemaking, indeed, the business was renamed McDonald's Wines.

Michael Cooper, whose *The Wines and Vineyards of New Zealand* (Hodder Moa Beckett Ltd, 1996) remains the best book on the subject, recounts that when André Simon visited Hawke's Bay in 1964, McDonald served him 1949 Château Margaux alongside his own 1949 Cabernet Sauvignon. Simon wrote this was 'rare and convincing proof that New Zealand can bring forth table wines of a very high quality.... The Margaux had a sweeter finish and a more welcoming bouquet, greater breed, but it did not shame the New Zealand cousin.' Moreover, he took a bottle with him as he moved on to Australia 'to show my Australian friends what New Zealand can do'.

McDonald died in 1987, but his memory lives on in the recently introduced super-premium wine called simply Tom, produced at The McDonald Winery which is now owned by Montana.

Simon wrote this was 'rare and convincing proof that New Zealand can bring forth table wines of a very high quality...'

Back in Australia, a series of incidents in the 1950s laid the basis for the wine industry of today. They occurred against the background of the end of beer shortages (which had fuelled domestic sales of fortified wine between 1940 and 1950) and other cultural and social changes.

▽ Len Evans at the Rothbury Estate he founded. The Evans Family winery, also in the Hunter Valley, now produces top wine from small vineyards

1962	**1963**	**1965**
Barossa and Coonawarra – linked here because these regions produced Penfolds Bin 60A Cabernet/Shiraz, regarded by many as the greatest Australian red wine made this century.	Max Lake plants the first vines at Lake's Folly.	A drought vintage in the Hunter Valley resulted in microscopic yields of ultra-ripe and concentrated Shiraz which produced Lindemans Bin 3100 and Bin 3110 Shiraz; luscious and brooding and promising eternal life.

First was the wave of immigration from Europe in the aftermath of the war. Unlike earlier ethnic migrations, which had tended to congregate in rural areas (the Italian community in the Riverland and Griffith region, for example), many of the immigrants stayed in the capital cities (notably Melbourne and Sydney). Many came from countries in which table wine was part of everyday life, and in which food was very different from the staple Anglo-Australian roast meat and veg dishes.

The watershed for red wine was prompted by Max Schubert's sojourn in Bordeaux.

Next, travel to Europe became faster and (in real terms) cheaper. After finishing school or university, it became increasingly common for young Australians to travel to Europe for a year or two, and to return with a very different view of life. There was a proliferation of restaurants and cuisines. Great French-inspired restaurants became increasingly commonplace in the 1970s, as did the restaurant-based business-man's lunch, at which wine tended to replace spirits and beer as the standard drink.

THE BORDEAUX EXPERIMENT

The watershed for red wine was prompted by Max Schubert's sojourn in Bordeaux, which led directly to the making of the first few barrels of experimental wine – now known as Penfolds Grange – in 1951. The 1952 satisfied Schubert that his approach was working. Cabernet Sauvignon seemed a logical choice of variety, but its shortage and the abundance of Shiraz (which responded equally well) led him to opt for the latter. Schubert's winemaking methods were known to only a few, and it was not until the mid-1960s that the first attempts were made to copy his technique – by Wolf Blass, an ebullient German emigre who had come to Australia to make sparkling wines for Kaiser Stuhl. The technique involved open fermenters which were drained of juice several times a day. Cooled juice was returned immediately, and the the must pressed while there was still active fermentation (around one to two *Baumé*). The wine, still incorporating the pressings, was taken direct to new American-oak barrels to complete its fermentation.

PEARLS BEFORE SWINE

The long interval before anyone copied the technique was due largely to the failure by Australian wine critics and judges to understand what this revolutionary wine style was about, and to appreciate its magnificent ageing potential. Nonetheless, the seed was sown, and blossomed into full flower in the 1980s and '90s.

The 1950s watershed for red wines was replicated with white wines. Import restrictions, a legacy of the war, were still stringent, and G Gramp & Sons (alias Orlando) managed to

1971

A disastrous vintage in South Australia, the second wettest on record, the crop decimated by mildew. To be avoided at all cost.

1979

One of those rare vintages in Hunter Valley when the rain fell when it should (winter and spring) and not when it shouldn't (vintage). Great, long-lived Semillon and Shiraz resulted.

beat S Smith & Sons (alias Yalumba) in a battle for an import licence for stainless-steel pressure-fermentation tanks from Germany.

The tanks were installed in time for the 1953 vintage, and resulted in dramatically improved wines. The wines were treated as aberrations by the show judges, but in 1955 the Orlando 1955 Barossa Riesling won first prize at the 1955 Adelaide Wine Show, causing a sensation because it was so different from the prevailing, bottle-aged 'hock-style' wines. Yalumba received its fermenters a year after Orlando, and after that, interest in the new technology spread quickly. Scientific developments in Europe were watched with interest.

The tanks had been invented in Germany for the storage for long periods of grape juice saturated with CO_2. After the war, a German wine chemist developed the idea of using the tanks as fermentation vessels to retain the primary aromas and flavours of Riesling.

Across the border in Austria, Professor Salter at Klosterneuburg had the same aim, but used a different method: refrigeration. Before long, Australian winemakers decided that refrigeration was the more effective technique and as a result the pressure tanks had a relatively short-lived reign before being converted for other uses.

In November 1956, Orlando's Barossa Pearl was released to coincide with the Melbourne Olympics. Guenter Prass, former chief executive of Orlando, recalls the event: 'This launch was without doubt one of the most successful launches of any wine style in the last 50 years in Australia. The wine instantly captured the imagination of the Australian public. For many years the supply of Barossa Pearl was rationed and after producing the five-millionth bottle, the company stopped counting.'

The next change was the arrival of the 'boutique' or 'weekend' winery. In 1963, Dr Max Lake planted the first vines at Lake's Folly,

and in 1967, released the first commercial vintage (following a tiny, foot-stamped experiment in 1966). He himself likened his move to opening Pandora's box, and he might well have had a point. By 1999, 550 Australian wineries (roughly

A German wine chemist developed the idea of using the tanks as fermentation vessels to retain the primary aromas and flavours of Riesling.

half the total) were crushing less than 50 tonnes (around 3,000 cases), and of these 316 were crushing less than 20 tonnes. Only a few could offer their owners a living; overwhelmingly they were part-time holiday or retirement ventures.

The fourth change has seen the varietal mix of classic varieties in the vineyards change (and grow) beyond all recognition:

VARIETY	PRODUCTION (tonnes)	
	1969	1999
Chardonnay	–	236,000
Riesling	2,600	31,000
Semillon	16,000	89,500
Sauvignon Blanc	–	23,300
Shiraz	18,000	207,000
Cabernet Sauvignon	1,250	133,500

(Source: Australian Bureau of Statistics)

In contrast to the above trends is the situation facing the white multipurpose grapes: Sultana and Muscat Gordo Blanco. These varieties are used variably in winemaking, for drying, or as table grapes, depending on demand. Overall, the multi-purpose grapes have declined from over 60 per cent to under 20 per cent of the total crush, but their presence has always provided a cushioning for the wine industry. With another 400,000 tonnes of the classic

1983

Over half of the planted area in New Zealand is Müller-Thurgau.

1986

A very dry, warm year in South Australia produced exceptional Shiraz and Cabernet Sauvignon across the length and breadth of the state; difficult to find a poor wine.

1987

A copybook season in Margaret River which produced the 1987 Leeuwin Chardonnay – a wine on a par with great white burgundy, with layer-upon-layer of complexity.

▷ John Buck's architect-
designed house looks out
on to Coleraine, one of
New Zealand's finest red
vineyards at Hawke's Bay's
prestigious winery Te Mata.

varieties due to feed through over the next two years or so, the outlook for the growers of multi-purpose grapes is bleak.

Across the Tasman Sea, the wine industry had been kept alive (just) by the descendants of

The wine industry had been kept alive (just) by the descendants of the tough Dalmatians who had arrived at the end of the 19th century to dig gum.

the tough Dalmatians who had arrived at the end of the 19th century to dig gum. George Mazuran was at the forefront of a campaign to liberalize the incredibly restrictive laws, which prevented any sale of wine in less than two gallon amounts as well as stipulating the hours

and days during which it could be sold. From 1955 to the end of the decade changes were made which set the scene for the major investment by both domestic and foreign companies in New Zealand.

McWilliam's and Penfolds both set up businesses; Seppelt invested in Vidal, and Gilbeys in Nobilo. By the 1970s, the ownership had returned to New Zealanders, but in 1973, Seagram acquired a 40 per cent share in Montana Wines. Between 1965 and 1970 vineyard plantings tripled, thanks to large-scale developments on the Gisborne plains. But the boom 'was achieved at the expense of quality', as campaigner George Mazuran observed in 1971. The law permitted the addition of both sugar and water to grape-must and there are

1990

Perfect growing season conditions in South East Australia produced perfectly ripened grapes and hence wines of flawless flavour and structure; Coonawarra was first among equals.

1993

Australian wine exports exceed 100 million litres (102 million) for the first time – heading to 215 million litres in 1999.

lurid stories of gross malpractice in the winery including adulteration and the inclusion of additions other than sugar and water. Taking into account the hybrid and *Vitis labrusca* plantings which dominated the scene at this time, the abysmal quality of much of the wine was hardly surprising.

Nonetheless, the forward momentum was there. Just as in Australia, between 1965 and 1990 table wine would grow from a 10 per cent to a 93 per cent market share, and wine consumption would increase tenfold.

It took longer to get the vineyard plantings in order. Hybrids and *Vitis labrusca* were rejected and new plantings led to the domination of Müller-Thurgau. The variety, named after Doctor Müller (of the Swiss canton Thurgau) who created it in 1883, was thought to be a crossing of Riesling and Sylvaner (*see* also p133), and was designed to combine the better characteristics of each. Much of New Zealand's Müller-Thurgau is labelled Riesling/Sylvaner. By 1983, when I was a judge at the Auckland Wine Show, it accounted for over half the plantings, giving rise to a procession of Müller-Thurgau classes, each a little sweeter than the last, and nary a drop of Riesling or Chardonnay to be seen.

Changes between 1984 and 1999 in New Zealand's vineyards were every bit as dramatic as those in Australia. Production grew from 41,700 tonnes in 1984 to 79,700 in 1999, while during the same period exports leapt from 720 litres to 16,618.

FORWARD LOOKING

Australia and New Zealand have very similar ambitions for the future of their wine industries, the only difference being one of scale. Australia left the blocks first, and has achieved a higher growth rate on a bigger base, but both countries are aiming to increase their exports enormously by 2003. The vines are already planted. If Australia were to achieve its target export figure of 401 million litres by 2003, the country would be fourth in the international exports league table lying behind Italy (1,511 million litres), France (1,229 million litres) and Spain (673

Australia and New Zealand have very similar ambitions for the future of their industries, the only difference being one of scale.

million litres). But there is a strong view that the 2003 forecast (made by the federal Australian Bureau of Agricultural Resource Economics) is conservative, and that by 2005 at the latest exports will reach 600 million litres.

New Zealand has forged an international reputation for its Sauvignon Blanc, courtesy of Montana Wines and Cloudy Bay, which are both renowned world brands. Its strongest weapon, however, will be the Pinot Noir grown between Central Otago (South Island) and Wairapa (North Island). The small scale of production in Burgundy has not proved to be a problem, so why should it in New Zealand?

If Australia were to achieve its target export figure of 401 million litres by 2003, the country would be fourth in the international exports league table.

But for Australia the challenge is every bit as great as the opportunity. It will need to maximize the benefits of growing each of the *Institut National des Appellations d'Origine* (INAO)-designated classic French varieties, find a way to incorporate the best grape aspects of Italy and Spain, and explore every combination of climate, soil, and variety. Its freedom to do so represents one of the greatest strengths of the New World.

1996

This vintage completes a trilogy of great red wine vintages in South Australia, joining 1986 and 1990. Once again, Coonawarra provided superb quality grapes.

1998

New Zealand has its vintage of the century, with a warm to hot and dry vintage providing superlative Pinot Noir from Martinborough to Central Otago, plus Cabernet Sauvignon and Merlot from Hawke's Bay, with all the colour, ripeness and richness of a top Australian red.

Key winemakers have revolutionized the wine industry again and again, capitalizing on success and adapting swiftly to meet new demands. Thanks to the absence of native winemaking tradition, the 20th century has been one of tumultuous change.

US & Canada

Brian St Pierre

In 1900, California was America's leading wine-producing state, having pulled far ahead of the 20 other states where vines had been planted, with high hopes and only intermittent success. California wine had become an international business, with sales in Japan, Canada, Mexico and South America. Many had won gold medals

Within about 60 years… the adolescent wine industry had lived up to its self-generated optimism and finally grown up.

in European competitions as well as the backhanded compliment of bearing counterfeit French labels in New York. Within about 60 years, despite economic depressions, surpluses, scarcities, frost, flood, spoilage, chicanery and incompetence, vine disease and phylloxera, the adolescent wine industry had lived up to its self-generated optimism and finally grown up. It is just as well that California winemakers, surveying a sunny economic horizon at last, had no idea that the worst sort of pestilence imaginable – the man-made kind – was heading their way.

California wine had begun haphazardly, in the wrong place (southern California) with the wrong raw material – a grape known as Mission, planted by Franciscan missionaries who first colonized California for God and Spain in 1769. The utilitarian vines thrived in hot weather, yielding delicious table grapes, mediocre but palatable wine and quite good brandy. For decades, they were the breeding stock of California vineyards, the mother lode of wine from the Mexican border to the upper reaches of Napa and Sonoma.

Central Europe was in a turmoil of wars and revolutions in the mid-19th century. Even without the lure of the Gold Rush and democracy, it was a good time to leave. The French, Germans and Italians especially poured in, joining the Americans and 'Californios' – the Mexicans who had stayed on when America annexed the territory. Many of the new immigrants came from countries with a wine culture. Before long, better European varieties were imported, and their planting in the cooler areas of northern California began the transformation and ascendancy of the state's wines.

1900	1906	1919
Thirty-six wines from California, Florida, North Carolina, Ohio, Virginia, and Washington DC, win medals at the Paris Exposition in France.	The San Francisco earthquake did enormous damage to the city and its wine cellars.	Prohibition was enacted across America by a party of urban temperance advocates.

The names of many of those pioneers still appear on labels – Beringer, Foppiano, Charles Krug, Paul Masson, Simi, Wente, for example – but they were often merely local heroes then.

The California system was similar to that of Bordeaux: most of the business was done by brokers who bought wines in bulk and blended them in their San Francisco cellars to be exported. Wineries that operated independently gambled; several pioneers died broke, devastated even before phylloxera began exterminating grape-vines. The bug did have one beneficial effect, however: it reduced the Mission grape to permanent minority status, clearing the decks for an eventual California wine renaissance.

The eastern states of America, settled much earlier than the west, had vineyards cultivated even while they were colonies. Thomas Jefferson, William Penn and other Founding Fathers grew grapes and tried to make wine, but were defeated by an array of moulds, bacteria, viruses and freezes, as were commercial winemakers later, in more than a dozen states.

Even varieties that thrived in the wild failed in the ordered proximity of vineyards; like children in school, when one got a bug, they all did. Still, a few winemakers persisted. They learned that water moderated the effects of winter freezes and spring frosts, and breezes reduced powdery mould and mildew, so they planted vines on the hilly, windswept shores of lakes and rivers, and in New York, Ohio, Missouri and Indiana. The native varieties, *Vitis labrusca*, produced wines notable for their musky aroma and flavour and a distinct tang of bracken and wet fur. When new strains of mildew and other diseases wiped out most of these industries in the late 19th century, it was an aesthetic blessing.

Several pioneers died broke, devastated even before phylloxera began exterminating grape-vines.

New York hung on with widespread planting of a hardy, disease-resistant variety known as Concord – a dark purple grape that is pleasant to eat, produces decent fresh juice and jelly (if sweetened), and barely tolerable wine (if heavily sweetened). Table grapes helped growers through hard times, but the wines eventually created more problems than they solved.

△ The 1906 earthquake devastated San Francisco: brokers in the region lost millions of gallons of wine and many their cellars too.

1933

Repeal put an end to 14 years of madness, but the Federal Law granted states the right to regulate production, sales, marketing and promotion of alcoholic beverages – many states stayed dry or imposed heavy taxes.

1936

First vintage of Beaulieu Reserve Cabernet Sauvignon.

Canada's small wine industry, on the opposite shore of Lake Ontario, went through the same awkward process, for the same reasons, and with the same long-term problematic results.

California entered the century confidently: business was good and profits were protected by the California Wine Association, a small network of powerful brokers known as the 'Wine Trust'. Replanting after phylloxera had often put better grapes in many of the right places, and technological progress ensured that most of the wines were at least soundly made. Business boomed until April 18th, 1906, when things suddenly went dreadfully wrong.

Replanting after phylloxera had often put better grapes in many of the right places.

Earthquakes and fires were nothing new in the San Francisco Bay area, but this was the Big One. More than 28,000 buildings were destroyed. More than 15 million gallons of wine stored in the brokers' cellars went down the drains as vats and barrels burst. Damage was extensive at either end of the bay, from Sonoma

to San Jose, where the stately Paul Masson winery lost its entire inventory and gained a long crack down its elegant façade.

The resulting wine shortage increased prices dramatically, which in turn brought in more capital investment; that and the insurance payout enabled brokers to build 'Winehaven', the world's largest winery and cellar, on the eastern shore of the bay, with its own railroad siding and piers for ocean-going boats. The Wine Trust grew, opened more markets worldwide, and created a slipstream that pulled smaller independents along, apparently ever upward.

A stumbling block lay ahead, however: Prohibition, a movement that had been growing across America for nearly 100 years. The most popular alcoholic beverages in America had always been whiskey and beer, and saloons were the front parlour, dining room and at times even the office of the American male. In the late 19th century, when American had no more frontiers, gentility began to call time; some states prohibited Sunday sales of liquor and many small towns banned it altogether. Vintners weren't too worried yet – they, too, were against whiskey ('noxious and poisonous liquors,' as one winemaker wrote). While many were amused by the saloon-smashing antics of Kansas matron Carry Nation, urbane temperance advocates formed the Prohibition Party, got out the 'Dry' Vote and, in 1919, Prohibition became the law all across America.

Amazingly, business immediately improved for grape-growers and wineries that owned vineyards, as there was a 33-word provision in the new law which permitted 'male heads of households' to make up to 200 gallons of fermented fruit juice a year (intended to placate apple growers who made a little cider on the side). Grape prices soared and vineyard acreage increased as a market for fresh wine-grapes boomed. Some wineries began making

1944

Joachim von Ribbentrop, Hitler's foreign minister, is revealed as secret owner of the American Wine Company in Missouri.

1957

The SS Angelo Petri, America's only wine tank ship, delivers 2.5-million gallons of California wine seven times a year for a decade.

grape concentrate, which was easier to ship to home winemakers; others funnelled 'tonic wine' (bolstered with beef extract) though a medical loophole. Altar wine was also exempted 'for sacramental purposes or like religious rites', which resulted in a surge of new 'non-hierarchical' congregations.

But overplanting soon led to grape surpluses and general collapse for the nation's wine industries. In California during the 1920s, the number of wineries dropped from more than 700 to 140; even fewer survived in New York. Many of the larger wineries simply adapted to the new tactics; smaller wineries where some real wine ambition burned got religion: Beaulieu Vineyards, Paul Masson, Sebastiani, Louis M Martini, and others sold sacramental wine to churches and synagogues, and got by until 1933, when another Constitutional amendment repealed Prohibition.

America's cultural shift during the 13-year gap had been huge. The Roaring Twenties had slipped into the Great Depression, hot jazz had turned into the dirge of 'Brother, Can You Spare a Dime?'. Criminalizing alcohol had created a large criminal class, and a stigma that lumped wine with whiskey as 'booze'. Even worse, America's taste had changed, tempted toward sweetness by the increased popularity of soft drinks and soda fountains. Most of the old-timers and many of the newcomers who revived the wine business in 1934 hit a wall of consumer resistance when their dry table wines came on to the market. The best sellers were sweet, heavy wines fortified with grape spirit, labelled 'port' or 'sherry' or 'madeira', though they bore no resemblance to the European originals

In order to secure Repeal, the Federal Law had granted the individual states of America the right to regulate production, sales, advertising and promotion of alcoholic beverages, which created a byzantine patchwork of repressive local laws and regulations. Many states and counties remained dry or restricted sales in various ways, and almost all imposed heavy taxes on wine.

Despite these obstacles, when the phoenix rose from the ashes it resembled the wine industry we know today – an odd bird at that awkward time, but poised to take flight at last. The century-old lack of a wine tradition now became an opportunity for the wineries that had survived, as well as for some enterprising newcomers.

The Roaring Twenties had slipped into the Great Depression, hot jazz had turned into 'Brother, can you spare a dime?'.

The situation at the end of the 1930s didn't change much for the next 20 years. In Napa, a few wineries were producing wines to the highest standards possible at the time. The aristocrats were Beaulieu Vineyards, whose founder Georges de Latour had recruited French-trained (but Russian-born) winemaker André Tchelistcheff; Inglenook, which was reopened by the founding family; and Beringer, mostly getting by on its reputation. Newcomers Cesare Mondavi and Louis M Martini had seen Napa's great potential, moved in and bought vineyards and cellars. The Christian Brothers, a Catholic teaching order, set up shop in the mountains after one of the brothers had taken a short course at the University of California's reorganized School of Viticulture and Enology.

Although Sonoma was where the fine wine business had really begun, its revival in 1934 was fairly muted. Sebastiani was the most successful, but continued to sell in bulk until after the Second World War, as did Foppiano and Pedroncelli; Simi and Korbel were well-known brands here and there, on a small scale. In Mendocino, Parducci had much the same profile. East of San Francisco Bay, in Alameda

1965	1966	1967	1968	1969
Schramsberg founded to make America's first classic-variety classic-method sparkling wines.	Robert Mondavi builds the first new winery in Napa Valley since Prohibition.	André Tchelistcheff commuted from Beaulieu to Washington State to 'midwife' a new industry.	Spring frosts and a late harvest made for a nervous season, but California Cabernets and Chardonnays were stunning, creating a strong new perception of the state's potential.	Karl Wente discovers mould on his Riesling grapes in Monterey County, correctly identifies it as *Botrytis cinerea*, and bottles the resulting sweet wine as California's first *'spätlese'*.

County, Wente and Concannon led the way; both founded in the 1880s, they had survived through church connections. To the south, Santa Clara Valley had been San Francisco's vegetable basket. Its high hills were perfect for grapes, but Paul Masson was the only producer of stature left. In the 1980s, the area was transformed into Silicon Valley.

The winery, estimated to be worth well over $500 million... launched with just $5,900 and a winemaking pamphlet from the library.

California had an abundance of proven vineyards waiting to be rediscovered or matched with the right grapes. Some, like To Kalon in Napa, had been cultivated since the 19th century, but others, like the Stags Leap district in Napa, had reverted to scrub woodland. Too many, especially in Santa Clara and Alameda, were paved over for suburbs.

Near the end of the 1930's, the University of California's role became more dynamic, beginning to transform the industry. Once again, the lack of tradition became an opportunity. Everything about viticulture and oenology was studied, questioned, quantified and debated. Heat-summation tables told vineyardists where they might best plant what grapes, cold-fermentation research suggested ways to make them into better wines; measured irrigation made viable vineyards of desert and dry lands (ie most of California). There were mistakes, as the university worked with an industry dominated by conservative, large-scale producers, but the progress was considerable.

The other transformation, a defining one, concerned varietal labelling. In the 19th century, wines were defined more or less by style, or by a calculated appeal to a particular audience – an old-timer once told me that his 'Burgundy' had contained slightly less Zinfandel than his 'Chianti', which he sold to Italian restaurants. 'Claret' was a popular name, as was 'Hock', made from every grape but Riesling; 'White Pinot', was usually Chenin Blanc and others. My personal favourite remains 'Nouveau Medoc', the more specific place-name signifying higher quality. Oddly enough, Zinfandel was also bottled under its own name, but the concept didn't really catch on until after Repeal.

The man who lit this fire was a journalist, Frank Schoonmaker. Sent to Europe by *The New Yorker* to write about wine after Prohibition, he returned to preach against indiscriminate blending and generic labelling, and for appellations of origin. A few wineries listened, and Schoonmaker began marketing wine himself, agreeing to sell some California wines nationally if the wineries would label their wines with honest appellations and varietal names. They were successful, and a trend began.

Out in the San Joaquin Valley, a huge basin where sunshine and irrigation ensure farming on an immense scale, commodity winemaking was conducted by cooperatives and agricultural corporations, with one notable exception: E&J Gallo. Almost everything about Gallo demands superlatives – the world's largest winery, it produces about 25 per cent of all the wine consumed in America. Its brandy (E&J) and several of its mass-produced jug wines are all the top-sellers in their categories. What makes the story so fascinating is that the winery, estimated to be worth well over $500 million, is a privately-held family company, launched with just $5,900 and a winemaking pamphlet from the library.

Ernest and Julio Gallo were young men when Prohibition ended, orphans with a little experience of grape-growing. They were self-reliant, hard-working, dedicated and driven, moving from bulk production to branded wine, dogging the footsteps of the other mass-

1970

Severe frost cut the crop and made wines of the decade – the promise was fulfiled, excitement national, especially for Napa Cabernet like Krug, Martini, Heitz and Beaulieu.

1974

A textbook vintage, and also a fairly large one, with opulent Cabernets (Robert Mondavi and Inglenook reserves stood out) and voluptuous Zinfandels; Ridge had both.

marketers, often imitating their products but also improving them and then selling them harder. They mostly followed trends rather than creating them, but with no shareholders to answer to, they could move quickly, and never far from the centre of any new development.

On the east coast, in Maryland, a courtly newspaperman and home-winemaker named Philip Wagner, who lost his California grape source after Repeal, ordered a batch of hybrid vines from Europe. They were crossbred from European and American varieties to withstand cold, and had lost the rank taste of the *labrusca* varieties. His wines were so successful that as well as a winery, he established a nursery to sell cuttings to others. These French-American hybrids were planted in hundreds of vineyards in dozens of eastern states and Canada, creating a middle ground for local wine industries. Later, after viticultural research and improved vine stock, many of those vineyards were at least partly converted to European varieties, some with considerable success. In New York and Canada, the hybrids were also used to make winter-harvested wines from frozen grapes, known as 'Icewines'. The best are thoroughly sweet, delicious dessert wines; their unique flavour has become a marketing virtue.

Through the 1940s, '50s and even the '60s, change was painstakingly slow. The large San Joaquin Valley and New York wineries brought out novelty wines, usually sweet, fruit-flavoured concoctions that sold alongside their table wines – 'Burgundy', 'Chablis', or 'Rhine' ('Rhine' generally being sweeter than 'Chablis'). Kosher vintners like Manischewitz and Mogen David sweetened their Concord-grape wines and created a national market. Then it all changed fairly suddenly. For consumers, as the generation that came of age after the Second World War, the 1960s brought optimism, prosperity, a boom in tourism thanks to cheap air fares to Europe, and a determination to live better; 'lifestyle' entered our vocabularies, and 'gourmet' became an adjective. Good wine was in demand, and California's smaller wineries did their best to meet the challenge.

Resources were limited. There was little Cabernet Sauvignon, most Pinot Noir was thin and uninspiring, there was so little Chardonnay that it was lumped with 'other white grapes' in vineyard statistics, as was Merlot in the red category. Zinfandel and Barbera were workhorse grapes that made fairly rough wine. Riesling and Chenin Blanc, both slightly sweet, were well regarded. On the other hand, there had been great progress in viticulture and oenology – hardly anyone outside winemaking circles had heard of cold fermentation, clonal selection, virus-free vines and other advances, but they were to matter a great deal in the next decade. The absence of any constraining tradition became a liberating opportunity, seized by old-timers and a rapidly swelling band of newcomers, who relished the very American combination of science, idealism, money, romance, commerce, art and a touch of glamour, required by this lofty enterprise.

Many newcomers moved into and renovated long-abandoned wineries, some of which were set in choice vineyard land. The pace picked

Many newcomers moved into and renovated long-abandoned wineries, some of which were set in choice vineyard land.

up: Joe Heitz scored a double coup, first by buying at auction a batch of Chardonnay that had been matured in French oak and ageing it a bit longer, then by selling it to an audience that recognized its similarity to white burgundy. Incredibly, this was California's first such wine. Heitz also released a vintage-dated Cabernet

1977	1978	1983	1984
Moët et Chandon releases Domaine Chandon Brut after four years of ageing and blending, making the first California-French connection for sparkling wine.	After two years of severe drought, a warm vintage brought botrytis – and fine Rieslings; and fleshy, showy reds Caymus and Robert Mondavi reserve Cabernets fully mature in 2000.	Pinot Noir takes centre stage on the West Coast: Carneros and Russian River do well, and Oregon vaults into the national spotlight with many fine, widely praised bottlings.	The first of four fine vintages in California: warm, dry and orderly. Clear styles emerge, leaning toward classical and restrained. Santa Barbara enters the fine wine arena.

◁ In 1925, speakeasies – illicit liquor stores during Prohibition – provided havens for Americans who still liked to imbibe.

▷ No mercy was shown when secret liquor stores were found. Here, in 1950, a United States Government official swings an axe to a shipment of untaxed alcohol.

◁ A woman demonstrates why Russian boots – incorporating a convenient flask pouch – achieved popularity in some circles in the early 1920s.

▷ Ingenious devices were used to smuggle alcohol into America during Prohibition; these steel torpedoes were towed, unseen, from the Scottish coast.

△ Raids were inevitably common, and this photograph captures a raid on a basement where it is said Orientals were making hooch.

◁ Prohibition lasted for 14 years (1919–33); here American entrepreneurs guard an elaborate still concealed in the woods.

Sauvignon made exclusively from one vineyard, which he called Martha's Vineyard; it too started a trend. Bob Mondavi broke away from his family's company and built the first new winery in the Napa Valley since Prohibition, a showplace filled with French oak barrels.

Another first was the revival of Jacob Schram's old winery, Schramsberg, by Jack and Jamie Davies, who were determined to make sparkling wine that could challenge Champagne. Most

High-powered absentee owners came and eventually went when they discovered that wine was different from pizza, soda pop and other packaged goods.

sparkling wine in California then was made by mass-production methods, or from marginal grapes. Davies wanted to make sparkling wine in the classical bottle-fermented manner, from classical varieties. By the early 1970s, he had not only succeeded but was joined by producers of fine sparkling wine from Champagne who began wineries in Napa and Sonoma.

But, the news wasn't all good. Napa Valley jewels Inglenook and Beaulieu were sold to corporate owners. The former steadily deteriorated, but the latter held on to a high standard. The pattern continued through the 1970s; most of the high-powered absentee owners came and eventually went when they discovered that wine was different from pizza, soda pop and other packaged goods.

The fine wine ambition wasn't burning only in California. In Oregon, two newcomers had planted vineyards in the early 1960s, the first *Vitis vinifera* varieties since the turn of the century. Richard Sommer had set vines out in mountainous southern Oregon, while David Lett had done the same in Willamette Valley. Sommer began with Riesling, while Lett favoured Pinot Noir. Today, there are about

8,000 acres of vines in Oregon, supplying more than 100 wineries, mostly with Pinot Noir.

In Washington, there was substantial grape acreage, mostly of Concord – the native American variety, which was made into dreadful sweet 'Port' and 'Sherry'. André Tchelistcheff, who had a consultancy business in addition to his job at Beaulieu, tasted some homemade wine from Washington *vinifera*, thought it excellent, and came north in 1967 to help launch a new industry. He persuaded the manager of American Wine Growers, the largest producer, to rehabilitate its overgrown *vinifera* vineyards, and supervised the harvest and fermentation. The wines turned out well, and the enterprise became the large, prestigious Chateau Ste Michelle group of wineries. In the same year, he encouraged a group of home-winemakers, who had been pooling their resources, to turn professional. They did, as Associated Vintners, which also became the equally notable Columbia Winery. Today, with more than 16,000 acres of vines and 100 wineries, Washington ranks second to California in United States wine production.

In 1968, table wine at last outsold fortified sweet wine in America. Winery touring became big business. Chardonnay plantings had increased exponentially through the decade, and now Merlot was emerging as a new star. Sutter Home introduced White Zinfandel, a new and sexy type of dry wine (later to become a mass-market success in a sweeter version); Fetzer was the first new winery established in Mendocino since Prohibition. In rapid succession, important new players appeared: Freemark Abbey, Spring Mountain, Sterling, Simi, Chalone and Joseph Swan, the last two specializing in thoroughly Burgundian Pinot Noir. Paul Draper at Ridge and Bob Travers at Mayacamas assumed control of hobbyist operations and elevated them to the first rank.

1985	**1986**	**1987**
Long, cool, relatively problem-free vintage, good enough to read like an all-star list from Washington, Oregon, and California. Stag's Leap Wine Cellars SLV, Freemark Abbey Bosché will be splendid in 2005.	Rain in winter, heat in spring; unwelcome widespread botrytis in Pinot Noir and Chardonnay. Cabernets are intense and rich, slightly soft, fully mature in 1999.	Mother Nature's remedy for complacency – a hot, dry August makes producers scramble. Among the best Cabernets: Far Niente, Robert Mondavi Reserve, deliciously mature in 2000.

Startled old-timers began replacing their semi-generic wines with vintage-dated varietals.

By the mid-1970s, the momentum was inexorable. In 1975, Gallo introduced a line of varietal wines with national television commercials starring Peter Ustinov. Paul Masson countered with Orson Welles, and later John Gielgud. Clearly, there would be no turning back.

Comparison with their French counterparts was inevitable. 'Blind' tastings became a popular pastime; California did well, but the French disdained the sport. Then, in 1976, in Paris, with a panel of experienced French experts, expatriate Englishman Steven Spurrier staged a blind tasting to celebrate America's Bicentennial. The California wines came out ahead on points and in favourable comments by the judges, who were horrified when the labels were shown. Several of the wineries were newly established, like Chateau Montelena, leader in the Chardonnay category, Stag's Leap Wine Cellars, which topped the list for Cabernet Sauvignon, and Clos du Val, which followed closely. The resulting deluge of worldwide publicity created a major shift in perception and acceptance of California wine. A few years later, *Gault-Millau* magazine staged a taste-off in Paris of hundreds of wines from around the world, and California wines again did extremely well. David Lett's Eyrie Vineyards Pinot Noir outshone numerous burgundies, and Oregon staked its claim on the wine map too. What few noticed then was that all the most successful California wines were from vineyards first identified as among the best in the 19th century.

The French concept of *terroir* was about to sidle into California's consciousness. In the late 1970s, reflecting some of this newest coming-of-age, the wine industry struggled with wine-labelling reform. Self-appointed experts and critics wrote articles and filed lawsuits. Just as a consensus was forming, the idea of creating appellations of origin was mooted. The new regulations which created the American Viticultural Appellations (AVAs) were manifold and represented a vast improvement on the previous 'non-system', but there is still work to be done. Much attention was paid to varietal definitions, but the linkage to appellations was the key to more sweeping change. There will likely never be a system of controls on varieties and yields, but the expectation is that market forces and an increasingly sophisticated public will provide incentives to keep standards high.

The 1970s saw a planting boom. California wine-grape acreage doubled and many new districts were created. Long Island became an important district in New York. A large majority of American states, including Hawaii, now contained wineries. Small wineries that specialized in *vinifera* wines, especially Riesling and Chardonnay, blossomed in the Canadian provinces of Ontario and British Columbia.

In the 1980s and into the '90s, consumption and growth slowed, but the value of wine sold increased hugely. Big wineries shifted their operations into the northern coastal districts, and the increased profitability brought in a new wave of entrepreneurs, especially in the Napa Valley and Sonoma, who thought nothing of charging top prices for their initial releases.

A new wave of entrepreneurs… thought nothing of charging top prices for their initial releases.

As the 20th century ended, American wine had become a firm favourite at home, and was greatly admired abroad. There was another outbreak of phylloxera, but this time it was quickly overcome. Given the wild ride of the 20th century, only a brave soul would attempt to predict developments over the next 100 years – but they will surely be fascinating to watch.

1990

Spring rains and variable summer heat were worrying, but autumn was a glorious Indian summer. Charming wines, with good varietal character. Phylloxera was discovered; replanting began.

1994

Soggy spring and cool summer did no favours for Zinfandel. Pinot Noir was variable to good, and later-ripening Cabernet was mostly superb, especially from Napa and Sonoma.

1995

An uneven summer, with warm spells promoting growth and prompting mid-season pruning (so-called 'green harvesting'). Cabernet fine, but Zinfandel swaggering y opulent.

Chile, its blessed vineyards already planted with Bordeaux varieties, learnt fast when it woke to international demand. And Argentina, given a determined pioneer plus foreign influence and investment, is now challenging at a quality the world can't ignore.

South America

Bob Thompson

In spite of being next-door neighbours, Chile and Argentina have taken such different paths in winemaking, in such different circumstances, that their convergences are more surprising than their usual seven leagues of separation.

Winemaking, based on classic French grape varieties, was 50 years old in Chile when the 20th century opened. The industry was already on a high: Chile had imported cuttings of all the major varieties from Bordeaux before phylloxera began its devastations along the Gironde. Bordeaux varieties turned out to be

Chile and Argentina have taken such different winemaking paths in such different circumstances.

excellent matches for Chile's sun and soil, particularly on Santiago's doorstep, where the wealthy were pleased to become gentlemen *vignerons* of the Maipo Valley. A fledgling industry attracted experienced Bordelais viticulturalists and oenologists before phylloxera, even more of them afterwards. And, greatest good fortune of all, the root louse did not come with the other imports.

Wines from those early years won major prizes at international competitions in Bordeaux (1882), Liverpool (1885) and Paris (1889). More usefully, phylloxera-diminished France left open shelves in international markets. Then bad luck came fast and hard. Anti-alcohol sentiments had grown in a country where many became alcoholics on cheap wine made from Pais – the old missionaries' grape first planted in the mid-16th century.

Outright Prohibition was unlikely in an intensely Catholic country but, in spite of all the saints invoked on labels, legal restrictions were not. Repressive taxation came in 1902. Strict limitations on production followed. In 1938, the government set a cap of 30 litres per head per year, and froze plantings at a maximum of 102,000 hectares (a cap not lifted until 1974). Protectionist laws redoubled the problems, intentionally locking foreign goods out, unintentionally shutting domestic products in.

In that climate, an artificially small industry drifted. Growers paid the bills by over-cropping. Oenologists lost the stimulus of outside voices and had to make do with declining equipment. International markets evaporated.

1902

Repressive taxation on wine in Chile results in strict regulation of production.

Argentina also broke from the starting gate in the mid-1800s, but without a tie to any particular place and with no apparent international aspirations. It did not need any. By the time the 20th century arrived, a huge, thirsty home audience did not care whether it paid its pennies per litre for wine from 50-tons-per-hectare Criolla, or from under-appreciated Malbec. Producers were happy to offer both types at the same price, so long as they could aim for maximum volume at minimum cost.

Mendoza became the region of choice because it had already been developed for irrigation, and its relentless sun ripened Brobdingnagian crops. Huge was becoming a synonym for excellent. The result: a long patch of dim wines in all save local eyes.

Both countries got their 20th century wake-up call at the same late hour. Chile opened one eye in 1974, and forthwith had it punched shut. The export campaign launched in that year was premature. The wines used had long since gone over every hill imaginable. But the Chileans took the lesson, withdrew, re-tooled their industry from top to bottom, and came back a decade later in very near the form that serves them so well now. Also in 1974, Argentina launched an equally ill-advised export drive, took the same punch, but didn't learn its lesson, or – given a wildly erratic economy – couldn't afford to. As late as 1990, winemakers clung to gigantic concrete tanks as their ageing vessel of choice, and still thought nothing of waiting 10 or 15 years before bottling.

Chile could move fast because of its more internationally minded winemaking community, and more stable economy. Among old-line Chilean firms, Concha y Toro, Santa Rita and Santa Carolina modernized in a trice. The proprietors of Discover Wine (Montes) were just as quick to organize a new company aimed only at the international market.

△ Stakes are prepared at the Curicó winery in Chile, part of the Miguel Torres empire that has seen a recent return to form with some fresh whites and attractive reds.

With local confidence came foreign investment. Miguel Torres from Spain was first (1979). France returned early and strongly: Lafite-Rothschild as a partner in Los Vascos (1988), Paul Pontalier and Bruno Prats with Domaine Paul Bruno (1990), William Fèvre-Chile (1991), Marnier-Lapostolle with Casa Lapostolle (1994), and so on through Mouton-Rothschild with Almaviva, a joint venture with Concha y Toro (1999). The United States was also useful if only supplementary: Robert Mondavi and his partner Errázuriz set up Caliterra, while Kendall-Jackson started up on its own with Calina. With money came modern wineries. In the blink of an eye stainless-steel tanks replaced wooden vats constructed from an indigenous tree called *rauli*. Pneumatic presses and membrane filters arrived with the steel. French oak barrels were right behind. And with modern wineries came skilled winemakers. An originally small pool of native talent grew so quickly that the names behind Chile's most-praised wines were often those of home-grown talent such as Aurelio Montes, Pablo Morande, María del Pilar Gonzales and Ignacio Recabarren.

1938

The government in Chile sets a cap on production of 30 litres/year and freezes further planting of vines.

If Argentina lagged on these scores at first, catching up in the cellars was relatively easy after 1989, when politics calmed down and the economy stabilized enough to bring in foreign investment (notably Moët et Chandon, Pernod Ricard, and Kendall-Jackson). With it came membrane presses, temperature-controlled stainless-steel tanks and French barrels. And 'fly-anywhere' winemakers were able to stand in while the locals were trained.

▽ The Cousiño Macul estate in Maipo, Chile was bought by the immensely rich Cousiño family in 1856 and was replanted with mostly French varieties.

Where Chile remains miles ahead is in the vineyard. Its greatest legacy from the latter half of the 19th century is its range of market-satisfying Bordeaux varieties, most especially the reds: Cabernet Sauvignon and Merlot, and now, potentially, Carmenère. Carmenère had always been in the vineyard mix, but was long thought to be a clone of Merlot.

In the wake of its unmasking in 1996 by French ampelographer Jean-Michel Boursiquot, some see in it the possibility of a signature red for Chile. At this point, Cousiño Macul's Cabernet Sauvignon Antiquas Reservas and Concha y Toro's Cabernet Sauvignon Don Melchor are purely Chilean classics to measure the rest by, while Monte's 'M' and Casa Lapostolle's Clos Apalta are the most internationalized reds.

The one trendy variety not in Chile's arsenal before the 1980s was Chardonnay. Again, luck was on its side. In 1982, Pablo Morande began planting it in a hitherto vineless valley – Casablanca – which turned out to be notably well suited. So, Chile had not only Chardonnay, but a new talking point to help sell it. Chardonnay has since proven well-adapted to the easterly edges of the Maipo Valley as well. Its emergence has been at the expense of traditional Sauvignon and Sémillon. Not everyone frets about that. Given Casablanca Sauvignon Blanc and Aventura Sémillon, maybe somebody should. Viña Casablanca and Pablo Morande under his Dueto label have shown what Chardonnay can do in Casablanca; Gilles Rollet at William Fèvre-Chile makes a striking case for the Maipo.

Except for Casablanca, Chile's grape-growing regions are well understood from long experience. A *Denominaciones de Origen* system established in 1995 helped Colchagua escape the shadow of Maipo as a premier source for reds, especially Cabernet Sauvignon. Otherwise the main thing DOs have done is formalize old understandings. They many have a greater role

1974	1979	1982	1989
Cap on planting in Chile is lifted. An export campaign is launched by both Chile and Argentina.	Miguel Torres is the first foreign investor to settle in Chile's wine industry.	In Chile, Pablo Morande plants Chardonnay in Casablanca, to great success.	Political upset in Argentina calms and foreign investors start to take interest in the wine industry.

to play as Pinot Noir and other experimental varieties come along, especially as vines march south into Bío Bío, and perhaps beyond.

To put it in a nutshell, plant vines in any conventional way, make wines according to the standard textbook, and Chile's sun and soil produce bright textures and fresh-fruit flavours from the whole gamut of popular international varieties. Do the same in Argentina, and vineyards turn out heavy, alcoholic, port-ripe wines that take years to evolve any real complexity. Such wines are so comfortable to Argentinians that many are reluctant to abandon them. Even now, export possibilities motivate many less than a shrinking domestic market: per capita consumption dropped in 20 years from 90 litres in the mid-1970s to 42 litres.

The crucial step was to break the old Mendoza mind-set. The hero of that revolution has to be Nicolas Catena, who came back from a professorship at the University of California at Berkeley convinced that Mendoza could compete with the rest of the New World – with Chardonnay. To make Argentinian Chardonnay respectable, he pushed vines higher into the Andean foothills than Mendoza vineyards had ever reached before, Tupungato and Gualtallery being thus far the new regional names to note.

His example has caused others to search out internal divisions within old Mendoza, even to look outside it. Producers and bibbers alike now distinguish readily among Lujan de Cuyo, Maipu, San Rafael and other Mendoza sub-zones. They also look outside old Mendoza to the sheltered Rio Negro Valley in cold, wind-swept Patagonia, and a desert-like upland valley (to 2,000 metres elevation) called Calchaquies, near the northern town of Cafayate. Tiny Rio Negro is a complete unknown, but is exploring both Sémillon and Pinot Noir. In climate and varietal range, small Calchaquies competes directly with Mendoza.

Chardonnay, being new to an Argentina that had never thought much about white wine, displaced no other white variety. But in their rush to internationalize with Chardonnay and Cabernet Sauvignon, Argentinians uprooted Malbec wholesale – around 38,000 hectares disappeared out of a total 50,000. Only after it was on the endangered species list did the industry realize that this is easily the country's best red variety and will remain so for years to come. At least its sudden rarity helped cause the more careful segmenting of Mendoza into sub-zones.

Chile's sun and soil produce bright textures and fresh-fruit flavours from the whole gamut of popular international varieties.

Beyond Malbec, and the now ubiquitous Cabernet Sauvignon, Bonarda (thought to be the French Charbonneau or a close relation) looks promising. Sangiovese and other Italian varieties also loom as likely future red alternatives because of Argentina's huge and powerful Italian population. Where Chardonnay will not go, the obscure, probably Iberian Torrontes would appear to be the alternative of choice, though its powerful aromas cause even its supporters to admit that it will be a hard sell in a Chardonnay world.

In the course of leading the revolution, Catena has built a considerable vinous empire during the 1990s, with Catena Alta, La Rural, Rutini and Trumpeter among its many labels. Other names to watch for include Etchart, Fabre Montmayour, Norton and Michel Torino. Chile and Argentina deservedly command the South America limelight now, but elsewhere on their continent Uruguay is on a bit of a roll with Tannat, and Peruvian Chardonnay has turned enough heads that the dawning of a new century is no time for the leaders to nod off again.

1995	1996	1997	1998
An outstanding vintage for Chilean reds. A *Denominaciones de Origen* system is established in Chile; it helps Colchagua escape the shadow of Maipo as a premier source for red wines.	The launch of Montes 'M', one of the leading super-premium Chilean reds. A French ampelographer unmasks the Carmenère variety – expected to be a signature red for Chile.	A second too vintage for reds from Chile.	Widely regarded as a disappointing year in South America.

In spite of a 340-year-old vine-growing history, the 'Rainbow Nation' re-entered international wine markets in the 1990s with a confused image. But foreign investment and expertise is helping to set a positive course, and a lively revival is well under way.

South Africa

John Platter

Wine, like much else in South Africa, has been deeply influenced by the country's history of conflict and pariah politics. But the liberation of the late 20th century – unlocking doors slammed during decades of international boycotts – confronted Cape wine with its greatest challenge in three centuries: remaking the national wine image after the shame of apartheid, and recovering wasted years of insularity during boom times in the wider wine world.

South Africa, the world's eighth-largest producer and now an old-age pensioner of the New World.

So opened the latest chapter in a long tale featuring Khoi herdsmen, Xhosa expansionists, Dutch colonialists, Malay slaves, British imperialists and French Huguenot refugees. Few, including the French, had any strong background in wine.

The Dutch pioneered the first vineyards and produced wine in 1659. Their Calvinist religion and the Afrikaner language and culture they developed continue to mould the Cape's wine and politics. By the early 1990s, South Africa,

the world's eighth-largest producer and now an old-age pensioner of the New World, faced momentous choices – whether to bury much of its past and restyle itself as a standard bearer of the modern wine revolution, or simply to dust off its traditional laurels.

The uneasy rebirth of Cape wine is best understood against the background of a century of dramatically mixed fortunes. Recovery from phylloxera – which hit vineyards from 1885 – had been exceptionally swift. But the craftsmanship that went into making the late 18th century Constantia dessert wines – rich, gold and red Muscat de Frontignans – was relegated to legend until it was revived in 1986 by Klein Constantia Estate, and then only on a minute scale of 800 cases a year.

For much of the first half of the 20th century, Cape table wine was a byword for mediocrity in England. The labels would be deemed outrageous 'passing off' today: Africander Claret, Cape Hock, Veldt Burgundy, Table Mountain Chablis. Little seemed to have changed since Cyrus Redding wrote in his *History and Description of Modern Wines* (1851):

1918	1923	1924	1925
Kooperatiewe Wijnbouers Vereniging (KWV), the wine farmers' organization, is established.	55 million litres of wine were deliberately drained into the Eerste River at Stellenbosch, due to large surpluses.	General Smuts, as prime minister, grants the KWV statutory powers to fix its own minimum distilling wine prices to the trade. The SFW (Stellenbosch Farmers' Winery) is founded by William Charles Winshaw and partners.	Professor Abraham Perold crosses Pinot Noir and Cinsaut to give birth to what will become South Africa's signature grape – Pinotage.

'Red Cape drunk at the proper age in the country is a sound wine. Who would believe this from the specimens drunk in England?'

Inevitably, with mediocrity also came plenty; huge surpluses between 1904 and 1924 – in 1923, some 55 million litres were drained into the Eerste River at Stellenbosch. Growers were in disarray as prices swung wildly. An austere war hero, General Jan Christian Smuts, rode to the farmers' rescue. He was born in the Cape winelands, a Cambridge law graduate, and a canny Boer War commander against the British. In 1924, as prime minister, he granted the wine farmers' organization the *Kooperatiewe Wijnbouers Vereniging* (KWV), established in 1918, statutory powers to fix its own minimum distilling wine prices to the trade. So was born a market-free, monopoly producer cooperative, that would shape the destiny of Cape wine. The persistent gluts dictated their own simple logic – distillation and fortification. Had wine become a by-product? *Dop en dam* (a tot of brandy and water) became, and remains, a staple white South African drink.

Some stability ensued. Grape-farmers were buffered from the realism of the market and the awkward 'problems of under-consumption', a quaint term for a wine-lake. The choice of grape varieties – predominantly white, chiefly Chenin Blanc, Colombard, Palomino, Clairette and Sémillon – stemmed from these expediencies, reflecting farmers' safety in bulk production and their dependence on distilling.

KWV's powers were extended in 1940 to include the annual price-fixing of table wines, and production-quota limits were imposed in 1957. These restricted vineyards to designated farms, mostly on the hot, alluvial, irrigable valley floors. There were no limits on yield or variety, and few on quality. Income was determined by yields and calculated on sugar production. But there was progress beyond the distillations. One surviving

◁ General Jan Christian Smuts who, as prime minister in 1924, granted statutory powers to the national cooperative the KWV, allowing it effectively to control prices and absorb surplus.

flag-bearer is Alto Estate, south of Stellenbosch. From the 1920s it made Alto Rouge, aged in large, old casks, a 'traditional' blend of low-yielding Cabernet, Shiraz and Cinsaut. The resulting wine was hailed for its excellence.

The Cape's major innovation in viticulture came in 1925. Professor Abraham Perold, the country's foremost viticulturalist, crossed Pinot Noir and Cinsaut to give birth to Pinotage. The new variety languished in obscurity for decades, but from the 1960s began to cause excitement. It is a moody grape tending to coarseness and excess – of acidity, of sharp fruity-sweet aromas – but a few consistently outstanding and long-lived wines were produced, notably from Kanonkop, and have been joined by Hidden Valley, Uiterwyk, Warwick, L'Avenir and Grangehurst.

There were newcomers among the cast of movers and shakers. William Charles Winshaw came to Cape Town from Kentucky in 1899. In 1924, he and partners formed Stellenbosch Farmers' Winery (SFW), which pioneered the first mass-market table wines – Lieberstein

1940	1945
The KWV's powers are extended to include the annual price fixing of table wines.	Acclaimed by old-timers as the vintage of the century, but scarcely any bottles remain. At 40 years old, these Cabernet-based blends were still dense and porty, despite the rustic winemaking.

▷ Tim Hamilton-Fussell, a leading reformer and award-winning producer, used his expertise in climatology to pinpoint the perfect spot for growing Chardonnay and Pinot Noir.

(semi-sweet Chenin) and Chateau Libertas (a Cabernet/Cinsaut). Both are still going strong.

Johann Graue, a German immigrant after the Second World War, developed cold fermentation on a commercial scale, which revolutionized white wine quality. His successor at Nederburg in Paarl was Günter Brözel from Württemberg. In 1967, he made the first – since much-copied – delectable Cape *botrytis* Chenin Blanc.

In 1967, a secretly pre-arranged defection brought to South Africa a feisty Hungarian called Julius László, who had been head of Romania's Wine Research Institute for 17 years. Probably no one galvanized the Cape more, in

In 1973, the authorities introduced the first comprehensive Wine of Origin (WO) system.

this sanctions-obscured period, than this perfectionist scholar-scientist. The *éminence grise* of the winelands, tobacco tycoon Anton Rupert, hired László to head his large Stellenbosch wine house, Die Bergkelder. But this great Afrikaner

philanthropist perhaps epitomises the carefree national attitude to wine. Rupert keeps no cellar, just a couple of boxes for current drinking. 'The difference between great and good wine is not so big,' he says. László was shocked by the Cape's backwardness: at the start of the 1980s there were only two or three experimental oaked Chardonnay labels (De Wetshof and Backsberg setting the pace), a few Sauvignon Blanc vineyards, and no *barrique*-aged Cabernets. The first Bordeaux-style blend appeared only in 1980. Officials had counselled against Chardonnay: the Cape's soils, they said, were insufficiently calcareous. This was nonsense. Chardonnay is as adaptable as Cabernet, but the only clone available before imports in 1982 was badly virus prone. And wine quotas fixed regions, preventing wider experiment with the vines in other climates and soils. However, progress in other directions was sharpening producers in important ways. In 1973, the authorities introduced the first comprehensive Wine of Origin (WO) system, which certified vintage, grape variety, area of origin and estate wine, though it fell short of purist notions of estate-bottling – 'estate' wines did not need to be matured, let alone bottled, on the estate.

TAKING STOCK

More progress came from 1980 when a Johannesburg advertising man, Tim Hamilton-Russell, defied convention – and a few regulations – by planting Pinot Noir and Chardonnay on a non-quota farm at the cool Walker Bay, far from traditional vine-growing areas. Hamilton-Russell was hounded for years by the establishment, which managed to convict him in court for mentioning Burgundy in his brochures, but he remained uncowed, eventually producing some of the first really fine Cape Chardonnays in 1983. His Pinot Noir won considerable acclaim abroad too.

1957

Quota limits on wine production are imposed by the KWV.

1969

A superb year for botrytised Chenin Blanc from Nederburg, a wine that is still going strong.

◁ The release of Nelson Mandela in 1990 paved the way for the return to international acceptance for South African wine; but growers still had to reverse the effects of years of isolation and under-investment.

By the time the Cape's political quarantine was lifted, a few independent producers were making wines in the modern idiom: riper, fruitier, more concentrated, fashionably oaked and stylishly packaged. In the vanguard were Klein Constantia, Buitenverwachting, Thelema, Mulderbosch, Cabrière, Neil Ellis, Hamilton-Russell and a few others who intended to play to an international audience. Several were harried and fined for quota contraventions. One or two long-established heavyweights hardly needed to dust themselves off to confirm their sought-after status – consistent and elegantly laid-back Meerlust, for example, and more robust Kanonkop; Hartenberg, Uiterwyk, Overgaauw, Backsberg, Fairview and Simonsig.

At about the same time, the wine scene was enlivened by heavy, sometimes showy, investment – on occasion complete with Napa-style flamboyance; at Plaisir de Merle, for example, Lanzerac, Neethlingshof, Saxenburg, Graham Beck, Rustenberg, Vergelegen, Steenberg and Boschendal (last three owned by Rand-based mining and industrial giants).

A headlong surge of expansion followed after 1992 when the absurd quota system was finally abandoned. Foreign capital liked the new openness; wineries and vineyards mushroomed, and interlopers boldly gate crashed the party. L'Avenir, Jordan, Ken Forrester, Grangehurst, and Veenwouden were among these bright newcomers.

Trophy-hunting tycoons also hit town, the Huguenot hamlet of Franschhoek became a roll-call of retired CEOs (Chief Executive Officer). Big foreign names joined the throng: the Rothschilds from Bordeaux (in partnership with the Ruperts in 'R & de R' at Fredericksburg Winery, the Cointreaus from Cognac, Pernod Ricard, Zelma Long from

1973
The Wine of Origin (WO) system is introduced.

1974
A warm, practically cloudless summer. Some fine Nederburg Cabernets (blended with Shiraz and aged in large vats) were still very much alive 20 years later.

1977
Poor vintages are rare in South Africa's mild and frost-free climate, but this was a washout, especially for Cabernet Sauvignon.

California, flying winemakers, and consultants such as Michel Rolland, Alain Moueix, and Paul Pontallier.

After Mandela's liberation and the lifting of sanctions, at least 20 new wineries opened doors each year, while the juggernaut cooperatives began to transform themselves into streamlined

Juggernaut cooperatives began to transform themselves into streamlined open roadsters.

open roadsters. They eagerly off-loaded workaday whites to chain buyers at price-points long since vacated by the Antipodeans, though at better than the borderline local distilling rates they had been receiving.

However, the industry's top-quality standard-bearers bottled probably no more than a million cases in an industry growing the equivalent of 90 million cases in 1999 – insufficient to re-launch a 'Super Cape' international wine image. And South Africa lacked world-class cult wines, with the following – and the prices – that so excited Americans about their Opus One, Dominus, and Harlan; and Australians about Grange and Henschke.

But this was perhaps not the industry's most serious problem. Vast swathes of vineyards remained riddled with viruses, which inhibit ripening especially in very hot years; hence the

The notorious Dop system – wine in lieu or partially in lieu of pay – which had produced centuries of addiction among vineyard labourers.

frequent green tannins and lack of flesh and fruit in many Cape reds. New, virus-tested material from approved nurseries was often quickly reinfested when planted out. There were also acute shortages of new plant material. Quality-conscious growers took action, hiring

outside viticulturalists and Australian and French consultants and winemakers. But others defended the 'structured leanness' as 'the national, traditional style', dismissing Australian wines as 'evanescent, fruity, here today, gone-tomorrow fruit juices'. They disdained the easier drinking styles, which offended Cape self-esteem, saying they preferred – and hoped the world eventually would, too – the harder, *dikvoet* (big foot) traditional reds.

There were other concerns in the vineyard. The mix of grape varieties – 101,000 hectares in 1998 for an annual harvest just below one million tons – was way adrift of world drinking trends. It lopsidedly favoured not only white grapes (78 per cent in 1998) but also bulk varieties processed by a vast cooperative network. Chardonnay and Sauvignon Blanc accounted for only 11 per cent of production.

To these structural imbalances were added deep-rooted social and racial disparities, which many industry leaders would have liked to file away as the 'baggage of the past'. But they continued to haunt the present. There was the enduring legacy of the notorious *Dop* system – wine *in lieu* or partially *in lieu* of pay – which had produced centuries of addiction among vineyard labourers. Declaring this illegal was not enough; some farmers and workers continued to flout the unpoliced law. In 1999, *The New York Times* reported research showing an exceptionally high incidence of Foetal Alcohol Syndrome among Cape mixed-race farm-workers' children.

These issues were brought into sharper focus by the fact that after six years of democratic rule, there was not one black vineyard or winery owner and only one university-qualified mixed-race winemaker. A half-dozen private partnership schemes with mixed-race and black partners – Backsberg, Fairview, Nelson, Paul Cluver and SFW were

1980	1982	1986	1987
Tim Hamilton-Russell plants Pinot Noir in Walker Bay against the wishes of the establishment.	Introduction and first imports of virus-free clones.	Klein Constantia revives the legendary dessert wine – Constantia.	Even vintages have tended to outclass the odd ones, but this year broke the pattern, yielding rich deep reds.

pioneers – led in changing the complexion of the winelands. For some it was too slow. 'This all-white industry should be on its knees thanking Mandela,' said Jabulani Ntshangase, a Zulu who had returned after 12 years in the New York wine trade. 'It was going nowhere before sanctions were lifted. I'm flabbergasted at how slow they've been to respond. Don't they understand it is in Cape wine's own interests to be racially inclusive at all levels?'

A rancorous exchange in 1997 between the new government and the KWV over restructuring the industry squandered some of the racial goodwill generated during Mandela's presidency. Over decades, the cooperative had used its statutory powers to amass considerable assets in plant, land, brandy stockpiles, brand names and other holdings that resulted in its virtually controlling 80 per cent of wine production, and much of the wine trade too.

The KWV announced it wished to privatize itself. The new government, while supporting deregulation and a degree of privatization in principle, said it wanted the public's share of its contribution to decades of protectionism. The KWV remained defiant.

The then Minister of Agriculture, Derek Hanekom, eventually capitulated in return for an industry contribution of R200 million to a new Wine Trust. The value of assets had been estimated at up to ten times this sum. The KWV, which demanded and got almost 50 per cent representation on the Trust, insisted the funds be used mainly for research and generic marketing campaigns; less than half of the already reduced sum was allocated to bringing mixed-race and black farmers into the industry.

The Cape wine regions remained one of the last redoubts of a colonial lifestyle. Criticism was all too often equated by the establishment with slighting Afrikaner culture itself – and these sensitivities were not entirely misplaced. Nor did the local wine press ask thorny questions. They have been a mild, even cowed lot. Wine publications have been advertising-driven, or even directly linked to the wine business.

Despite all the difficulties, volume figures were impressive. Between 1992 and 1998, exports quintupled to 13.1 million cases, about 45 per cent going to Britain. In 1991, only 46 per cent of the harvest was made into table wine; by 1998 this had risen to 66 percent, the varietal composition staying more or less stable.

RE-EMERGENCE

It is curious that after 340 years of vine-growing, there still isn't a stronger wine culture throughout South Africa. National per capita wine consumption in 1998 was 8.7 litres per year – less than half that of Australia and almost one-seventh that of France. South Africa's two million mixed-race and 4.5 million whites make up only 15 per cent of its total population of 42 million and the majority black population has an enduring preference for beer.

Against the backdrop of confused historical legacies, vineyard viruses, varietal imbalances

There was now at least a growing number of exciting wines, and sounder business and social ethics bridging the complex historical divides.

and a racial quagmire three centuries in the making, South Africa performed creditably enough in the hectic decade of 're-emergence'. If it was still refining its wine identity, there was now at least a growing number of exciting wines, and sounder business and social ethics bridging the complex historical divides, to redeem the lustre of old Constantia and assert South Africa's place among the great wine nations of the world.

1991	1992	1994	1997	1998
An exceptional vintage for reds, dark and densely packed, blossoming into wines with balanced ripe tannins. The Thelema Mountain Cabernet was memorable, with unusually friendly tannins.	The quota system on production is abandoned, allowing a surge of expansion in the industry.	A very dry year, giving concentrated reds.	A cool year with a long ripening season, yielding elegant wines for the long haul that are worth cellaring.	Very dry and hot, with alcohols often above 14 per cent. Wineries practicing careful vineyard management and cellar handling delivered sound fruit and elegance in the bottle.

The accelerating pace of change in the vineyard, the winery and the market place has profoundly affected every variable in the once-simple winemaking equation. But a century of progress has left the wine world at the threshold of yet more dramatic change.

Wine in the 21st Century

Stephen Brook

If in 1900 an observer of the international wine scene had been asked how the industry would develop over the next 100 years, I suspect he or she would have been puzzled by the question. A hundred years ago little seemed to change, except when disease ravaged the vineyards. Treatments were developed to combat mildew and oidium, but the microscopic louse *Phylloxera vastatrix* demonstrated human powerlessness

'Climate stations' and computerized irrigation systems will allow the winemaker to make informed decisions without even setting foot in the vineyard.

against natural phenomena. By and large the picture was one of continuity, of the perpetuation of tradition, of perennial struggle against the vagaries of nature.

At the beginning of the 21st century, the wine world can survey with some pride the achievements of the last 100 years. New techniques in vineyard and winery ensure that totally disastrous vintages are rare exceptions. Viticulturalists have largely succeeded in combining healthy yields with good quality fruit. Whereas low yields were often caused by missing or diseased vines, today they are more usually a matter of choice. Clonal selection and

proliferating rootstocks have given the grower greater control over the kind of fruit his vines are likely to yield. In traditional vineyard areas, where massal selections (cuttings from existing vines) are still an option, this is less of an issue than in most parts of the New World, where few suitable ancient vineyards exist. Mechanical harvesting, its advocates insist, gives growers greater choice regarding when and how to harvest than they had when they relied on itinerant teams of workers whose availability – and sometimes expertise – was uncertain.

What lies ahead? Mechanization in the vineyard will surely become more widespread, except on the most privileged sites. But even at these top vineyards, where inaccessible slopes or the necessity of highly selective picking preclude the use of machines, technology will play its part. 'Climate stations' and, in some areas, computerized irrigation systems will be installed, allowing the winemaker to make informed decisions and act on them without even setting foot in the vineyard.

Genetic modification is likely to be less of a threat to the integrity of grape varieties than might be feared at present – not just because of widespread public suspicion. Steve Smith MW, an experienced New Zealand viticulturalist, argues: 'There are limits to the ingenuity we can

◁ The space-age *cantina* at Villa Banfi in Tuscany, provides the ultimate controlled environment for wines from its huge plantings in Montalcino. But, does such technological precision ultimately raise standards or simply homogenize the wines?

practise as vine-breeders. Any grower can tell you that Gewürztraminer is a notoriously poor setter after flowering, and sure enough a clone has been developed that sets perfectly. The only problem is that the wine it yields lacks the variety's hallmark spicy character. So I would guess that for the next 50 years or so we will be working with the existing gene pool rather than seeking to modify it. Soy is soy and maize is maize, but vines are all about nuance. Where genetic modification may play a part is in producing yeasts that can control fermentation precisely. Today, despite the variety of yeasts at our disposal, we can't be certain how efficiently they will function, but in future the conversion performed by yeasts will be completely predictable.'

It might be possible to use genetic modification to remove seeds from fashionable white varieties such as Chardonnay and Viognier, thus eliminating the risk of the extraction of harsh tannins in the vinification of white wines; on the other hand alternatives to costly techniques such as whole-cluster pressing, which is currently used to overcome the problem, may be developed.

Organic viticulture will surely become more fashionable and feasible. Already a substantial proportion of the grapes cultivated in Mendocino County in California are cultivated organically by Fetzer and other growers. The more climatically marginal areas – such as the Mosel or the Loire – may conclude that organic viticulture is too risky an enterprise in regions where disease and rot are routine hazards, but in drier, more predictable

We will be working with the existing gene pool rather than seeking to modify it. Soy is soy, maize is maize, but vines are all about nuance.

climates – predominantly the New World zones where autumnal rainfall is rare – there is no such impediment to an organic approach. Biodynamic farming, however, will continue to be reserved for prestigious sites, simply because of the enormous cost involved. It would be wrong, suggests Steve Smith, to think of organic viticulture as a sentimental throwback. He predicts a growth in what is becoming known as 'scientific organics'. He cites an example from his native New Zealand: 'Scientists have found a way to extract a compound generated in compost which, when sprayed on vines, causes the plants' natural defence to botrytis to kick in.

Legions of ambitious winemakers will continue to make hand-crafted wines that reflect the terroir as well as the skill and personality of the winemaker.

The vines are conned into acting as though they have been attacked, so their defence mechanisms are activated before, rather than when, botrytis attacks. This makes it an ideal system for protecting the vine. This scientific approach to organic viticulture is bound to develop in the years ahead.'

COMPUTERIZED CONTROL

In the winery too, the key word is control. A large modernized winery can process tens of thousands of gallons of wines with a mere handful of operatives to survey computerized temperature-control systems. An entire vintage can be programmed in advance and then simply monitored. Such mechanization may not give the most exciting wines in the world, but it can at least ensure that they will be clean and relatively fault-free. Yeasts, primary fermentation temperature curves, malolactic fermentation, choice of oak in all its permutations – all these elements give the modern winemaker an element of choice and control that was impossible a century ago. None of this wizardry will be of much use if the fruit harvested is of mediocre quality, but it has meant that the overall standard of basic wines for mass consumption is at least of an acceptable level.

It seems the next century can bring only an intensification of this trend. As James Halliday has pointed out in his essay on wine technology (*see* pp52–65), it is important to separate industrial from 'boutique' winemaking, though many wine producers have a foot in both camps. I think it is safe to predict that there will always be a distinction between these two types of wines, and the number of winemakers choosing to operate in both spheres is likely to increase. Mechanical pruning and harvesting will allow growers to cultivate vast swathes of vineyard, planted with a multiplicity of clones, which will form the basis of good-quality mass-produced wines. But much of it will be bland, and the legions of ambitious winemakers will continue to make hand-crafted wines that reflect the *terroir* as well as the skill and personality of the winemaker.

With immense new wine regions coming on stream – no visitor to California or South East Australia can fail to be amazed by the vast acreage that will soon be supplying tonnes of grapes to industrial wineries – it is possible that the price of decent if unexceptional wine will fall. At the other end of the market, trends such as those in Napa Valley, Pomerol, or Yarra Valley are likely to intensify: those owning the finest sites will employ sophisticated consultants to ensure the wine matches the current vogue in taste and style, and will also employ marketing firms to promote an exclusive image and price for their wines. If this two-tier system seems a depressing development, there will, no doubt, continue to be large New World wine companies such as Beringer in California and Southcorp in Australia, as well as *négociants* such as Jadot or Guigal in France, who will perform the most difficult feat of all: making large volumes of wine at an indisputably high quality level.

CENTRALIZED OPERATIONS

The 'flying winemaker', demonized by some, glamorized by others, will diminish in importance. Increasingly sophisticated computer systems will permit ever greater centralization of operations for mass-producing wineries. There will no longer be much need for the flying winemaker to board an aeroplane. Detailed climatic data, (including reliable weather forecasting) and grape content analyses will allow these super-technicians to make crucial decisions about harvesting and fermentation from afar; perhaps instructing a colleague on the spot to take care of trouble-shooting as required. Before long, expert winemakers on contract to supermarkets worldwide will oversee harvesting and winemaking operations in a dozen countries or regions from a central office. The best laid plans will, of course, continue to be undermined by the vagaries of nature. In the past vines were often planted at the limits of their ability to ripen – a risky course, but the vines' struggle to attain ripeness resulted, in successful years, in wines of intensity and distinction. But who can say whether those regions will remain stable? Climate change does seem to be taking place, with gradual warming the long-term trend. Should this trend continue, then by 2030 the chalky slopes of southern England may prove ideal sites for the production of *méthode champenoise* sparklers, while the poor growers in the ever-warmer Champagne region will struggle to avoid flabbiness in wines made from ripe grapes with negligible acidity.

PREDICTING DEMAND

With substantial new plantings will come economies of scale that may well see a welcome fall in wine prices. But the grape varieties will have to be chosen with great care and foresight: executive winemakers, corporate financiers, and marketing directors will all have to be consulted. Those investors who, reflecting on the white-wine boom of the early 1980s, put their money on white wine varieties received a nasty shock when the 'French paradox' swung consumer preference, almost overnight, toward red wines.

Now that a large part of the Western world is more concerned with 'lifestyle' than subsistence, consumers can indulge in the moral/medical dilemma crudely represented by health versus hedonism. Most will continue to respond to medical fad and fashion, and our tastes for food and drink will fluctuate according to the scientists' latest pronouncement on carcinogens, cholesterol levels and the ubiquitous RDA (Recommended Daily Allowance). As our sketchy scientific understanding of the chemical components of wine – its aromas, flavours, tannins and mineral traces – develops, so those new discoveries will influence what kinds of wines are produced and consumed.

It is tempting to look forward to the year when Chasselas or French Colombard is scientifically proven to be the world's healthiest grape variety – a veritable elixir – and supermarkets find themselves unable to shift the glut of Montrachet on their shelves.

International patterns of wine consumption will also continue to change. The European mantra of 'smaller quantity, higher quality' will persist, and large-scale producers will look more and more towards burgeoning Asian markets. The extent to which those growing Asian markets will compensate for dwindling European markets, however, is harder to predict. In the 1990s, the Asian market showed great volatility.

The European mantra of 'smaller quantity, higher quality' will persist, and large-scale producers will look more towards burgeoning Asian markets.

After the financial crisis of July 1997, wine imports into Thailand fell to less than one third of their peak level in 1996. The devaluation of Asian currencies further diminished demand, since it more or less doubled the cost of imported products. In the long term, however, the sheer size of the Asian market and the energy of the leading entrepreneurs, not to mention an increasingly globalized economy, is likely to ensure that overall wine consumption will continue to grow. Japan, admittedly more accustomed to wine than other major Asian markets, has seen phenomenal growth despite having been dogged by economic recession. In the last three years of the 20th century wine imports to Japan trebled in volume.

The vast and largely untapped Chinese market will continue to grow, but forecasters remain sceptical about the proportion of that colossal population that will be regular wine

Japan has seen phenomenal growth despite having been dogged by economic recession. In the last three years of the 20th century wine imports to Japan trebled in volume.

drinkers. But with a total population numbering over one billion, even a modest assessment of the size of the sector with disposable income and a liking for fermented grape juice would suggest a market of more than 100 million individuals. Sales of Cognac and whiskey have diminished in favour of wine, especially red wine. Whether there will be a surge in domestic

▷ China's modern wine industry began in the early 1980s and expanded quickly through the '90s to meet a huge growth in demand. The Shandong peninsula especially has produced Riesling and Chardonnay of acceptable international quality.

production is less certain. Chinese entrepreneurs may well further develop regions within China, such as the Shandong Peninsula south of Beijing, that are suited to viticulture, but until the monolithic political system is modified, it is likely that its wines will be predominantly for domestic consumption.

Consumer demand can certainly be influenced by political and humanitarian considerations. South African wines were shunned by most

It is unlikely that Chinese wines, or indeed any others produced using cheap or enforced labour, will find favour with international buyers.

British consumers during the apartheid era, and it is unlikely that Chinese wines, or indeed any others produced using cheap or enforced labour, will find favour with international buyers. Stricter laws regarding content and production methods will also need to be in place before such wines can make an impact on the international market. Lack of refrigerated storage and the lame requirement that 'wine' need contain no more

than 70 per cent grape juice will impede swift progress. The spread of conservative Islam, or indeed its possible decline, could also influence international wine consumption. As countries such as Malaysia and Indonesia adopt stricter observance of Moslem law and custom, any moves towards greater wine consumption by the kind of sophisticated consumer who already enjoys wine in Singapore, Hong Kong and Japan are likely to be frustrated. However, Moslem traditions in these eastern countries are far from extreme or unduly proscriptive, so it is not inconceivable that wine consumption could grow there too.

Eastern Europe will continue, in the short term at least, to provide supermarket fodder. This is not because its vineyards lack potential, but because during the latter half of the 20th century, the region's nationalized vineyards were developed in flat sites geared to mechanization and mass-production rather than on the hillside sites traditionally cultivated in the pre-communist era. Ambitious and proud growers will revive the old vineyards and traditional grape varieties, perhaps with financial backing from Western entrepreneurs, but volumes will remain relatively small. This process will echo the changes seen in the 1980s and '90s in southern France, where the vineyards that once the supplied the EU wine lake now provide some of the country's more characterful and sensibly priced wines.

Within Western Europe and the Americas the trend toward consuming better-quality wines will continue. There may well be glitches, even slumps, in international economies that will hit wineries – especially if they have been over-ambitious or plain greedy – but if the overall global economy remains buoyant, so will wine consumption. Regions that have under-performed for decades, such as much of Spain, Portugal and southern Italy, will continue to distance themselves from mass-produced wines, and, with the help of international expertise (the flying winemakers reincarnate, as well as the canny investor looking for diversification) set their sights on producing flavoursome wines at reasonable prices. The growing internationalization of wine will deal further blows to the cherished European appellation systems. While New World producers are revelling in their freedom to plant the varieties they favour in the sites they choose, Italian and other European wine-producing countries are

The growing internationalization of wine will deal further blows to the cherished European appellation systems.

busily adding to an already over-complicated appellation system. This may help to preserve certain local traditions, but is unlikely to foster long-term advantage in the marketplace. In non-traditional markets, it will be surely be the New World countries, with their clear varietal labelling, that will win over those who have understandable difficulty in distinguishing a Borba from a Portalegre, or a Franciacorta from a Valcalepio. The mysteries of Burgundian *crus* and German *Einzellagen* may well enhance

▽ Irrigating the vineyards at Indage, southeast of Bombay. The Chardonnay and Pinot Noir-based sparkling wines made here have earned India's tiny industry international recognition.

connoisseurs' pleasure in wine, but for many new consumers, such subtleties are less significant than brand and price. However the world wine atlas of the future will be shaded in terms of plantation and favoured varieties, the development of two parallel markets will continue. The market for the fashionable and rare – whether from Bordeaux, Burgundy, or the

The wine-lovers of the 21st century will be scouring the internet for their specific requirements – be they cases of bargain buys or rare obscurities.

▽ Wine has been grown since at least the 8th century in Japan, but production is tiny. However, there is a luxury market for Japanese wines made from European varieties.

boutique wineries of Napa Valley, Barolo, and Ribera del Duero – will grow. Instability is likely to increase too, as financially over-stretched wineries are superseded by newcomers with a catchier label and more fashionable winemaker.

At the other end of the scale, technological improvements and mechanization will improve the quality and probably lower the price of wines for everyday drinking. Underperforming cooperatives in southern Europe will either find

new investors to help replace outmoded and inefficient equipment, allowing them to compete with the sophisticated wineries of Chile and Australia – or they, too, will go the wall.

Both producers and consumers will also have to adapt to the rolling revolution in wine marketing and distribution. In the last years of the 20th century wines were being sold in ways inconceivable to earlier generations. The rise of supermarkets, at the expense of traditional wine merchants and high-street chains, will be less powerful. The wine-lovers of the 21st century will be scouring the internet for their specific requirements – be they cases of bargain buys or rare obscurities – and taking increasing advantage of online auctions. By the end of 1999 the American-based online wine auctioneer Winebid was reporting a growth rate of 70 per cent per quarter, as were other comparable companies. Growth in internet retailing will accelerate, although it will in the short term be hampered by restrictive shipping regulations and high delivery costs to certain markets. If it is now possible to bid for wines on the internet,

it is even simpler to order directly from producers and retailers with websites. In California, many wineries have such sites and more European-based companies will start to set up their own. The varying duty and VAT rates that currently exist make cross-European online purchasing a complex and frustrating business, but it surely will not be long before such discrepancies are ironed out. In the United States there is considerable tension between wineries that are prepared to ship direct to customers and local retailers who want to hang on to their captive market. Such difficulties may well surface in Europe too. Clearly, if it becomes possible for the Beaujolais fancier to order a selection of wines from a Georges Duboeuf website, for example, then the role of the importer and agent will have to change or will disappear completely.

FUTURISTIC GADGETRY

Other futuristic technological aids will doubtless be developed, such as the self-decanting wine bottle, which expels sediment through a straw-like insert. Keypads on restaurant tables could render the *sommelier* obsolete: just tap in your price limits and the codes of the dishes you wish to order, and a selection of appropriate wines will arrive from the cellar, at the correct temperature, through the inverse dumb waiter. At home, the 'oenochest' could hold two dozen bottles of wine, each at a different, 'correct', temperature. Corks and other solid stoppers may become obsolete too: bottles will be sealed with a layer of gas, which has to be 'melted' using a pocket laser-pencil before pouring. The success of such gadgetry would of course depend on the wine-lover's tastes evolving away from the earthy, personal and intimate enjoyment many derive from handling and discussing the merits of the bottle in the first place. By 2090, it is rumoured, the self-fermenting grape will have eliminated the need for controlled fermentation. But that's still in the realms of speculation.

Whatever the advances in viticulture and vinification, however welcome or insidious the influence of genetic modification, or sophisticated the new forms of distribution and gadgetry, at the end of the day wine will continue to be made in the world's vineyards. Steve Smith, adept at the latest techniques of wine manipulation, concedes: 'Technology will never eliminate the mysteries of the vineyard. We still don't fully understand the link between the land and the wine. Technicians who believe they can control all that happens in the vineyard and winery are deceiving themselves by ignoring the mysterious way in which parcels of land express themselves.'

That strikes me as true and just. Nature, whether benign or malicious, will upset the best laid plans. A drought here, a hailstorm there, a pesky mite or an unexpectedly troublesome clone in this vineyard, all these will subtly alter the resulting wine. We should welcome the technical advances that will ensure that the average quality of wine will improve, but the essential mystery of wine – a gnarled vine on a poor patch of earth undergoing the miraculous transformation into an infinitely subtle glass of wine – will, fortunately, persist well beyond the end of the 21st century.

△ Websites devoted to selling and auctioning wines proliferate almost daily; it remains to be seen how many the market will accommodate.

Tap in your price limits and the codes of the dishes you wish to order, and a selection of appropriate wines will arrive from the cellar, through the inverse dumb waiter.

Index

Page numbers in *italic* refer
to the illustrations